SIMULATING NEURAL NETWORKS

with
Mathematica

James A. Freeman
Loral Space Information Systems
and
University of Houston–Clear Lake

ADDISON-WESLEY PUBLISHING COMPANY
Reading, Massachusetts • Menlo Park, California
New York • Don Mills, Ontario • Wokingham, England
Amsterdam • Bonn • Sydney • Singapore • Tokyo
Madrid • San Juan • Milan • Paris

Mathematica is not associated with Mathematica Inc., Mathematica Policy Research, Inc., or MathTech, Inc.

Many of the designations used by manufacturers and sellers to distinguish their products are claimed as trademarks. Where those designations appear in this book, and Addison-Wesley was aware of a trademark claim, the designations have been printed in caps or initial caps.

The programs and applications presented in this book have been included for their instructional value. They have been tested with care, but are not guaranteed for any particular purpose. The publisher does not offer any warranties or representations, nor does it accept any liabilities with respect to the programs or applications.

Library of Congress Cataloging-in-Publication Data

Freeman, James A.
    Simulating neural networks with Mathematica / James A. Freeman.
        p.   cm.
    Includes bibliographical references and index.
    ISBN 0-201-56629-X
    1. Neural networks (Computer science) 2. Mathematica (Computer
    program)   I. Title.
    QA76.87.F72 1994
    006.3–dc20

                                                                92-2345
                                                                CIP

Reproduced by Addison-Wesley from camera-ready copy supplied by the author.

1 2 3 4 5 6 7 8 9 10-DOC-97 96 95 94 93

Preface

I sat across the dinner table at a restaurant recently with a researcher from Los Alamos National Laboratory. We were discussing a collaboration on a neural-network project while eight of us had dinner at a quaint restaurant in White Rock, just outside of Los Alamos. Fortified by a few glasses of wine, I took the opportunity to mention that I had just reached an agreement with my publisher to write a new book on neural networks with *Mathematica*. My dinner companion looked over at me and asked a question: "Why?"

I was somewhat surprised by this response, but reflecting for a moment on the environment in which this person works, I realized that the answer to his question was not necessarily so obvious. This person had access to incredible computational resources: large Crays, and a 64,000-node Connection Machine, for example. Considering the computational demands of most neural networks, why would anyone working with them want to incur the overhead of an interpreted language like *Mathematica*? To me the answer was obvious, but to him, and possibly to you, the answer may require some explanation.

During the course of preparing the manuscript for an earlier text, *Neural Networks: Algorithms, Applications, and Programming Techniques* (henceforth *"Neural Networks"*), I used *Mathematica* extensively for a variety of purposes. I simulated the operation of most of the neural networks described in that text using *Mathematica*. *Mathematica* gave me the ability to confirm nuances of network behavior and performance, as well as to develop examples and exercises pertaining to the networks. In addition I used *Mathematica*'s graphics capability to illustrate numerous points throughout the text. The ease and speed with which I was able to implement a new network spoke highly of using *Mathematica* as a tool for exploring neural-network technology.

The idea for *Simulating Neural Networks with Mathematica* grew along with my conviction that *Mathematica* had saved me countless hours of programming time. Even though *Mathematica* is an interpreted language (much like the old BASIC) and neural networks are notorious CPU hogs, there seemed to me much insight to be gained by using *Mathematica* in the early stages of network development.

I explained all of these ideas (somewhat vigorously) to my dinner companion. No doubt feeling a bit of remorse for asking the question in the first place, he promised to purchase a copy of the book as soon as it was available. I hope he finds it useful. I have the same wish for you.

This book will introduce you to the subject of neural networks within the context of the interactive *Mathematica* environment. There are two main thrusts of this text: teaching about neural networks and showing how *Mathematica* can be used to implement and experiment with neural-network architectures.

In *Neural Networks* my coauthor and I stated that you should do some programming of your own, in a high-level language such as C, FORTRAN, or Pascal, in order to gain a complete understanding of the networks you study. I do not wish to retract that philosophy, and this book is not an attempt to show you how you can avoid eventual translation of your neural networks into executable software. As I stated in the previous paragraph, most neural networks are computationally quite intensive. A neural network of any realistic size for an actual application would likely overwhelm *Mathematica*. Nevertheless, a researcher can use *Mathematica* to experiment with variants of architectures, debug a new training algorithm, design techniques for the analysis of network performance, and perform many other analyses that would prove far more time-consuming if done in traditional software or by hand. This book illustrates many of those techniques.

The book is suitable for a course in neural networks at the upper-level undergraduate or beginning graduate level in computer science, electrical engineering, applied mathematics, and related areas. The book is also suitable for self-study. The best way to study the material presented here is interactively, executing statements and trying new ideas as you progress.

This book does not assume expertise with either neural networks or *Mathematica*, although I expect that the readers will most likely know something of *Mathematica*. If you have read through the first chapter of Stephen Wolfram's *Mathematica* book and have spent an hour or two interacting with *Mathematica*, you will have more than sufficient background for the *Mathematica* syntax in this book.

I have kept the *Mathematica* syntax as understandable as possible. It is too easy to spend an inordinate amount of time trying to decipher complex *Mathematica* expressions and programs, thereby missing the forest for the trees. Moreover, many individual functions are quite long with embedded print statements and code segments that I could have written as separate functions. I chose not to, however, so the code stands as it is. For these reasons, some *Mathematica* experts may find the coding a bit nonelegant: To them I extend my apologies in advance. I have also chosen to violate one of the "rules" of *Mathematica* programming: using complete English words for function and variable names. As an example, I use bpnMomentum instead of the more "correct" backpropagationNetworkWithMomentum. The former term is easily interpreted, requires less space leading to more understandable expressions, and is less prone to typographical errors.

Readers with no prior experience with neural networks should have no trouble following the text, although the theoretical development is not as complete as in *Neural Networks*. I do assume a familiarity with basic linear algebra and calculus. Chapter 1 is a prerequisite to all other chapters in the book; the material in this chapter is fairly elementary, however, both in terms of the neural-network theory and the use of *Mathematica*. Readers who possess at least a working knowledge of each subject can safely skip Chapter 1. If you have never studied the gradient-descent method of learning, then you should also study Chapter 2 before proceeding to later chapters. The discussion of the Elman and Jordan networks in Chapter 6 requires an understanding of the backpropagation algorithm given in Chapter 3.

The text comprises eight chapters; each one, with the exception of the last, deals with a major topic related to neural networks or to a specific type of network architecture. Each chapter also includes a simulation of the networks using *Mathematica* and demonstrates the use of *Mathematica* to explore the characteristics of the network and to experiment with variations in many instances.

The last chapter introduces the subject of genetic algorithms (GAs). We will study the application of GAs to a scaled-down version of the traveling salesperson problem. To tie the subject back to neural networks, we will look at one method of using GAs to find optimum weights for a neural network. A brief description of the chapters follows.

Chapter 1: **Introduction to Neural Networks and** *Mathematica*. This chapter contains basic information about neural networks and defines many of the conventions in notation and terminology that are used throughout the text. I also introduce the concept of learning in neural networks, and that of Hinton diagrams, and show how to construct them with *Mathematica*.

Chapter 2: **Training by Error Minimization**. This chapter introduces the topic of gradient descent on an error surface as a method of learning in a simple neural network. The chapter begins with the Adaline, showing both the theoretical calculation of the optimum weight vector, as well as the least-mean-square algorithm. I also describe techniques for simulating the Adaline using *Mathematica* and for analyzing the performance of the network.

Chapter 3: **Backpropagation and Its Variants**. In this chapter we develop the generalized delta rule and apply it to a multilayered network generally known as a backpropagation network. To demonstrate how *Mathematica* can be used to experiment with different network architectures, we investigate several modifications to the basic network structure in an attempt to improve the performance of the network. We also study a related network known as the functional link network.

Chapter 4: **Probability and Neural Networks**. In this chapter we explore the use of probability concepts in neural networks using two different types of networks. After describing the deterministic Hopfield network, we examine some concepts in the thermodynamics of physical systems and see how they relate to the Hopfield network. Then we use a technique called simulated annealing to develop a stochastic Hopfield network. We also examine the probabilistic neural network, which is an example of a network that implements a traditional classification algorithm based on Bayesian probability theory.

Chapter 5: **Optimization and Constraint Satisfaction with Neural Networks**. In this chapter we explore the concept of constraint satisfaction using the familiar traveling salesperson problem. Then we illustrate how this problem, and other constraint-satisfaction problems, map onto the Hopfield network.

Chapter 6: **Feedback and Recurrent Networks**. In this chapter we describe and simulate networks that depart from the simple feedforward structures typical of the backpropagation network. We begin with a two-layer network called a bidirectional associative memory (BAM). We then proceed to networks that can recognize and reproduce time-sequences of input patterns. Specifically, we look at the networks described by Jordan and Elman.

Chapter 7: **Adaptive Resonance Theory.** Adaptive Resonance Theory (ART) defines a class of neural networks that includes several different, but related, types, including ART1, ART2, ART3, ArtMap, Fuzzy ART, and other variations. This chapter explores ART1 and ART2. ART2 is distinguished from ART1 primarily by its ability to accommodate other than binary input vectors.

Chapter 8: **Genetic Algorithms.** In this final chapter, I depart from the neural network field to describe the basics of a data-processing technique called genetic algorithms (GAs). Like some neural networks, GAs are good at solving optimization problems of many types. Since determining weight vectors in a neural network is an optimization problem in its own right, a discussion of GAs is appropriate in a book on neural networks.

Beginning with Chapter 2, each chapter has associated with it a set of *Mathematica* functions. A complete listing of the functions for each chapter appears in the Appendix. The Bibliography contains a list of reference books from which you can obtain additional information about the neural networks described in this book, as well as many other neural networks. I have also included a few references on *Mathematica* and genetic algorithms.

Because this text is supposed to convey a spirit of exploration, I have not attempted to include only the best, or most efficient neural-network techniques. In fact, some of the experiments presented result in networks that do not actually work very well, but such is the nature of experimentation. We can learn from these attempts as well as from those that are successful. The best way to study the material is interactively, executing statements and trying new ideas as you progress. I trust that you will be able to accept a text that does not always give the "right" answer and that you will forgive any lingering errors, for which I accept full responsibility.

Source Code Availability

The source code for all of the functions in this text is available, free of charge, from MathSource. MathSource is a repository for *Mathematica*-related material contributed by *Mathematica* users and by Wolfram Research, Inc. To find out more about MathSource, send a single-line email message: "help intro" to the MathSource server at mathsource@wri.com. For information on other ways to access MathSource, send the message "help access" to ms-request@wri.com.

If you do not have direct electronic access to MathSource, you can still get some of the material in it from Wolfram Research. Contact the MathSource Administrator at: Wolfram Research, Inc. 100 Trade Center Drive, Champaign, Illinois, 61820-7237, USA, (217) 398-0700.

Acknowledgments

First, I would like to correct a grievous omission from my previous book. Dr. Robert Hecht-Nielsen was my first and only formal instructor of neural networks. I owe to him much of my appreciation and enthusiasm for the subject. Thanks Robert! Of course, many others have contributed to this project and I would like to mention several of those individuals.

In particular, I would like to thank Dr. John Engvall, of Loral Space Information Systems, who has been a continuing source of support and encouragement. Don Brady, M. Alan Meghrigian, and Jason Deines, who I met through the CompuServe AI Expert and Wolfram Research forums, reviewed portions of the manuscript and software in its early stages. I thank them greatly for their efforts and comments.

I initially wrote the manuscript as a series of *Mathematica* notebooks, which had to be translated to TEX. I want to thank Dr. Cameron Smith for providing software and many hours of consultation to help with this task.

I wish to express my appreciation to Alan Wylde, previously of Addison-Wesley Publishing Company, for his support early on in the project. I also want to thank Peter Gordon, Helen Goldstein, Mona Zeftel, Lauri Petrycki and Patsy DuMoulin, all of Addison-Wesley, for their support, assistance, and exhortations throughout the preparation of this manuscript.

Finally, I dedicate this book to my family: Peggy, Geoffrey, and Deborah, without whose support and patience this project would never have been possible.

J.A.F.
Houston TX

Contents

Chapter 1

Introduction to Neural Networks and *Mathematica*

More times than I care to remember, I have had to verify, using a calculator, the computations performed by a neural network that I had programmed in C. To say that the process was laborious will bring a chuckle to anyone who has had the same experience. Then came *Mathematica*. For a while, *Mathematica* became my super calculator, reducing the amount of time spent doing such calculations by at least an order of magnitude. Before long I was using *Mathematica* as a prototyping tool for experimenting with neural-network architectures. The answer to the question, "Why use *Mathematica* to build neural networks?" will, I trust, become self-evident as you see the tool used throughout this book.

Those of you to whom neural networks is a new technology may be asking a different question that requires answering before the issue of using *Mathematica* ever arises: "Why neural networks?" I would like to spend a little time discussing the answer to that question in the first section of this chapter. In Section 1.2, we will begin to use *Mathematica* to perform some basic neural-network calculations and to do some simple analyses. The techniques and conventions that I introduce in that section will form the basis of the work we do in subsequent chapters.

1.1 The Neural-Network Paradigm

Ask someone who is doing research or applications development in neural networks why neural networks are worth pursuing. The ensuing discussion will probably include comments about how well humans perform tasks such as vision and language, which are difficult to program a computer to perform. The short form of the argument is that humans do some things well (e.g., vision and language), and computers do some things well (e.g., numerical integration) and never the twain shall meet.

The fact is that computers do little useful work that a human cannot also do; computers just do it significantly faster. After all, a human must develop the algorithm and write the program that enables a computer to perform its function. In order to perform this development, humans must think in a serial fashion because most computers execute instructions one after the other.

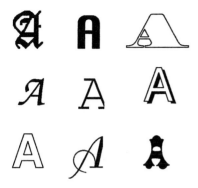

Figure 1.1 We can recognize all of these letters as variations of the letter "A." Writing a computer program to recognize all of these, and all other possible variations, is a formidable task.

1.1.1 Neural Networks vs. Traditional Algorithms for Pattern Classification

Take a look at the letters in Figure 1.1. Think about how you might construct a computer program that can take as its input a picture of a letter, and that produces an output indicating the identity of the letter.

One approach to writing the program is to store all of the possible patterns in a database, and to do a bit by bit comparison of the letter in question with all of the stored templates. If the pattern matches one of the templates to within a certain degree of error, we can conclude that the letter is in fact an "A."

This approach is not satisfactory, however, for a number of reasons. First, the number of templates that you would have to store would be large, especially if you wanted to recognize all letters, both upper and lower case, and all numerals. Try to imagine all of the possible variations. There could be variations in size and in angle of rotation, as well as in the style of the letter. If you added the complication of wanting to recognize handwritten characters, the number of templates could be astronomical.

The situation may not be hopeless, however, since we could add a bit of intelligence to our computer program. For example, we could study all of the ways that the letter "A" is formed, and attempt to discern commonalities — features, as they are often called — that distinguish one letter from another. Then we could program an intelligent system

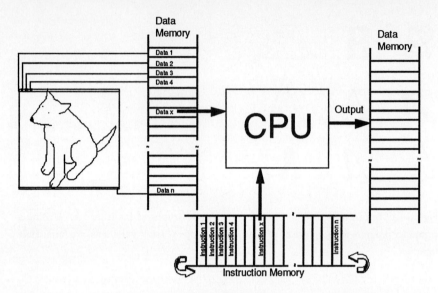

Figure 1.2 In a program designed to identify what appears in the picture, each picture element, or pixel, becomes a single entity in data memory. The central processing unit (CPU) reads instructions sequentially and operates on individual data elements, storing the results, which can themselves be operated on by the CPU. In order for the CPU to correctly classify the image, we must specify exactly the correct sequence of operations that the CPU must perform on the data.

to search systematically for those features and match them against the known list for the various letters. While this approach might work for some letters, variations in writing style and typography would still necessitate a huge information base and would likely not account for all possibilities.

The problem with these approaches and with others that have been tried in the past is that they depend on our ability to systematically pick apart the picture of the letter on a pixel-by-pixel, or feature by feature, basis. We must look for specific information in the picture and apply rules or algorithms sequentially to the data, hoping that we are smart enough to be able to write down in sufficient detail what it is exactly that makes an "A" an "A" and not some other letter. The solution to this problem has proved elusive. Figure 1.2 shows a simple schematic of how data processing of this type takes place in a sequential computing environment.

It is curious that, although we can identify letters and objects visually with great speed and accuracy, we have trouble writing down an algorithm that will allow a computer program to accomplish the same task. Perhaps we are not just stupid; instead, it may be that we have trouble translating our ability into a sequential program because we do not perform the task sequentially ourselves.

Look again at one of the letters in Figure 1.1. Think about the process you went through to identify the letter. Did you scan the letter from left to right and top to bottom? Did you assemble information about the angle of lines and the intersection between line segments? Did you pick apart the letter's features and logically conclude that, on the basis of the information, the letter must be an "A"? Probably not, at least not consciously, and certainly not in a long sequence of individual steps that treat each feature or pixel sequentially: The brain's processing elements (neurons) are much too slow to account for the almost instantaneous recognition. What then accounts for our remarkable ability to recognize almost any handwritten or printed letter without the slightest effort? The answer, I believe, lies in the massive parallelism of the brain, and the way in which the brain processes data.

When you look at one of the letters in Figure 1.1, information from every point reaches your retina simultaneously. That information is transformed into electrical impulses that travel along nerves to locations deep within your brain. There, the information from all of the pixels is processed. Features are extracted from various parts of the image, and information from one part of the image is combined with information from other parts, allowing the brain to rapidly form a hypothesis about the identity of the letter. It is likely that some of this processing is serial in nature: Simple features are extracted first, then these features are combined to identify more complex features, etc. The main point, however, is that much of this work is done in parallel, with the brain operating on the whole image at once, sharing information among neurons about features in all parts of the image. This massive parallelism gives the brain its ability to process data so quickly and efficiently; the existence of that same parallelism frustrates our attempts to render the process in a sequential algorithm.

A neural network, as we use the term here, is a computational paradigm inspired by the parallelism of the brain. Using this paradigm we can begin to build computers that mimic those functions that humans do so easily, but for which sequential algorithms either do not exist or

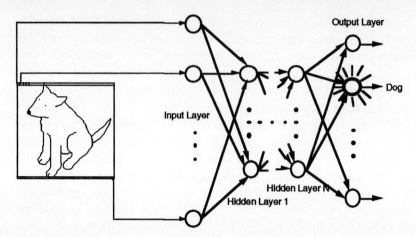

Figure 1.3 This figure shows a simple example of a neural network that is used to identify the image presented to it. Imagine that the input layer is the retina. The neurons on this layer respond simultaneously to data from various parts of the image. In hidden-layer 1, data from all parts of the retina are combined at individual neurons. The output layer generates a hypothesis as to the identity of the input image, in this case a dog. In this particular network, each neuron on the output layer corresponds to a particular hypothesis concerning the identity of the pattern on the input layer. While there is some serial processing, much of the work is done in parallel by neurons on each layer.

are so hard to discover that they are impractical. As a simple example, Figure 1.3 shows how we might translate the picture-recognition task from Figure 1.2 into one that uses the neural-network paradigm.

The example of Figure 1.3 illustrates some general characteristics of the neural-network models that we shall study in this text; although not all models share all of the same characteristics. Individual neurons, which we shall call **processing elements** (PEs), **nodes**, or **units**, are represented by the circles. Arrows show the direction of data flow from one unit to the next. Notice that a unit can have numerous inputs and can send data to numerous other units. Although not explicitly indicated in the figure, each unit has only a single output value, which can be sent to many other units. Also typical of most neural-network models is the layered structure apparent in Figure 1.3.

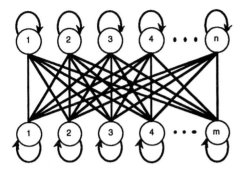

Figure 1.4 In this two-layer network, units are connected with bidirectional connections, illustrated as lines without arrows. Also notice that each unit has a feedback connection to itself. In this network the distinction between input and output layer is ambiguous, since either layer can act in either capacity, depending on the particular application.

1.1.2 Example Neural-Network Architectures

So that you do not get the idea that all neural networks look alike, Figures 1.4, 1.5, and 1.6 show examples of possible neural-network architectures. Even these examples, however, do not exhaust the possibilities.

1.2 Neural-Network Fundamentals

Having now spent some time discussing the neural-network paradigm and its value, I would like to move on directly into some of the prelim-

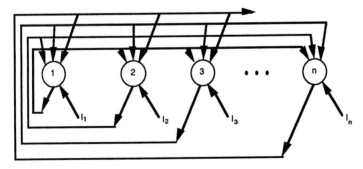

Figure 1.5 This network architecture has only a single layer of units. The output of each unit becomes an input to other units.

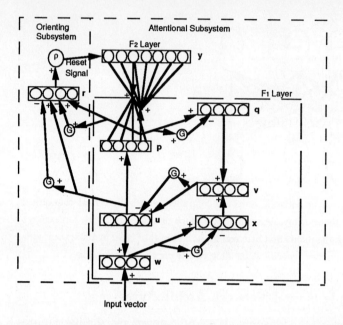

Figure 1.6 This network architecture is an exampe of a complex, multilayered structure. For the sake of clarity, all of the individual connections between units are not shown explicitly. For example, in the layer labeled "F2 Layer," all of the units are connected to each other by inhibitory connections. These connections are implied by the nature of the processing that takes place on this layer, but the connections themselves are not shown.

inary technical information without stopping to elaborate further on the earlier question of why *Mathematica* is a useful tool in this environment. It is better that you become convinced as you see *Mathematica* put to use to build and experiment with neural networks.

The neural-network paradigm has, at its core, the notion of individual units. These units share some basic characteristics with real, biological neurons, although to say that they are simulations of real neurons would overstate the reality.

Like their biological counterparts, individual units generally have many inputs but only one output. Moreover, this output can be fanned out to many other units, again in analogy to actual neurons. In a neural network, real numbers suffice to represent the strength of electrical signals sent from one neuron to the other. Synapses, the junction between neurons, are called **connections** in neural-network models. In real neural networks, signals pass across synapses from one neuron to another. During this passage, the efficiency with which the synapse transfers the signal differs from synapse to synapse. In our neural-network models, this difference manifests itself as a multiplicative factor that modifies the incoming signal. This factor is called a **weight** or **connection strength**. Each connection has its associated weight value. As you will see shortly, these weight values contain the information that lets the network success-fully process its data. Building a neural network to perform a specific task often depends on the development of a set of weights that encodes the appropriate data-processing algorithm. Fortunately, many neural-network models can learn the required weight values, so that we do not have to specify them in advance.

1.2.1 The General Neural-Network Processing Element

Figure 1.7 shows a schematic of a typical processing element in a neural network. This unit is somewhat more general than we will need for most networks, but it is intended to cover the majority of cases.

Generally speaking, output values from units will be positive num-bers. Weights can be either positive or negative. This situation leads us to categorize the inputs to a unit according to their effect. Inputs whose connections have a positive weight contribute a net positive value to the overall excitation of the unit. Those inputs whose connections have neg-ative weights detract from the overall excitation. We refer to the former type as **excitatory connections**, and the latter as **inhibitory connections**. Other types of connections are possible as we shall see in later chapters.

We shall refer to the overall excitation of a unit as its **net-input value**, or simply, the **net input**. We usually calculate that value by summing the products of the input values and the weights on the associated con-nections. For the ith unit, the net input is:

$$\text{net}_i = \sum_{j=1}^{n} x_j w_{ij} \tag{1.1}$$

where n is the number of units having connections to the ith unit, x_j is the output of the jth unit, and w_{ij} is the weight on the connection *from* the jth unit *to* the ith unit.

Let's use *Mathematica* to perform this calculation for a single unit. First, we must set up vectors for the weights and inputs. For this exam-ple, we shall assume that the inputs are all binary numbers.

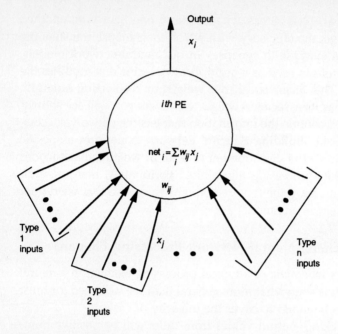

Figure 1.7 This figure shows a representation of a general processing element of a neural network; in this case the ith unit.

`xj = Table[Random[Integer,{0,1}],{10}]`

`{1, 0, 0, 1, 1, 1, 1, 1, 1, 0}`

For weights, we shall assume random values between -0.5 and 0.5.

`wij = Table[Random[Real,{-0.5,0.5}],{10}]`

`{-0.435611, 0.294576, -0.36385, 0.0753376, 0.472324, -0.437153,`
`   -0.440387, -0.394219, -0.033852, -0.311905}`

Finding the net-input value is simply a matter of multiplying the vectors using the dot product. Remember that the vectors must be of the same length.

` neti = xj . wij`

`-1.19356`

In some neural-network models, units transform their net-input value into an **activation value** as an intermediate step before producing an output value. Many architectures skip this intermediate step and proceed directly to the generation of an output value. We shall ignore the complication of activation values for the moment, taking them up again in a later chapter. For now we shall just be interested in the output value. We can express the output value of a unit in the form of a differential equation. Like their biological counterparts, the outputs of our units are dynamic functions of time. The simplest form of the equation for the outputs in which we shall be interested is the following:

$$\dot{x}_i = -x_i + f(\text{net}_i) \qquad (1.2)$$

where $f(\text{net}_i)$ is a function that we shall refer to as the **output function**.

The function $f(\text{net}_i)$ can take many different forms. For now we shall look at a simple case where $f(\text{net}_i)$ is the identity function; that is, $f(\text{net}_i) = \text{net}_i$. Then we can write Eq. (1.2) as

$$\dot{x}_i = -x_i + \text{net}_i \qquad (1.3)$$

We can use *Mathematica* to integrate this differential equation in order to study the behavior of the variable x as a function of time. To do this integration, we approximate the derivative as

$$\dot{x}_i \approx \Delta x_i / \Delta t$$

and rewrite Eq. (1.3) as

$$\Delta x_i \approx \Delta t (-x_i + \text{net}_i)$$

and finally

$$x_i(t+1) = x_i(t) + \Delta t (-x_i(t) + \text{net}_i) \qquad (1.4)$$

The loop in Listing 1.1 iterates Eq. (1.4) and appends each value to a list, along with the timestep index, in such a way that we can easily plot the results when the calculation is finished. In the **If** statement, we anticipated the fact that the value of x would asymptotically approach the value of net_i. You can see this fact easily by setting the derivative in Eq. (1.3) equal to zero to find the equilibrium value for x.

$$x_i^{eq} = \text{net}_i$$

Let's plot the results of our calculation.

```
xlist = {};                (* define list to hold results *)
done = False;           (* initialize flag *)
deltaT = 0.01;        (* pick value for timestep size *)
xi = 0.0;                   (* initialize variables *)
neti = 2.0;               (* pick value for net input *)
For[i=1,done==False,i++,          (* until flag is true *)
    xi = xi + deltaT (-xi + neti);  (* update xi *)
    AppendTo[xlist,{i deltaT,xi}];     (* append to list *)
    If[Abs[xi-neti]< 0.005,done=True,Continue];(* stop ? *)
        ]                      (* end of For *)
```

Listing 1.1


```
xiList = ListPlot[xlist];
```

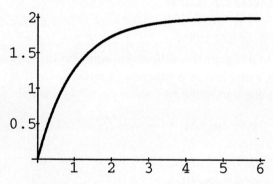

To see how close we came to the expected equilibrium value, look at the last element in xlist.

```
Last[xlist]
```

{5.97, 1.99504}

Both the time step, deltaT, and the value of the stopping criterion in the If statement affect the integration. Since Eq. (1.2) is easy to integrate in closed form, we can compare the results of the numerical integration with the actual solution.

Let's let *Mathematica* do the integration for us. We first clear the value of neti so that *Mathematica* will include this parameter symbolically in the result. We have to include the initial condition, **xi[0]==0**, in order to prevent *Mathematica* from adding an unknown constant of integration.

```
Clear[neti]
DSolve[{xi´[t]==-xi[t]+neti,xi[0]==0},xi[t],t]
```

```
                    t
          -neti + E  neti
{{xi[t] -> ---------------}}
                 t
                E
```

Now let's assign the result to the variable **xi**

```
xi = xi[t] /. First[%]
```

```
          t
-neti + E  neti
---------------
       t
      E
```

and put the result into a more familiar form

```
xi = Simplify[xi]
```

```
        neti
neti - ----
         t
        E
```

We would most likely choose a slightly different form for the solution, such as Eq. (1.5):

$$x_i(t) = \text{net}_i(1 - e^{-t}) \qquad (1.5)$$

Next, we can assign a value to **neti** and do the plot.

```
neti=2;
xiPlot = Plot[xi,{t,0,10}];
```

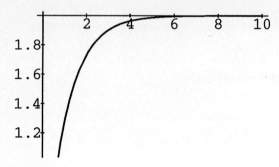

Mathematica's choice of axes makes comparison of the two plots a little difficult. We can get an idea of the accuracy of the numerical integration by showing both graphs plotted on the same set of axes.

```
Show[{xiList,xiPlot}];
```

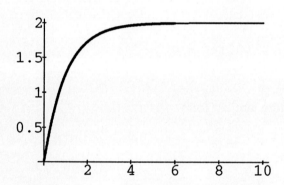

On my computer the numerical integration of Eq. (1.2) required a fair number of seconds to compute. We can generally assume that the units always have enough time to reach their equilibrium state; thus, we can forego the numerical integration step altogether for many of our experiments.

1.2.2 Output Function

As of yet, we have not considered any form of the output function other than the identity function. Let's look at some other forms for the output function.

For reference, let's plot the identity function:

```
out1 = Plot[neti,{neti,-5,5}];
```

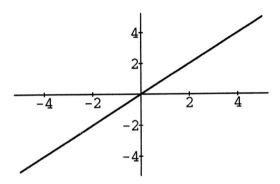

We can change the slope and position of this graph by including some constants in the output function. For example, consider the function

$$f(\text{net}_i) = c\,\text{net}_i + d$$

where c and d are constants. If we pick some numbers for c and d, we can plot the resulting function.

```
c=2;
d=-0.5;
out2 = Plot[c neti + d, {neti,-5,5}];
```

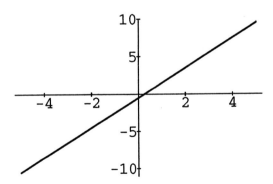

Plot them together to see the difference.

```
Show[{out1,out2}];
```

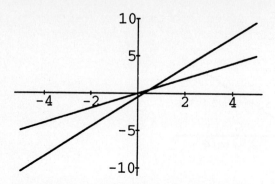

A particularly useful output function is one called a **sigmoid**. One version of a sigmoid function is defined by the equation

$$f(x) = \frac{1}{1 + e^{-x}} \tag{1.6}$$

To see the general shape, plot the function. First, however, let's define a function for the sigmoid, since we will be using it often.

```
sigmoid[x_] := 1/(1+E^(-x))
```

Now the plot:

```
sig1 = Plot[sigmoid[x],{x,-10,10}];
```

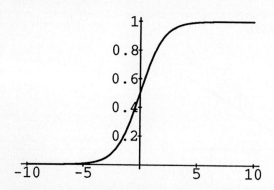

Notice that the sigmoid function is limited in range to the values between zero and one. Also notice that if the net input to a unit having a sigmoid output is less than about negative five or greater than about positive five, the output of the unit will be approximately zero or one, respectively. Thus, a unit with a sigmoid output saturates at these net-output values and cannot distinguish between, for example, a net input of 8 or 10.

We can change the shape and location of the sigmoid curve by including parameters in the defining equation. Consider this example:

```
r = 2;
s = 2.0;
sig2 = Plot[1/(1+E^(-r neti)) + s,{neti,-10,10}];
```

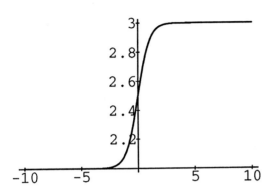

By adjusting the value of r we can change the slope of the sigmoid. Consider the following three plots where we have set s=0:

```
r = 20.0;
sig3 = Plot[1/(1+E^(-r neti)),{neti,-10,10}];
r = 0.5;
sig4 = Plot[1/(1+E^(-r neti)),{neti,-10,10}];
r = 0.1;
sig5 = Plot[1/(1+E^(-r neti)),{neti,-10,10}];
```

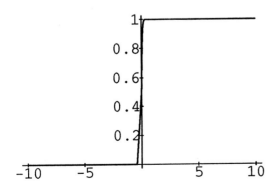

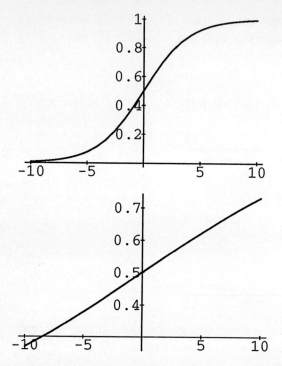

Let's plot them together with the original sigmoid graph:

Show[{sig1,sig3,sig4,sig5}];

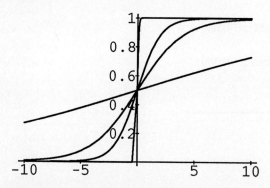

Plot **sig3** is almost a threshold function. A **threshold function** is one defined by an equation such as the following:

$$f(x) = \begin{cases} 1 & x \geq \theta \\ 0 & \text{otherwise} \end{cases} \qquad (1.7)$$

where θ is the threshold value. The larger the value of r in the sigmoid equation, the closer the function will approximate a threshold function. Plot sig5 is essentially a linear function over the domain of interest.

The parameter s can shift the position of the graph along the ordinate. For example,

sig6 = Plot[sigmoid[x]-0.5,{x,-10,10}]

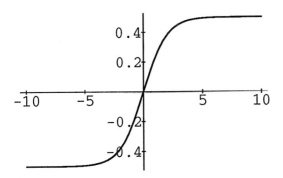

The above plot shows the sigmoid shifted so that it passes through the origin. The limiting values are ±0.5. One of the important features of the sigmoid function is that it is differentiable everywhere. We will see the importance of this characteristic in Chapter 3.

If the output function of a unit is a sigmoid function, then the following relationship holds:

$$f'(\mathrm{net}_i) = f(\mathrm{net}_i)(1 - f(\mathrm{net}_i))$$

If we define $o_i = f(\mathrm{net}_i)$, then we can write

$$f'(\mathrm{net}_i) = o_i(1 - o_i) \tag{1.8}$$

Equation (1.8) will be useful during the discussion of the backpropagation learning method in Chapter 3.

1.2.3 Layers and Weight Matrices

If you look back at Figures 1.3 through 1.6, you will notice the characteristic layered structure of the networks. This structure is general: You can always decompose a neural network into layers. It may be true that

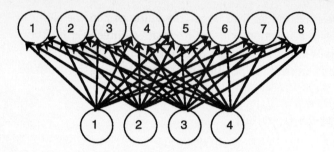

Figure 1.8 This figure shows two layers of a neural network. The bottom layer sends inputs to the units in the top layer. The layer is fully interconnected; that is, all units on the bottom layer send connections to all units on the upper layer.

some layer has only a single unit, or that some units are members of more than one layer, but, nevertheless, layers are the rule.

We shall impose a constraint on our layers that requires all units on a layer to have the same number of incoming connections. This constraint would seem to be in keeping with the networks in Figures 1.3 through 1.6. On the other hand, not all neural networks are structured so that all units that form the logical grouping of a layer have the same number of input connections. As an example, a network may have units that are connected randomly to units in previous layers, making the number of connections on each unit potentially different from that on other units. Nevertheless, we can force any such network to appear as though all units on a layer have the same number of connections by adding connections with zero weights. Any data flowing across these connections would have no effect on the net input to the unit, so it is as if the connection did not exist. The reason that we go to this trouble is for convenience in calculation.

Consider the small network shown in Figure 1.8. Each unit in the top layer receives four input values from the units in the previous layer.

Each unit on the bottom layer sends the identical value — its output value — to all units in the upper layer. Each unit in the upper layer has its own weight vector with one weight for each input connection. The easiest way to deal with these individual weight vectors is to combine them into a **weight matrix**. Let's define such a weight matrix for the network in Figure 1.8, using random weight values.

```
w = Table[Table[Random[Real,{-0.5,0.5},3],{4}],{8}]
```

```
{{0.364, -0.273, -0.453, -0.425},
 {-0.159, -0.489, 0.379, -0.471},
 {-0.196, -0.297, -0.0228, 0.148},
 {-0.411, -0.385, -0.0487, -0.354},
 {-0.0832, 0.177, 0.00528, 0.194},
 {-0.362, -0.129, -0.0755, -0.208},
 {-0.0372, 0.388, 0.31, -0.442},
 {-0.11, 0.0686, -0.278, -0.431}}
```

We can access the weight matrix for each individual unit by indexing into the matrix at the proper row. For example, the weight matrix on the third unit in Figure 1.8 is given by

w[[3]]

```
{-0.196, -0.297, -0.0228, 0.148}
```

Similarly, the weight from the second unit on the first layer to the third unit on the upper layer is given by

w[[3,2]]

```
-0.297
```

or alternatively

w[[3]][[2]]

```
-0.297
```

We will sometimes find it advantageous to view the weight matrix in a more familiar form. We can do the transformation with the **MatrixForm** command:

MatrixForm[w]

```
0.364    -0.273   -0.453    -0.425
-0.159   -0.489   0.379     -0.471
-0.196   -0.297   -0.0228   0.148
-0.411   -0.385   -0.0487   -0.354
-0.0832  0.177    0.00528   0.194
-0.362   -0.129   -0.0755   -0.208
-0.0372  0.388    0.31      -0.442
-0.11    0.0686   -0.278    -0.431
```

To calculate the net inputs to all of the upper-layer units, all we need do is to perform a vector-matrix multiplication using the output vector of the bottom layer, and the weight matrix of the upper layer. First, we must define the output vector of the bottom layer. Let's keep it simple:

```
out1 = {1,2,3,4}
```

```
{1, 2, 3, 4}
```

The net-input calculation results in a vector of net-input values for the upper layer.

```
netin2 = w . out1
```

```
{-3.24135, -1.88379, -0.268188, -2.74074, 1.0637, -1.68074,
  -0.0994623, -2.53006}
```

Note that we could reverse the order of multiplication in the above expression, provided we first transpose the weight matrix.

```
netin2a = out1 . Transpose[w]
```

```
{-3.24135, -1.88379, -0.268188, -2.74074, 1.0637, -1.68074,
  -0.0994623, -2.53006}
```

I should point out a fundamental difference between vectors as they appear in *Mathematica* and vectors as they might appear in another text. In *Mathematica*, a vector is the same as a list; that is, the vector appears as though it were a row vector.

```
VectorQ[{1,2,3,4}]
```

```
True
```

A list, however, is actually a vector in column form.

```
MatrixForm[{1,2,3,4}]
```

```
1
2
3
4
```

This convention is in keeping with other texts that assume vectors are column vectors. For example, in *Neural Networks,* I would write the vector **out1** as $(1, 2, 3, 4)^t$, where the t superscript represents the transpose operation. In fact, if you attempt to transpose the **out1** vector, you will get an error. Try it.

Let's return to the issue of randomly-connected networks. With the above convention, connections that do not exist should have zeros at those locations in the weight matrix. The following matrix is an example.

```
 0.364  0.000 -0.450  -0.425
-0.159 -0.489  0.000  -0.471
 0.000 -0.297 -0.022   0.148
 0.000  0.000  0.000  -0.354
-0.083  0.177  0.005   0.194
-0.362 -0.129  0.000   0.000
 0.000  0.388  0.310   0.000
-0.110  0.000 -0.278  -0.431
```

In some high-level programming languages, such as Pascal, it might be more advantageous to use a linked-list approach to layers that are not fully connected, especially when the connection matrix is sparse. Here, however, we shall stay with the weight-matrix approach. We may suffer a bit in performance due to the number of additional multiplications that do not contribute anything to the net input, but the ease in notation that this approach affords is well worth the price. Bear in mind, however, that when translating to a high-level language where performance is more of an issue, there may be benefits to using the linked-list approach when the connection matrix is sparse.

1.2.4 Hinton Diagrams

By now, it should come as no surprise to you that the weight values play a crucial role in neural networks. It is the weights that encode the processing algorithm that allows a network to transform its inputs into some meaningful output value. In the next section we shall begin to look at how we can go about determining the proper set of weights to encode a particular processing function. In this section, we shall examine an interesting way of displaying weight values that often will allow us to infer certain facts about how the weights accomplish their task. That method of display is called a **Hinton diagram,** after Geoffrey Hinton,

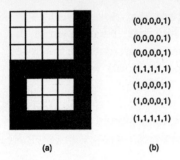

(0,0,0,0,1)

(0,0,0,0,1)

(0,0,0,0,1)

(1,1,1,1,1)

(1,0,0,0,1)

(1,0,0,0,1)

(1,1,1,1,1)

(a)   (b)

Figure 1.9 (a) This figure shows a 5 by 7 array of inputs to a neural network. Each array location, or pixel, may be either on (black) or off (white). (b) This binary representation of the image on the input array are the 35 numbers used as inputs to the neural network.

who first used them.

Assume that we have constructed a neural network with 35 input units, arranged in a rectangular array of 5 inputs by 7 inputs. Furthermore, assume that the input values can take on only the values of zero or one. Figure 1.9 shows an example of such an input array along with one possible input pattern.

We shall assume that the 35 input values of the array in Figure 1.9 are sent to two units of a neural network. Let's examine hypothetical weight vectors on those two units. For the first unit, assume the weight vector is

```
w1 = {0.8,0.3,0.5,0.1,0.1,0.6,-0.5,-0.7,-0.5,0.6,
     0.6,-0.5,-0.7,-0.3,0.5,0.4,0.3,0.6,0.5,0.4,
     0.5,-0.5,-0.6,-0.1,0.3,0.4,-0.4,-0.5,-0.2,0.4,
        0.4,0.5,0.3,0.7,0.2};
```

Notice that I have used a semicolon after the above expression in order to suppress the output from *Mathematica*, which I shall do when I do not feel that showing the output adds anything to the discussion.

Assume the second unit has the weight vector

```
w2 = {-0.4,-0.7,-0.5,-0.6,0.8,-0.5,-0.4,-0.7,-0.6,0.8,
        -0.4,-0.3,-0.7,-0.4,0.6,0.4,0.5,0.4,0.7,0.4,
        0.7,-0.5,-0.6,-0.1,0.4,0.5,-0.4,-0.5,-0.2,0.6,
        0.4,0.7,0.7,0.6,0.4};
```

The input vector is

```
in = {0,0,0,0,1,0,0,0,0,1,0,0,0,0,1,
      1,1,1,1,1,0,0,0,1,1,0,0,0,1,1,1,1,1,1};
```

As a point of reference, let's find the net-input value for each of these two units. For unit 1:

```
net1 = in . w1
```

7.1

and for the second:

```
net2 = in . w2
```

9.6

The second unit has a somewhat larger net input; that is, unit number 2 is excited more strongly by the input pattern than unit 1. Just looking at the weight vectors, however, would not easily lead you to that conclusion until you actually calculated the results.

Let's rewrite the weight vectors as rectangular weight matrices having a row-column structure the same as that of the input pattern. Weight 1 becomes

```
w1 = Partition[w1,5]
```

```
{{0.8, 0.3, 0.5, 0.1, 0.1}, {0.6, -0.5, -0.7, -0.5, 0.6},
 {0.6, -0.5, -0.7, -0.3, 0.5}, {0.4, 0.3, 0.6, 0.5, 0.4},
 {0.5, -0.5, -0.6, -0.1, 0.3}, {0.4, -0.4, -0.5, -0.2, 0.4},
 {0.4, 0.5, 0.3, 0.7, 0.2}}
```

In matrix form:

```
MatrixForm[w1]
```

```
0.8   0.3   0.5   0.1   0.1
0.6  -0.5  -0.7  -0.5   0.6
0.6  -0.5  -0.7  -0.3   0.5
0.4   0.3   0.6   0.5   0.4
0.5  -0.5  -0.6  -0.1   0.3
0.4  -0.4  -0.5  -0.2   0.4
0.4   0.5   0.3   0.7   0.2
```

Similarly, weight vector two yields:

```
w2 = Partition[w2,5]
```

```
{{-0.4, -0.7, -0.5, -0.6, 0.8}, {-0.5, -0.4, -0.7, -0.6, 0.8},
  {-0.4, -0.3, -0.7, -0.4, 0.6}, {0.4, 0.5, 0.4, 0.7, 0.4},
  {0.7, -0.5, -0.6, -0.1, 0.4}, {0.5, -0.4, -0.5, -0.2, 0.6},
  {0.4, 0.7, 0.7, 0.6, 0.4}}
```

```
MatrixForm[w2]
```

```
-0.4   -0.7   -0.5   -0.6   0.8
-0.5   -0.4   -0.7   -0.6   0.8
-0.4   -0.3   -0.7   -0.4   0.6
 0.4    0.5    0.4    0.7   0.4
 0.7   -0.5   -0.6   -0.1   0.4
 0.5   -0.4   -0.5   -0.2   0.6
 0.4    0.7    0.7    0.6   0.4
```

The matrix forms of w1 and w2 are still not so transparent. Let's apply the command `ListDensityPlot` to both.

```
ListDensityPlot[Reverse[w1]];
```

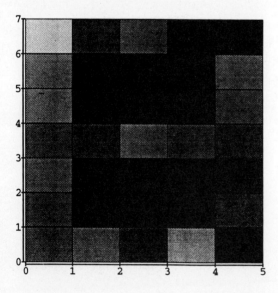

```
ListDensityPlot[Reverse[w2]];
```

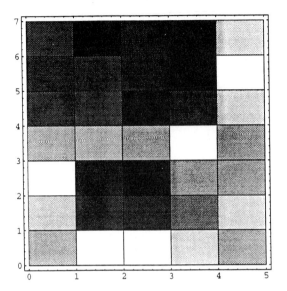

Each square in either of these two plots corresponds to one weight value, and each row corresponds to the weight vector on a single unit. If you stand back from these graphics, you should notice that the first one contains an image of an upper-case "B," and the second contains an image of a lower case "d." In these pictures, the larger the weight, the lighter the shade of the square.

Notice that the second weight matrix has large values in the same relative locations in which the input vector has a 1. This correspondence leads to a larger dot product than in the case where the large weight values and large input values do not match. This analysis assumes that the weight vectors are normalized in some fashion, so that there is no false match resulting from an unusually large weight-vector length.

Notice in the plots of the weight matrices that we had to **Reverse** the matrices before plotting. If we had not done this reversal, the image of the letters would have appeared upside down in the plot.

It is certainly not always the case that the weight matrix mimics one of the possible input vectors. When this does happen, we say that the corresponding unit has encoded the pattern, which itself is often called an **exemplar**. Nevertheless, it is often true that we can gleen some insight from looking at the weights in this manner, even though their meaning

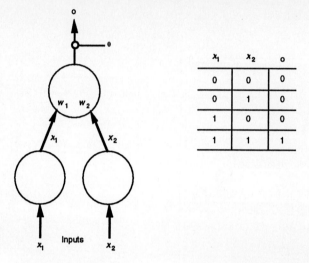

x_1	x_2	o
0	0	0
0	1	0
1	0	0
1	1	1

Figure 1.10 This figure illustrates a simple network with two input units and a single output unit. The table on the right shows the AND function. We wish to find weights such that, given any two binary inputs, the network correctly computes the AND function of those two inputs.

may not be so obvious.

1.2.5 Learning in Neural Networks

Learning in neural networks involves finding a set of weights such that the network performs correctly whatever data-processing function we intend. There are many different ways to determine a proper set of weights, and there is often more than one set of weights that will encode a particular function. In much of the remainder of this book, we investigate various methods of determining weights. For the moment, however, let's look at a couple of examples.

Some Simple Examples   For very simple cases, we might be able to arrive at weights by a trial-and-error procedure. Let's consider constructing a single-unit system that computes the AND function of two binary inputs (see Figure 1.10).

The unit in Figure 1.10 has two weights and a threshold output function, as in Eq. (1.7). We can rewrite the threshold condition in the following way: The network will have an output of one if

$$\sum_{i=1}^{n} w_i x_i - \theta > 0 \qquad (1.9)$$

and otherwise, the output will be zero. n refers to the number of inputs.

If we replace the inequality in Eq. (1.9) with an equality, the equation becomes the equation of a line in the $x_1 x_2$ plane. If we position that line properly, we can determine the weights that will allow the network to solve the AND problem. Look at the following plot:

```
Show[{Graphics[{PointSize[0.03],{Point[{0,0}],Point[{0,1}],
Point[{1,0}],Point[{1,1}]}}],Graphics[Line[{{0,1.2},
        {2.4,0}}],Axes->Automatic]}];
```

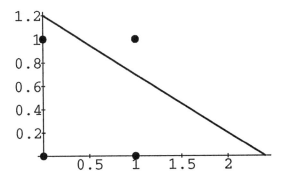

The line is the plot of the equation: $x_2 = -0.5x_1 + 1.2$. Let $\theta = 1.2$, $w_1 = 0.5$, and $w_2 = 1.0$. Rewrite the equation in the form of Eq. (1.9): $0.5x_1 + 1.0x_2 = 1.2$. If $x_1 = x_2 = 1$, the left side of the equation is equal to 1.5, which is greater than 1.2; thus giving the correct output. For all other cases, we get an answer less that 1.2, giving zero as the result. So, by an astute placement of a line, we have determined a set of weights that solves the AND problem. There are an infinite number of other lines that also yield weights that solve this problem.

The line in the preceding problem is an example of a **decision surface** (even though it is a line, we refer to it as a surface for the sake of generality). Notice how the line breaks up the space into two regions, one where the points in the region, when used as inputs, would satisfy the threshold condition, and one where the points in the region would not satisfy the threshold condition.

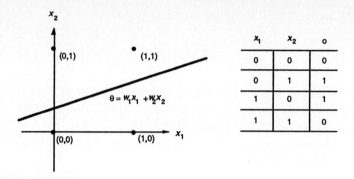

Figure 1.11 This figure shows the four input points for the XOR problem, a line representing a decision surface, and the XOR truth table. Note that there is no way to position the line so that it separates the points (0,0) and (1,1) from the points (0,1) and (1,0).

The device in Figure 1.10 is often refered to as a **perceptron**. Perceptrons were an early development in neural networks, dating from the late 1950s. They were invented by a psychologist named Frank Rosenblatt, who actually referred to collections of the above devices, rather than the individual unit, as perceptrons. Rosenblatt favored random connectivity among layers of these devices in his models of perception and vision. Unfortunately, the individual unit has a serious flaw that limits its use. Because of this flaw, early optimism in the perceptron soon gave way to extreme pessimism, and the field of neural-networks languished for many years.

We can explain the limitation of the perceptron with the following simple example. Consider once again a single unit, as in Figure 1.10. This time, however, we wish to solve the XOR problem. Figure 1.11 shows the truth table and the space of input points for this problem.

There is no orientation of the decision surface (line) that will correctly separate the points having an output of zero from the points having an output of one. The linear decision surface is a characteristic of the perceptron unit. We say that the perceptron unit can only separate categories, or classes, if they are naturally **linearly separable**. This characteristic is considered by many to be a serious weakness, since many real problems, of which the XOR is a very simple example, do not have classes that are linearly separable.

Although this problem appears formidable, there are actually one or two easy ways of overcoming it. One way is to construct a third input to

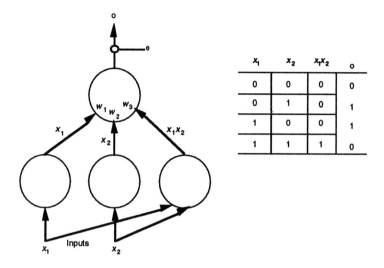

x_1	x_2	$x_1 x_2$	o
0	0	0	0
0	1	0	1
1	0	0	1
1	1	1	0

Figure 1.12 This figure shows a three-input unit where the third input is the product of the first two. The truth table still computes the XOR of the first two inputs; the network uses the third input to help distinguish between the two classes.

the network using the other two inputs. For example, we could multiply the two inputs together and use the result as a third input. Such a system appears in Figure 1.12.

Let's plot the set of points made up by the three-dimensional points from the truth table in Figure 1.12.

```
xor3d=Show[Graphics3D[{ PointSize[0.02],{Point[{0,0,0}],
    Point[{0,1,0}],Point[{1,0,0}],Point[{1,1,1}]}},
    ViewPoint->{8.474, -2.607, 1.547}]];
```

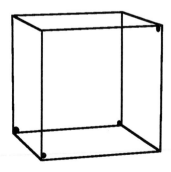

Notice how the point (1,1,1) is elevated above the $x_1 x_2$ plane. We can now separate the two classes of input points by constructing a plane to divide the space into the two proper regions.

```
Show[{%,Graphics3D[{GrayLevel[0.3],Polygon[{{0.7,0,0},
    {0,0.7,0},{1,1,0.8}}]}]}];
```

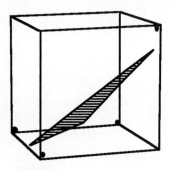

As with the AND example, there are an infinite number of decision surfaces that will solve correctly this modified XOR problem. Increasing the dimension of the input space forms the basis for a particular type of network architecture, called the functional-link network, that we will study in Chapter 3.

We can construct a second solution to the XOR problem by using a network of the type shown in Figure 1.13. Notice in this case that we have constructed a hidden layer of units between the input and output units. It is this hidden layer that facilitates a solution. Each hidden-layer unit produces a decision surface, as shown in the figure. The first hidden-layer unit (the one on the left) will produce an output of one if either or both inputs are one. The hidden-layer unit on the right will produce an output of one only if both inputs are one.

The output unit will produce a one only if the output of the first hidden unit is one AND the output of the second hidden unit is zero; in other words, if only one, but not both, of the inputs are one.

To verify the correct operation of this network, let's calculate the output value for each of the possible input vectors. Although the calculation is simple enough to perform by hand (or in your head), we shall write *Mathematica* code (Listing 1.2) for practice. To keep the routine simple, we shall perform the calculation for one input vector at a time. Here is the result for one input vector:

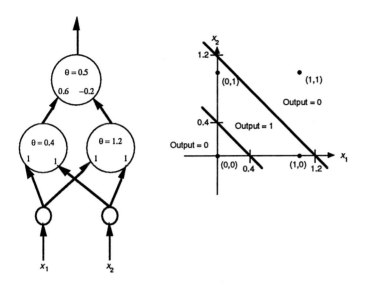

Figure 1.13 The figure on the left shows a network made up of three layers: an input layer, a hidden layer comprising two units, and a single-unit output layer. All units are threshold units with the value of θ as the threshold in each case. The two hidden-layer units construct the two decision surfaces shown in the graph on the right. The output unit performs the logical function: (hidden unit 1) AND (NOT (hidden unit 2)).

```
Net inputs to hidden layer = {2, 2}
Outputs of hidden layer = {1, 1}
Input vector= {1, 1} Output= 0
```

By changing the value of the **input** vector, you can verify that the network computes the XOR function correctly.

This example also serves to establish some notational conventions that we shall use throughout the text. The input vector will always be **inputs**, and the output vector will always be **outputs**. Other quantities will generally have compound names, such as **hidWt**, **outNetin**, etc. In each case, the first part of the name will refer to the layer, as in **hid** for hidden layer, and **out** for output layer. The second part of the name will refer to the particular quantity, as in **Netin** for net input value, and **Threshold** for threshold value. Moreover, the second part of any name will be capitalized for readability. If a third part of any name is necessary, the conventions will be the same as for the second part. I will abbreviate some names when I feel there will be no uncertainty in the intended

```
inputs = {1,1} (* input vector, change for each input *)
hidWt = { {1,1},{1,1} }    (* hidden layer weight matrix *)
outWt = { 0.6,-0.2}        (* output layer weight matrix *)
hidThreshold = {0.4,1.2}   (* thresholds on hidden units *)
outThreshold = 0.5         (* thresholds on output units *)
hidNetin = hidWt . inputs  (* net inputs to hidden layer *)
Print["Net inputs to hidden layer = ",hidNetin]
      (* good idea to print intermediate values for debug *)
hidOut = Module[{i},
   Table[If[hidNetin[[i]] > hidThreshold[[i]],1,0],
            {i,Length[hidNetin]}] ]        (* apply threshold *)
Print["Outputs of hidden layer = " ,hidOut]
outNetin = hidOut . outWt (* net input of output unit *)
outputs = If[outNetin > outThreshold,1,0] (* apply threshold *)
Print["Input vector= ",inputs," Output= ",outputs ]
```

Listing 1.2

meaning.

Let's turn our attention now to another type of learning that has its basis in an early theory of how brains actually learn. The theory was first described by a psychologist, Donald Hebb, and the learning method bears his name: Hebbian learning.

Hebbian Learning   First we must digress briefly to discuss a few facts concerning neurobiology. In the introduction to this section, we mentioned the concept of synapses, and the fact that electrical impulses are transferred from one neuron to another across these junctions. The two connecting neurons do not actually come into physical contact at the synapse; instead, there is a region between the cells called the **synaptic cleft**. When an electrical impulse, traveling down the axon of a neuron, reaches the area of the **presynaptic membrane**, it causes the cell to release certain chemicals into the synaptic cleft. We refer collectively to these chemicals as **neurotransmitters**. These neurotransmitters diffuse across the synaptic cleft and bond with receptor sites on the **postsynaptic membrane** of the receiving cell. These chemicals cause changes in the permeability of the postsynaptic membrane to certain ionic species resulting ultimately in changes in the electrical polarization of the fluid

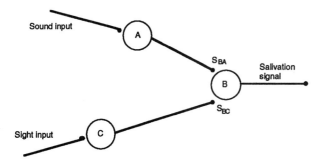

Figure 1.14 In this figure, which represents a schematic of the classical conditioning process, each lettered circle corresponds to a neuron cell body. The long lines from the cell bodies are the axons that terminate at the synaptic junctions. S_{BA} and S_{BC} correspond to the two synaptic junctions. Although we have represented this process in terms of a few simple neurons, we intend this schematic to convey the concept of classical conditioning, not its actual implementation in real nerve tissue.

in the receiving neuron. If the change in polarization is sufficient, the receiving neuron may itself become excited and send electrical impulses down its axon toward other neurons.

The type and strength of the effect that the **presynaptic cell** has on the **postsynaptic cell** depends on the identity and amount of neurotransmitter released and absorbed at the synapse. Hebb theorized that learning consisted of the modification of the strength of the effect that one cell had on the other. In particular, he felt that if a presynaptic cell and a postsynaptic cell were simultaneously on — that is, they were both transmitting pulses down their respective axons — then the strength of the synaptic connection between the two cells would be increased. Hebb put it this way in his 1949 book *The Organization of Behavior*:

> When an axon of cell A is near enough to excite a cell B and repeatedly or persistently takes part in firing it, some growth process or metabolic change takes place in one or both such that A's efficiency as one of the cells firing B is increased.

This theory can be used directly to explain the behavior known as **classical conditioning**, or **Pavlovian conditioning**. Refer to Figure 1.14.

Suppose that the sight of food is sufficient to excite cell C, which in turn, excites cell B and causes salivation. Suppose also, that in the absence of the sight of food, sound input from a ringing bell is insufficient to excite cell B, as we might expect. Now let's apply simultaneous sight and sound stimulation and analyze the result in accordance with Hebb's theory.

The strength of the synapse, S_{BC} is such that sight alone excites cell B; but notice that cell A is also being excited due to the sound input. Thus, cells A and B are on simultaneously, and, according to Hebb, the strength of the synapse S_{BA} will increase. If we repeat this experiment often enough, the strength of S_{BA} may increase to the point where the excitation from cell A is sufficient *by itself* to excite cell B and cause salivation, even in the absence of excitation from cell C.

There is an additional convention embedded in this example that I should explain. Notice that the synaptic strengths have symbols such as S_{BC}. In all cases the subscript has a "to-from" connotation. In other words, S_{BC} is the strength of the connection *to* cell *B from* cell *C*. Another example is w_{ij}, which refers to the weight on the connection *to* the *i*th unit *from* the *j*th unit.

Using this notation, we can describe the mathematical formulation of Hebbian learning. If x_i and x_j are the outputs of the *i*th and *j*th units respectively, then we can express Hebbian learning with the differential equation

$$\dot{w}_{ij} = -aw_{ij} + \eta x_i x_j \qquad (1.10)$$

where η is a proportionality constant, usually less than one, and a is also a constant less than one.

There is actually more in Eq. (1.10) than Hebbian learning as expressed in the quotation cited above. Consider, for example, what happens when either or both of the units have an output of zero. In that case, the weight will decrease (we assume that η, x_i, and x_j are all nonnegative quantities). This situation would correspond to *forgetting* rather than learning. Moreover, the appearance of the $-aw_{ij}$ term limits the magnitude of the resulting weight. Let's use *Mathematica* to solve Eq. (1.10) for the weight as a function of time.

```
DSolve[{wij'[t] == -a wij[t] + eta xi xj, wij[0]==0}, wij[t],t]


                         a t
             -1. eta + 1. E     eta
{{wij[t] -> 0. + ----------------------}}
                         a t
                     E      a
```

Plot the result assuming typical values for the various parameters. The
value asymptotically approaches the value η/n; in this case, 1.6.

```
wij = wij[t] /. First[%]
eta = 0.8
a = 0.5
xi = xj = 1.0
Plot[wij,{t,0,10}];
```

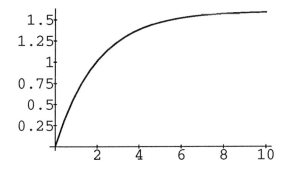

Many variations of the basic Hebbian learning law exist, and we shall
encounter a few of them in other places in this book. Moreover, we have
not yet addressed the issue of how a network, made up of multiple units,
learns to perform a particular function. This topic will consume most of
the remainder of this book.

Summary

In this chapter, we began our study of neural networks using *Mathematica*
by considering the rationale behind the neural-network approach to data
processing. We looked at the fundamentals of processing for individual
units including the net input and output calculations. We also introduced
the concept of learning and decision surfaces in neural networks. Along
the way, we introduced many of the *Mathematica* functions and methods
that we will use in the remaining chapters of this book. Both the neural
network and the *Mathematica* concepts covered in this chapter will serve
as the basis for the material in the chapters that follow.

Chapter 2

Training by Error Minimization

In the previous chapter, we discussed the fact that we train neural networks to perform their task, rather than programming them. In this chapter and the next, we shall explore a very powerful learning method that has its roots in a search technique called **hill climbing**.

Suppose you are standing on a hillside on a day that is so foggy, you can see only a few feet in front of your face. You want to get to the highest peak as quickly as possible, but you have no reference points, map, or compass to assist you on your journey. How do you proceed?

One logical way to proceed would be to look around and determine the direction of travel that has the steepest, upward slope and to begin walking in that direction. As you walk, you change your direction so that, at any given time, you are walking in the direction with the steepest upward slope. Eventually you arrive at a location from which all directions of travel lead downward. You then conclude that you have reached your goal of the top of the hill. Without instrumentation (and assuming the fog does not lift) you cannot be absolutely sure that you are at the highest peak, or instead, at some intermediate peak. You could mark your passage at this location and begin an exhaustive search of the surrounding landscape to determine if there are any other peaks that are higher, or you could satisfy yourself that this peak is good enough.

The method of training that we shall examine in this chapter is based on a technique similar to hill-climbing, but in the opposite sense; that is, we will seek the lowest valley rather than the highest peak. In this chapter we look at the training of a system comprising a single unit. In Chapter 3 we extend this method to cover the case of multiple units, and multiple layers of interconnected units.

2.1 Adaline and the Adaptive Linear Combiner

The Adaline comprises two major parts, as illustrated in Figure 2.1: an **adaptive linear combiner** (ALC), a unit almost identical in structure to the general processing element described in Chapter 1, and a bipolar output function, which determines its output based on the sign of the net-input value of the ALC. **Adaline** is an acronym for ADAptive LINear Element, or ADAptive LInear NEuron, depending on how you feel about calling these units neurons.

Notice the addition of a connection with weight, w_0, which we refer to as the **bias** term. This term is a weight on a connection that has its

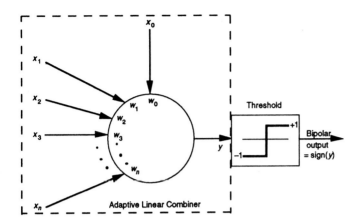

Figure 2.1 The complete Adaline consists of the adaptive linear combiner, in the dashed box, and a bipolar output function. The adaptive linear combiner resembles the general processing element described in Chapter 1.

input value always equal to one. The inclusion of such a term is largely a matter of experience.

The net input to the ALC is calculated as usual as the sum of the products of the inputs and the weights. In the case of the ALC, the output function is the identity function, so the output is the same as the net input. If the output is y, then

$$y = w_0 + \sum_{i=1}^{n} w_i x_i$$

where the w_i are the weights and the x_i are the inputs. If we make the identification $x_0 = 1$, then we can write

$$y = \sum_{i=0}^{n} w_i x_i$$

or in terms of the vector dot product

$$y = \mathbf{w} \cdot \mathbf{x} \qquad (2.1)$$

The final output of the Adaline is

$$o = \text{Sign}(y)$$

where the value of the Sign function is +1, 0, or −1, depending on whether the value of y is positive, zero, or negative. *Mathematica* contains a built-in function **Sign[]** that performs the appropriate calculation. For example:

Sign[2]

1

Sign[-2]

-1

In the remainder of this chapter, we shall be concerned only with the ALC portion of the Adaline. It is possible to connect many Adalines together to form a layered neural network. We refer to such a structure as a **Madaline** (Many ADALINEs), but we do not consider that network in this book.

2.2 The LMS Learning Rule

Suppose we have an ALC with four inputs and a bias term. Furthermore, suppose that we desire that the output of the ALC be the value 2.0, when the input vector is $\{1, 0.4, 1.2, 0.5, 1.1\}$ where the first value is the input to the bias term. We can represent the weight vector as $\{w_0, w_1, w_2, w_3, w_4\}$. There is an infinite number of weight vectors that will solve this particular problem. To find one, simply select values for four of the weights at random and compute the fifth weight. Let's do an example to illustrate the use of the **Solve** function.

```
o = 2.0                    (* desired output value *)
x = {1, 0.4, 1.2, 0.5, 1.1}   (* input vector *)
w = Append[Table[Random[],{4}],w5]
                    (* weights, with one unknown *)
Solve[o==w.x,w5]
```

```
{{w5 -> 0.496487}}
```

The weight vector is

```
w = w /. %
```

{{0.342886, 0.491887, 0.35746, 0.970542, 0.496487}}

Verify the calculation:

w.x

{2.}

Suppose we have a set of input vectors, $\{x_1, x_2, ..., x_L\}$, each having its own, perhaps unique, *correct* or *desired* output value, $d_k, k = 1, L$. The problem of finding a single weight vector that can successfully associate each input vector with its desired output value is no longer simple. In this section we develop a method called the **least-mean-square** (LMS) learning rule, or the **delta rule**, which is one method of finding the desired weight vector. We refer to this process of finding the weight vector as *training* the ALC. Moreover, we call the process a **supervised learning** technique, in the sense that there is some external teacher that knows what the correct response should be for each given input vector. The learning rule can be embedded in the device itself, which can then *self-adapt* as inputs and desired outputs are presented to it. Small adjustments are made to the weight values as each input–output combination is processed until the ALC gives correct outputs. In a sense, this procedure is a true training procedure, because we do not calculate the value of the weight vector explicitly.

2.2.1 Weight Vector Calculations

Before we develop the LMS rule, we can gain some insight into the procedure by looking at a method with which we can calculate the weight vector. To begin, let's restate the problem: Given examples (also called **exemplars**), $(x_1, d_1), (x_2, d_2), \ldots , (x_L, d_L)$, of some processing function that associates (or *maps*) input vectors, x_k, with output values, d_k, what is the *best* weight vector, w_{min}, for an ALC that performs this mapping? We shall assume $L > n + 1$, where n is the number of inputs and there is one additional weight for the bias term. This assumption means that we cannot find the weight vector by solving a system of simultaneous equations because such a system is overdetermined.

The answer to the question posed in the previous paragraph depends on how we define the word *best* within the context of the problem. Once we find this best weight vector, we would like the application of each input vector to result in the precise, corresponding output value. Since it may not be possible to find a set of weights that allows this mapping to be performed without error, we would like at least to minimize the error. Thus, we choose to look for a set of weights that minimizes the mean-squared error over the entire set of input vectors. If the actual output value for the kth input vector is y_k, then we define the error as

$$\varepsilon_k = d_k - y_k \qquad (2.2)$$

and the mean-squared error is

$$\xi = \langle \varepsilon_k^2 \rangle = \frac{1}{L} \sum_{k=1}^{L} \varepsilon_k^2 \qquad (2.3)$$

where the angled brackets indicate the mean, or expectation, value.

Substituting Eqs. (2.1) and (2.2) into Eq. (2.3) shows that the mean-squared error is an explicit function of the weight values:

$$\xi = \langle d_k - \mathbf{w} \cdot \mathbf{x}_k \rangle^2 \qquad (2.4)$$

Expanding this equation we find

$$\xi = \langle d_k^2 \rangle + \mathbf{w}^t \langle \mathbf{x}_k \mathbf{x}_k^t \rangle \mathbf{w} - 2 \langle d_k \mathbf{x}_k^t \rangle \mathbf{w} \qquad (2.5)$$

The fact that ξ is a function of the weights means that we should be able to find weights that minimize ξ. To visualize our approach, let's plot the function, $\xi(\mathbf{w})$, for the case of an ALC with only two inputs and no bias term. Using the following definitions

$$d = \langle d_k^2 \rangle, \quad \mathbf{R} = \langle \mathbf{x}_k \mathbf{x}_k^t \rangle \text{ and } \mathbf{p} = \langle d_k \mathbf{x}_k^t \rangle$$

and without specifying the actual input vectors, we can construct the graph.

```
ClearAll[R,p,w1,w2,wt,d];
wt = {w1,w2}
R = {{3,1},{1,4}};
p = {4,5};
d = 10;
wtPlot=Plot3D[d+wt.R.wt-2 p.wt,{w1,-50,50},
      {w2,-50,50}];
```

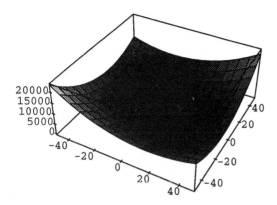

To view the graph from a slightly different perspective, use Show.

Show[%, ViewPoint->{8.578, -2.639, 0.671}];

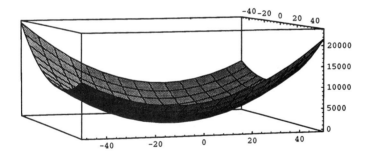

Although it may not be apparent to you from these graphs, the surface is a paraboloid. The function has a single minimum point. The weights corresponding to that minimum point are the best weights for this example. You may find it more instructive to look at a contour plot of the function.

ContourPlot[d+wt.R.wt-2 p.wt,{w1,-10,10},
        {w2,-10,10}];

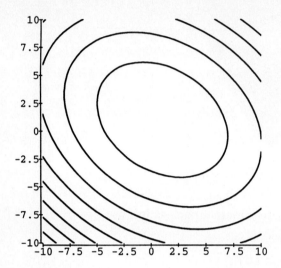

We can find the minimum point by taking the derivative of Eq. (2.5). The result is the weight vector that gives the minimum error:

$$\mathbf{w}_{min} = \mathbf{R}^{-1} \cdot \mathbf{p} \qquad (2.6)$$

For our example:

```
minWt = Inverse[R].p
```

```
{1, 1}
```

and the minimum error is

```
minError = d+minWt.R.minWt-2 p.minWt
```

```
1
```

2.2.2 Gradient Descent on the Error Surface

Given the knowledge of **R**, also called the **input correlation matrix**, and **p**, we saw how it was possible to calculate the weight vector directly. In many problems of practical interest, we do not know the values of **R** and **p**. In these cases we must find an alternate method for discovering the minimum point on the **error surface**.

Consider the situation shown in Figure 2.2. To initiate training, we assign arbitrary values to the weights, which establishes the error, ξ,

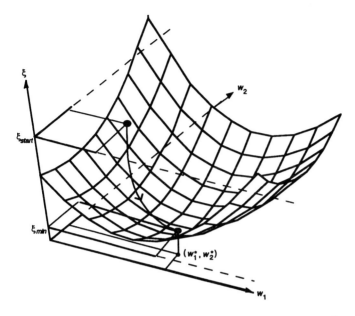

Figure 2.2 This figure illustrates gradient descent down an error surface toward the minimum weight value.

at a certain value. As we apply each training pattern to the network, we can adjust the weight vector slightly in the direction of the greatest downward slope. This procedure is exactly opposite to the hill-climbing procedure described at the beginning of this chapter.

To perform this gradient descent, we must know the equation of the surface, in which case we could calculate the weight vector directly. The point of this discussion is to help you to understand the principles of gradient descent, so that the idea will not be foreign when, in the next section, we discuss how to approximate the process in the absence of complete knowledge of the error surface.

2.2.3 The Delta Rule

Suppose we cannot specify the **R** matrix or **p** vector in advance, or suppose that the number of input vectors is so large as to make the calculations excessively time consuming. There may also be a case in which the distribution function of the input vectors changes as a function of time.

We can still take advantage of the gradient descent method by employing a local approximation to the error surface which is valid for a particular input vector.

First, apply a particular input patter, say the kth, and note the output, y_k. Then determine the error ε_k. Instead of applying other patterns and accumulating the squared error, we use this error value directly. As an approximation to the mean-squared error in Eq. (2.3), we can use the local value of the squared error for a particular pattern. That is:

$$\xi = \langle \varepsilon_k^2 \rangle \approx \varepsilon_k^2 = \xi_k \qquad (2.7)$$

Since ξ_k is a function of the weights we can compute the gradient:

$$\xi_k \approx \left(d_k - \sum_{i=1}^{n} w_i(x_i)_k \right)^2$$

$$\frac{\partial \xi_k}{\partial w_i} = -2 \left(d_k - \sum_{i=1}^{n} w_i(x_i)_k \right) (x_i)_k = -2\varepsilon_k(x_i)_k$$

We then adjust the weight value, in this case w_i, by a small amount in the direction opposite to the gradient. In other words, we update the weight value according to the following prescription:

$$w_i(t+1) = w_i(t) + \eta\varepsilon(x_i)_k \qquad (2.8)$$

or in vector form:

$$\mathbf{w}(t+1) = \mathbf{w}(t) + \eta\varepsilon(\mathbf{x})_k \qquad (2.9)$$

where η is called the **learning rate parameter** and usually has a value much less than one.

Equations (2.8) and (2.9) are expressions of a learning law called the LMS rule, or delta rule. By repeated application of this rule using all of the input vectors, the point on the error surface moves down the slope toward the minimum point, though it does not necessarily follow the exact gradient of the surface. As the weight vector moves toward the minimum point, the error values will decrease. You must keep iterating until the errors have been reduced to an acceptable value, the definition of *acceptable* being determined by the requirements of the application.

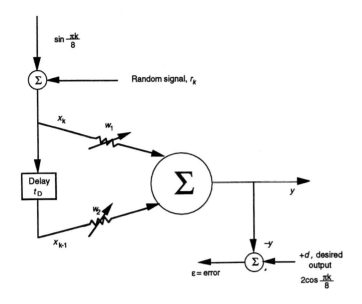

Figure 2.3 This diagram shows the ALC in the transversal filter configuration. In this case, there are two inputs. At each iteration the first input is shifted down to become the second input. The kth input is the sine function shown. The desired output value is twice the cosine of the argument of the kth input. We have also added a random noise factor to the inputs. We show the weights as variable resistors to indicate that they will change as training proceeds.

2.2.4 A Delta-Rule Example

Let's consider how to apply this learning rule by trying a specific example. We shall use an example from the text *Adaptive Signal Processing*, by Bernard Widrow and Samuel D. Stearns[1]. The ALC is a two-input unit arranged in a configuration known as a **transversal filter**. In this configuration, one input is simply a time-delayed copy of the other input. Figure 2.3 shows the ALC for this case.

At the kth timestep, the input value is given by

$$x_k = \sin\left(\frac{\pi k}{8}\right)$$

---

[1] Widrow, Bernard and Samuel D. Stearns. *Adaptive Signal Processing.*, Prentice Hall: Englewood Cliffs, NJ, 1985.

and the desired output value is

$$d_k = 2\cos\left(\frac{\pi k}{8}\right)$$

To each input value we shall add a random noise factor with a random signal power, $\phi = 0.01$, where

$$\phi = \langle r_k^2 \rangle$$

We can look at the input function by creating a table of points and then plotting those points.

```
Table[{k,Sin[Pi k/8.] //N},{k,0,24}]
```

{{0, 0.}, {1, 0.382683}, {2, 0.707107}, {3, 0.92388}, {4, 1.},

$\qquad\qquad\qquad\qquad\qquad\qquad\qquad\qquad -19$

{5, 0.92388}, {6, 0.707107}, {7, 0.382683}, {8, 3.79471 10 },

{9, -0.382683}, {10, -0.707107}, {11, -0.92388}, {12, -1.},

{13, -0.92388}, {14, -0.707107}, {15, -0.382683},

$\qquad\qquad\qquad -19$

{16, -7.58942 10 }, {17, 0.382683}, {18, 0.707107}, {19, 0.92388},

{20, 1.}, {21, 0.92388}, {22, 0.707107}, {23, 0.382683},

$\qquad\qquad -18$

{24, 1.35525 10 }}

```
ListPlot[%];
```

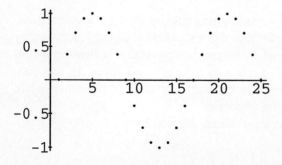

Adding a random value to the function disturbs the plot somewhat. Here is a rendering of the function with the random value, plotted with the points joined with lines.

```
inPlot = ListPlot[Table[{k,Sin[Pi k/8.]+Random[Real,
    {0, 0.175}] //N},{k,0,24}], PlotJoined->True];
```

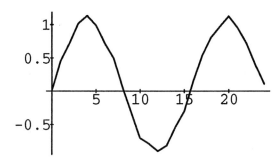

The desired output looks like this:

```
ClearAll[k]
outputs = Table[{k,2 Cos[Pi k/8]//N},{k,0,24}]
```

```
{{0, 2.}, {1, 1.84776}, {2, 1.41421}, {3, 0.765367}, {4, 0.},
  {5, -0.765367}, {6, -1.41421}, {7, -1.84776}, {8, -2.},
  {9, -1.84776}, {10, -1.41421}, {11, -0.765367}, {12, 0.},
  {13, 0.765367}, {14, 1.41421}, {15, 1.84776}, {16, 2.},
  {17, 1.84776}, {18, 1.41421}, {19, 0.765367}, {20, 0.},
  {21, -0.765367}, {22, -1.41421}, {23, -1.84776}, {24, -2.}}
```

```
outPlot = ListPlot[outputs, PlotJoined->True];
```

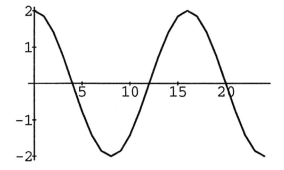

Shown together, the inputs and outputs look like this:

```
Show[{inPlot,outPlot}];
```

```
SeedRandom[4729]
wts = Table[Random[],{2}]    (* initialize weights *)
inputs = {0,Random[Real,{0, 0.175}]}(* initialize input vector *)
eta = 0.2                    (* learning rate parameter *)
k=1
errorList=Table[
    inputs[[1]] = N[Sin[Pi k/8]]+Random[Real,{0, 0.175}];
    outDesired = N[2 Cos[Pi k/8]]; (* desired output *)
    outputs = wts.inputs;    (* actual output *)
    outError = outDesired-outputs; (* error *)
    wts += eta outError inputs; (* update weights *)
    inputs[[2]]=inputs[[1]]; (* shift input values *)
    k++;                     (* increment counter *)
    outError,{250}
        ]                            (* end of Table *)
Print["Final weight vector = ",wts]
ListPlot[errorList,PlotJoined->True] (* plot the errors *)
```

Listing 2.1

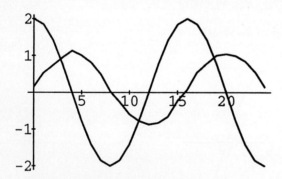

Listing 2.1 shows the *Mathematica* code for the ALC. The output giving the final weight vector and plot of the errors is as follows:

```
Final weight vector = {3.81539, -4.34484}
```

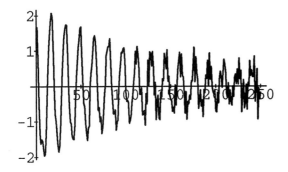

Note that by setting the input vector equal to {0,Random} initially, all that we need do to prepare the first valid input vector is replace inputs[[1]] with Sin[Pi/8], which is accomplished the first time through the loop. After the weight updates, the value in inputs[[1]] is shifted forward to inputs[[2]], and inputs[[1]] is recalculated at the beginning of the loop.

The actual optimum weight vector for this problem is 3.784, -4.178. You can see from the plot of the error values, that initially, the errors appear quite sinusoidal in character. As the ALC learns, the error is reduced to its random component.

We can make a slight modification to our code, as shown in Listing 2.2, and look at how the weight vector moves as a function of iteration step. The output from the code in Listing 2.2 is as follows:

```
Final weight vector = {3.81539, -4.34484}
```

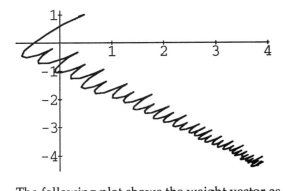

The following plot shows the weight vector as it converges on the known optimum weight value, depicted as a large dot. If we continued iterating the weight values, they would bounce around the optimum point. We could get closer by decreasing the learning rate parameter, at the cost

```
SeedRandom[4729]
wts = Table[Random[],{2}]    (* initialize weights *)
inputs = {0,Random[Real,{0, 0.175}]}(* initialize input vector *)
eta = 0.2                     (* learning rate parameter *)
k=1
wtList=Table[
   inputs[[1]] = N[Sin[Pi k/8]]+Random[Real,{0, 0.175}];
   outDesired = N[2 Cos[Pi k/8]]; (* desired output *)
   outputs = wts.inputs;    (* actual output *)
   outError = outDesired-outputs; (* error *)
   wts += eta outError inputs; (* update weights *)
   inputs[[2]]=inputs[[1]]; (* shift input values *)
   k++;                     (* increment counter *)
   wts,{250}                (* add wts value to table *)
   ]                        (* end of Table *)
Print["Final weight vector = ",wts]
ListPlot[wtList,PlotJoined->True]; (* plot the errors *)
```

Listing 2.2

of more iterations. For our purposes here, the current parameters are sufficient to illustrate the concepts involved with this type of training.

```
Show[{wtPlot,Graphics[{PointSize[0.03],
     Point[{3.784,-4.178}]}]}];
```

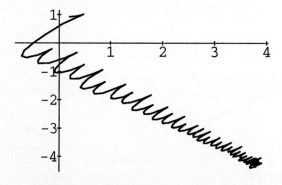

Widrow and Stearns have calculated the exact equation for the error surface for this example:

```
ClearAll[xi,wt1,wt2];
xi[wt1_,wt2_] := 0.51 (wt1^2+wt2^2) +
        wt1 wt2 Cos[N[Pi/8]] + 2 wt2 Sin[N[Pi/8]] + 2
```

(Be careful where you break an expression for a function definition. If you break the above expression before one of the + signs, *Mathematica* will think the function definition ends there.)

The error surface looks like this:

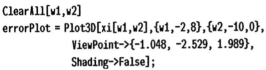

```
ClearAll[w1,w2]
errorPlot = Plot3D[xi[w1,w2],{w1,-2,8},{w2,-10,0},
            ViewPoint->{-1.048, -2.529, 1.989},
            Shading->False];
```

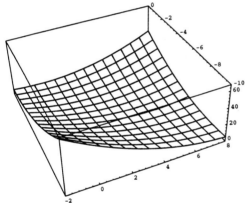

We can superimpose the contour plot with the plot of the movement of the weight vector as the ALC learns. The crosshair indicates the position of the actual optimum weight value.

```
ContourPlot[xi[w1,w2],{w1,-2,8},{w2,-10,0},
 ContourLevels->20, Epilog->{Line[wtList],
    Line[{{2,-4.178},{6,-4.178}}],
    Line[{{3.784,-3},{3.784,-5}}]}];
```

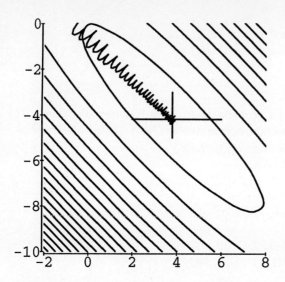

If you wish to experiment with different parameters, I suggest you construct a function based on the code. The example in Listing 2.3 allows you
to set the learning-rate parameter and the number of iterations through
arguments passed in the function call. The number of iterations defaults
to 250. Some examples of the use of the **alcTest** function follow:

alcTest[0.1,10]

```
Starting weights = {0.232585, 0.222531}
Learning rate = 0.1
Number of iterations = 10
Final weight vector = {0.0926947, -0.330191}
```

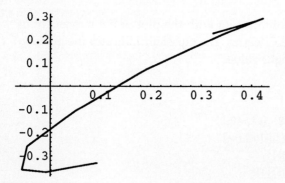

```
alcTest[learnRate_,numIters_:250] :=
Module[{eta=learnRate,wts,k,inputs,wtList,outDesired,outputs,outError},
  wts = Table[Random[],{2}];    (* initialize weights *)
  Print["Starting weights = ",wts];
  Print["Learning rate = ",eta];
  Print["Number of iterations = ",numIters];
  inputs = {0,Random[Real,{0, 0.175}]};(* initialize input vector *)
  k=1;
  wtList=Table[
    inputs[[1]] = N[Sin[Pi k/8]]+Random[Real,{0, 0.175}];
    outDesired = N[2 Cos[Pi k/8]]; (* desired output *)
    outputs = wts.inputs;    (* actual output *)
    outError = outDesired-outputs; (* error *)
    wts += eta outError inputs; (* update weights *)
    inputs[[2]]=inputs[[1]]; (* shift input values *)
    k++;    wts,{numIters}];                 (* end of Table *)
  Print["Final weight vector = ",wts];
  wtPlot=ListPlot[wtList,PlotJoined->True] (* plot the weights *)
]       (* end of Module *)
```

Listing 2.3

```
alcTest[0.1,200]
```

```
Starting weights = {0.232585, 0.222531}
Learning rate = 0.1
Number of iterations = 200
Final weight vector = {2.38218, -2.9718}
```

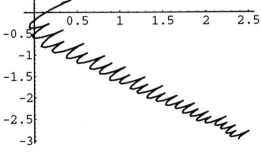

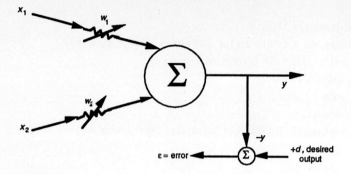

Figure 2.4 This diagram shows the ALC in its standard configuration. For the XOR example, there are two inputs.

```
alcTest[0.3]

Starting weights = {0.232585, 0.222531}
Learning rate = 0.3
Number of iterations = 250
Final weight vector = {4.22935, -4.81559}
```

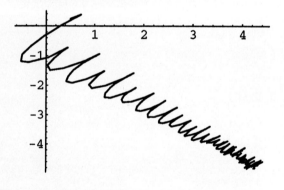

2.2.5 The XOR Problem and the ALC

As a second example, let's attempt to solve the XOR problem using a two-input ALC. (See Section 1.2.5 for a discussion of this problem.) We shall configure the ALC in its standard form, rather than as a transversal filter, as Figure 2.4 illustrates.

To run this example we shall construct a single function: alcXor appearing in Listing 2.4. We will need to define a list called the ioPairs

```
alcXor[learnRate_,numInputs_,ioPairs_,numIters_:250] :=
  Module[{wts,eta=learnRate,errorList,inputs,outDesired,ourError,outputs},
    SeedRandom[6460];        (* seed random number gen.*)
    wts = Table[Random[],{numInputs}];   (* initialize weights *)
    errorList=Table[     (* select ioPair at random *)
       {inputs,outDesired} = ioPairs[[Random[Integer,{1,4}]]];
       outputs = wts.inputs;   (* actual output *)
       outError = First[outDesired-outputs]; (* error *)
       wts += eta outError inputs;
       outError,{numIters}];    (* end of Table *)
    ListPlot[errorList,PlotJoined->True];
    Return[wts];
    ]; (* end of Module *)
```

Listing 2.4

list, or ioPairs vector, outside of the function. This list should contain the inputs and desired output values for the problem. The function, alcXor, takes the learning rate and the ioPairs vector as an argument, as well as the number of inputs and the number of iterations, which once again defaults to 250. The function returns the weight matrix for use later. For two inputs, the ioPairs vector is

ioPairsXor2 = {{{0,0},{0}},{{0,1},{1}},{{1,0},{1}},{{1,1},{0}}};

Let's execute the function with this ioPairs vector. The output will be a plot of the error value as a function of iteration.

wtsXor = alcXor[0.2,2,ioPairsXor2];

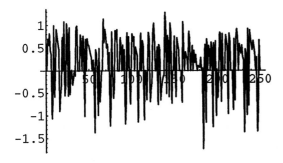

As you might expect, the error value shows no tendency to decrease. You can convince yourself further by trying more iterations, or varying the parameters, but the results will be the same.

Notice a couple of things about the code. We have introduced a new convention with the symbol ioPairs, and variation of that name used to identify specific examples. The format for the ioPairs table is:

ioPairs={{{input vector 1},{output vector 1}}, . . . }

In other words, ioPairs is a list of pairs of lists. Each pair of lists comprises a list of input values (the input vector) and a corresponding list of desired output values (the output vector). We shall use this convention throughout the text.

Let's add a third input to the ALC as we suggested in Section 1.2.5. The modification to the code is easy. All we need do is add the third input value to the ioPairs table, and initialize three weights instead of two.

```
ioPairsXor3 =
    {{{0,0,0},{0}},{{0,1,0},{1}},{{1,0,0},{1}},
    {{1,1,1},{0}}};
```

Once again, let's execute the function; this time with the new ioPairs vector.

```
wtsXor = alcXor[0.2,3,ioPairsXor3];
```

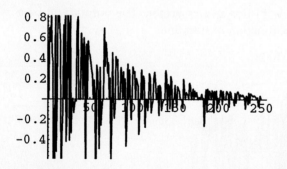

Notice in this case that the error decreases as the iteration proceeds. To see how close we are to an acceptable solution, we can write a simple function — testXor in Listing 2.5 — to run through the ioPairs and determine the error of the ALC for each input. Executing this function shows

```
ClearAll[testXor]
testXor[ioPairs_,weights_] :=
    Module[{errors,inputs,outDesired,outputs,wts,mse},
        inputs = Map[First,ioPairs]; (* extract inputs *)
        outDesired = Map[Last,ioPairs];  (* extract desired outputs *)
        outputs = inputs . weights; (* calculate actual outputs *)
        errors = outDesired-outputs;
        mse=
          Flatten[errors] . Flatten[errors]/Length[ioPairs];
        Print["Inputs = ",inputs];
        Print["Outputs = ",outputs];
        Print["Errors = ",errors];
        Print["Mean squared error = ",mse]
        ]
```

Listing 2.5

the explicit results, rather than just the errors.

```
testXor[ioPairsXor3,wtsXor]

Inputs = {{0, 0, 0}, {0, 1, 0}, {1, 0, 0}, {1, 1, 1}}
Outputs = {0, 0.956687, 0.972699, 0.0177852}
Errors = {{0}, {0.0433128}, {0.0273013}, {-0.0177852}}
Mean squared error = 0.000734417
```

In the examples that we have done so far, we have performed weight updates for a certain number of iterations. At the beginning of the section, we derived the delta rule based on a minimization of the mean-squared error; or rather its approximation, ε_k^2. Let's modify the code from the previous example to include a test of the mean-squared error, and a conditional termination based on its value.

We shall also write a function that calculates the mean squared error. The ALC code will call this function every four iterations. Even though we choose the input vector randomly, after a few iterations, the ALC should be learning all four patterns about equally. The code for the mean-squared error calculation appears in Listing 2.6. The code for the complete simulation appears in Listing 2.7. Finally, we execute the code, using 0.01 as the error tolerance value. The function returns the list of final weight values, which appear following the error plot.

```
calcMse[ioPairs_,wtVec_] :=
   Module[{errors,inputs,outDesired,outputs},
      inputs = Map[First,ioPairs]; (* extract inputs *)
      outDesired = Map[Last,ioPairs]; (* extract desired outputs *)
      outputs = inputs . wtVec; (* calculate actual outputs *)
      errors = Flatten[outDesired-outputs];
      Return[errors.errors/Length[ioPairs]]
      ]
```

Listing 2.6

```
wtsXor = alcXorMin[0.2,3,ioPairsXor3,0.01]
```

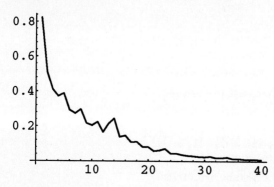

{0.843864, 0.920131, −1.68958}

The value of the coordinate on the abscissa of the resulting graph is the number of cycles rather than the number of iterations. We define a **cycle** to be equal to the number of exemplars; in this case four. Even though we pick inputs at random rather than choosing the four exemplars in sequence, we still consider a cycle to be four iterations. You could modify the code to present the four exemplars in sequence: Typically, you would use nested loops. As long as you have enough cycles so that all exemplars are presented approximately the same number of times, random selection is adequate.

   Once again, we can test the network performance:

```
testXor[ioPairsXor3,wtsXor]
```

```
Inputs = {{0, 0, 0}, {0, 1, 0}, {1, 0, 0}, {1, 1, 1}}
```

```
alcXorMin[learnRate_,numInputs_,ioPairs_,maxError_] :=
  Module[{wts,eta=learnRate,errorList,inputs,outDesired,
          meanSqError,done,k,ourError,outputs,errorPlot},
    wts = Table[Random[],{numInputs}];    (* initialize weights *)
    meanSqError = 0.0;
    errorList={};
    For[k=1;done=False,!done,k++,    (* until done *)
                      (* select ioPair at random *)
      {inputs,outDesired} = ioPairs[[Random[Integer,{1,4}]]];
      outputs = wts.inputs;    (* actual output *)
      outError = First[outDesired-outputs]; (* error *)
      wts += eta outError inputs; (* update weights *)
      If[Mod[k,4]==0,meanSqError=calcMse[ioPairs,wts];
          AppendTo[errorList, meanSqError];    ];
      If[k>4 && meanSqError<maxError,done=True,Continue];    (* test for done *)
        ];                      (* end of For *)
    errorPlot=ListPlot[errorList,PlotJoined->True];
    Return[wts];
    ] (* end of Module *)
```

Listing 2.7

```
Outputs = {0, 0.920131, 0.843864, 0.0744141}
Errors = {{0}, {0.079869}, {0.156136}, {-0.0744141}}
Mean squared error = 0.00907371
```

Before moving on, let's look at one item in the ALC simulation code. Notice that we did not use the Table function this time; rather, we used the For loop, as you might in a normal computer program. The reason for this switch is that we no longer know in advance how big the final array will be. When you know this value in advance, the Table construction is a better choice.

2.3 Error Minimization in Multilayer Networks

Before we take up the study of the backpropagation network in the next chapter, I wish to motivate that topic by posing a question: How would we do a gradient-descent search for optimum weight values in a neural

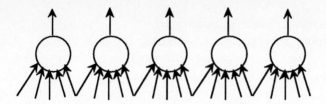

Figure 2.5 This figure shows a single layer of ALCs. Each ALC receives the identical input vector, but responds with a different output value.

network with multiple units and multiple layers?

The question of multiple units is not, in and of itself, so difficult to deal with. Suppose we had the situation as depicted in Figure 2.5.

In this situation, we presume that each of the five ALCs receives the same input vector and is supposed to produce some output value, different for each of the five units. Instead of having a single, desired-output value, we have a desired-output vector having, in this case, five components. Since we know the desired-output value for each of the ALCs, we can apply the delta rule individually for each ALC, and adjust the weights accordingly.

Consider, however, the network shown in Figure 2.6. Presumably the same logic that applied above still applies to the layer of units called the output layer: We still know what the desired outputs are — even though the inputs now come from the hidden layer — and can use the delta rule directly to update weights on the output-layer units.

The problem arises when we try to determine weight updates on the hidden-layer units. We do not know what the outputs of these units should be for any given input vector.

We can resolve this problem by realizing that the actual output values of the output-layer units *do* depend on the hidden-layer weights, because these weights form part of the calculation of the hidden-layer outputs, which subsequently are used in the calculation of the output-layer outputs. Therefore, it is possible to determine the local gradient of the error surface with respect to the hidden-layer weights and to use this value to update these weights.

We shall not carry through with such a derivation in this chapter because this type of layered architecture turns out to be not very interesting when made up only of ALCs. A more useful network results when we use units with a nonlinear output function, such as the complete Adaline.

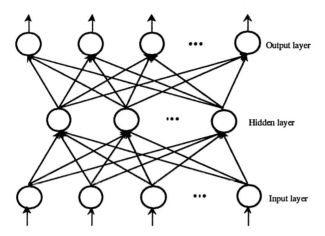

Figure 2.6 This figure shows a general, feed-forward neural network.

Unfortunately, the threshold output function is nondifferentiable because of the discontinuity, and therefore, we cannot derive an equivalent of the delta rule in this case. Other training paradigms are possible for a network of Adalines, but we shall not consider them further in this text.

There are other nonlinear output functions that are differentiable and do yield interesting network architectures. We shall look at such a network in the next chapter.

Summary

In this section, we used the single-unit adaptive linear combiner to develop a powerful learning method called the least-mean-square method. This method forms the basis of the multi-unit, multi-layer learning algorithm called backpropagation, which we shall introduce in the next chapter. We also saw that we can view the learning process geometrically as finding the minimum point on a surface that represents the error plotted as a function of the weight values. In the case of the ALC, the error surface is always a concave-upward hyperparaboloid. In multi-unit, multi-layer networks, we can still think of the learning process as finding the minimum value on a surface, but the topology of that surface is not usually as simple as the one for the ALC.

Chapter 3

Backpropagation and Its Variants

In the previous chapter we used a learning paradigm, known as the delta rule, to calculate an approximation to the optimum weight vector that would allow an ALC to correctly map input vectors to output values in accordance with certain examples used during the training process. In the last section of Chapter 2, we described how we could extend the delta rule to cover the case of multiple ALCs on a single layer. Extending the rule to multiple-layer networks requires that we add a nonlinear output function to the units, and this fact complicates the situation. Moreover, since we have no foreknowledge of the *correct* output values for units on any layer other than the output layer, we have to resort to other methods to determine the weight updates.

In this chapter we shall study a method for calculating weight updates that is commonly known as the method of **backpropagation of errors**, or more simply, **backpropagation**. By using this method, we can train a multilayered network to perform a great many processing functions. Because it is so powerful, the **backpropagation network** (BPN) has become an industry standard.

First we describe the architecture and develop the training algorithm. As a part of that development, we shall see that the BPN is quite expensive computationally, especially during the training process. Many people have attempted, therefore, to modify the basic backpropagation algorithm to speed training. We examine a few of these methods, not only for their relative value for neural-network applications, but also as examples of the ease with which we can use *Mathematica* to experiment with variation on a theme. Finally, we shall describe a backpropagation-like network called the **functional link network** which, in some cases, can eliminate the need for a hidden layer (as with the XOR problem discussed in Chapters 1 and 2).

3.1 The Generalized Delta Rule

In this section we extend the delta rule to multi-layered networks. Before we perform the derivation of the **generalized delta rule** (GDR) let's review the architecture of multi-layered neural networks and point out the features particular to the BPN.

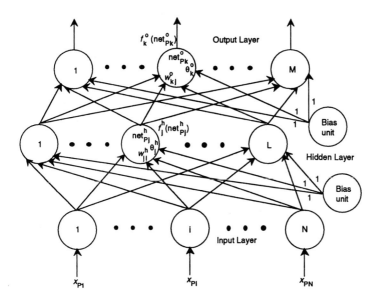

Figure 3.1 This diagram shows a typical structure for a BPN. Although there is only one hidden layer in this figure, you can have more than one. The superscripts on the various quantities identify the layer. The p subscript refers to the p th input pattern.

3.1.1 BPN Architecture

The standard BPN architecture appears in Figure 3.1. The **bias units** shown in that figure are optional. Bias units always have an output of one and they are connected to all units on their respective layer. The weights on the connections from bias units are called **bias terms** or **bias weights.**

Units on all layers calculate their net-input values in accordance with the standard sum-of-products calculation described in Chapter 1. For the hidden-layer units:

$$\text{net}_{pj}^h = \sum_{i=1}^{N} w_{ji}^h x_{pi} + \theta_j^h \tag{3.1}$$

and for the output-layer units

$$\text{net}_{pk}^o = \sum_{j=1}^{L} w_{kj}^o i_{pj} + \theta_k^o \tag{3.2}$$

where i_{pj} is the input from the jth hidden-layer unit to the output layer units for the pth input pattern, and the θs are the bias values. N and L refer to the number of units on the input and hidden layers respectively.

Unlike the ALC discussed in Chapter 2, the output function of these units is not necessarily the simple identity function, although it can be in the case of the output units. Most often, the output function will be the sigmoid function described in Chapter 1. Then the outputs of the units are

$$i_{pj} = f_j^h(\text{net}_{pj}^h) = \frac{1}{1 + e^{-\text{net}_{pj}^h}} \tag{3.3}$$

for units on the hidden layer, and

$$o_{pk} = f_k^o(\text{net}_{pk}^o) = \frac{1}{1 + e^{-\text{net}_{pk}^o}} \tag{3.4}$$

for units on the output layer.

We can use the identity function on the output-layer unit, in which case we have

$$o_{pk} = \text{net}_{pk}^o$$

If we were to use the identity function on the hidden-layer units, then the network would not be able to perform many of the complex input-output mappings that it could otherwise.

When we propagate data through the network from inputs to outputs, we can streamline the calculation by putting all of the weight values for a single layer into a **weight matrix**. Each row of the matrix represents the weights on a single unit on the layer. There would then be L rows, where L is the number of units on the layer. If there are N inputs, there would be N or $N+1$ columns, the latter figure including a place for the bias weight.

Let's look at a sample calculation for a single layer with four units, each having five inputs. To calculate the net inputs for all of the units on a layer, we can multiply the weight matrix by the input vector. First, define a five-element input vector with random components.

```
inputs = Table[Random[],{5}]
```

```
{0.775091, 0.324416, 0.724447, 0.596067, 0.662368}
```

Since there are five inputs, the weight matrix should have five columns (assuming no bias term). If there are four units on the layer, one possible (but highly unlikely) weight matrix may appear as follows:

```
wts = { {1,0,0,0,0},{0,1,0,0,0},{0,0,1,0,0},{0,0,0,1,0} };
```

Or in matrix form:

```
MatrixForm[%]
```

```
1 0 0 0 0
0 1 0 0 0
0 0 1 0 0
0 0 0 1 0
```

The net inputs are

```
netIn = wts.inputs
```

{0.775091, 0.324416, 0.724447, 0.596067}

We shall once again require the sigmoid function.

```
sigmoid[x_] := 1/(1+E^(-x))
```

The output values are

```
outputs = sigmoid[netIn]
```

{0.684621, 0.5804, 0.673586, 0.644756}

Notice that we can supply the sigmoid function with a list of values as an argument, rather than just a single value. *Mathematica* automatically applies the function to each element in the list. Now that we have described the basic feed-forward propagation in the BPN, let's move on to a derivation of the GDR.

3.1.2 Derivation of the GDR

As we did with the ALC, let's begin by stating the problem in slightly more formal terms. Suppose we have a set of P vector-pairs (exemplars), $(x_1, y_1), (x_2, y_2), \ldots , (x_P, y_P)$, that are examples of a functional mapping

$$\mathbf{y} = \Phi(\mathbf{x}), \ \mathbf{x} \in \mathrm{R}^N, \ \mathbf{y} \in \mathrm{R}^M$$

where $\mathbf{x}$ and $\mathbf{y}$ are N- and M-dimensional real vectors respectively. We wish to train a neural network (i.e., find a set of weights) to learn an approximation to that functional mapping. To develop the training algorithm we use the same approach that we used for the ALC in Chapter 2: gradient descent down an error surface.

The error that we choose to minimize by our training algorithm is

$$E_p = \frac{1}{2}\sum_{k=1}^{M} \delta_{pk}^2 \qquad (3.5)$$

where

$$\delta_{pk} = (y_{pk} - o_{pk}) \qquad (3.6)$$

The subscript, p, refers to the pth exemplar, o_{pk} is the output of the kth output-layer unit for the pth exemplar, and there are M output-layer units.

Equation (3.5) represents a local approximation to the global error surface

$$E = \sum_{p=1}^{P} E_p$$

Using the local approximation simplifies the calculation here, as it did in Chapter 2.

Substituting Eq. (3.6) into Eq. (3.5), and using Eq. (3.4), we find

$$E_p = \frac{1}{2}\sum_{k=1}^{M}(y_{pk} - f_k^o(\mathrm{net}_{pk}^o))^2$$

The gradient of E_p with respect to the output-layer weights is

$$\frac{\partial E_p}{\partial w_{kj}^o} = -(y_{pk} - o_{pk})\frac{\partial f_k^o(\mathrm{net}_{pk}^o)}{\partial(\mathrm{net}_{pk}^o)}\frac{\partial(\mathrm{net}_{pk}^o)}{\partial w_{kj}^o}$$

For now we shall write the partial derivative of the output function as

$$\frac{\partial f_k^o(\mathrm{net}_{pk}^o)}{\partial(\mathrm{net}_{pk}^o)} = f_k^{o\prime}(\mathrm{net}_{pk}^o)$$

Using Eq. (3.4) we can show that

$$\frac{\partial(\text{net}_{pk}^o)}{\partial w_{kj}^o} = i_{pj}$$

Finally, we can write the gradient of the error surface as

$$\frac{\partial E_p}{\partial w_{kj}^o} = -(y_{pk} - o_{pk})f_k^{o\prime}(\text{net}_{pk}^o)i_{pj} \qquad (3.7)$$

By a similar, and only slightly more complicated analysis, we can find the gradient of the error surface with respect to the hidden-layer weights:

$$\frac{\partial E_p}{\partial w_{ji}^h} = -f_j^{h\prime}(\text{net}_{pj}^h)x_{pi}\sum_{k=1}^{M}(y_{pk} - o_{pk})f_k^{o\prime}(\text{net}_{pk}^o)w_{kj}^o \qquad (3.8)$$

The reason that I left the derivatives of the output functions as "primed" functions instead of explicitly calculating the derivative, is because the value of that derivative depends on the form of the output function. The two primary cases of interest are the sigmoid and the identity function. In these two cases, the derivatives of the functions for output-layer units are

$$f_k^{o\prime}(\text{net}_{pk}^o) = o_{pk}(1 - o_{pk}) \qquad (3.9)$$

for the sigmoid, and

$$f_k^{o\prime}(\text{net}_{pk}^o) = 1 \qquad (3.10)$$

for the identity function.

As each training pattern is presented to the network, we first propagate the information forward to determine the actual network outputs. Then we calculate the error terms on the output layer, and the gradient of the error surface with respect to each of the output-layer weights. Next, we calculate the gradient of the error surface with respect to each of the weights on the hidden layer. If you look carefully at Eq. (3.8) you will notice that, for any given unit on the hidden layer, the gradient of the error surface depends on *all* of the errors on the output layer. This dependency is reasonable, since any change on a hidden-layer weight will have an effect on all of the output values of the output layer. Here is where the concept of *backpropagation* enters formally: We calculate errors on the output layer first, then bring those errors *back* to the hidden layer to calculate the surface gradients there.

Once we have calculated the gradients, then we adjust each weight value a small amount in the direction of the negative of the gradient. The proportionality constant is called the **learning-rate parameter,** just as it was for the ALC in Chapter 2. Next, we present the next input pattern and repeat the weight-update process. The process continues until we are satisfied that all output-layer errors have been reduced to an acceptable value.

Before moving on to some examples, we can simplify the notation somewhat through the use of some auxiliary variables. Define the **output-layer delta** as

$$\delta^o_{pk} = (y_{pk} - o_{pk})f^{o'}_k(\text{net}^o_{pk}) = \delta_{pk}f^{o'}_k(\text{net}^o_{pk}) \tag{3.11}$$

and the **hidden-layer delta** as

$$\delta^h_{pj} = f^{h'}_j(\text{net}^h_{pj})\sum_{k=1}^{M}\delta^o_{pk}w^o_{kj} \tag{3.12}$$

Using these definitions, the weight-update equations on both layers take on a similar form:

$$w^o_{kj}(t+1) = w^o_{kj}(t) + \eta\delta^o_{pk}i_{pj} \tag{3.13}$$

on the output layer, and

$$w^h_{ji}(t+1) = w^h_{ji}(t) + \eta\delta^h_{pj}x_{pi} \tag{3.14}$$

on the hidden layer. η is the learning-rate parameter, and we have assumed that it is the same on all units on all layers. This assumption is typically a good one, and we will employ it exclusively in this book.

3.2 BPN Examples

In this section we will write the *Mathematica* code for the standard BPN and use it to look at two specific examples. Because the BPN is so intensive computationally, we shall be restricted to fairly small networks. Nevertheless, we shall be able to experiment with several network parameters to see their overall effect on the performance of the BPN.

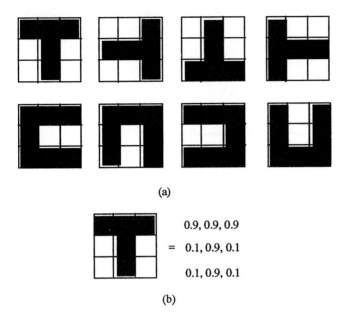

(a)

0.9, 0.9, 0.9

= 0.1, 0.9, 0.1

0.1, 0.9, 0.1

(b)

Figure 3.2 This figure shows the data-representation scheme for the T-C problem. (a) Each letter is superimposed on a 3 by 3 grid. (b) Filled grid-squares are represented by the real number 0.9, and empty ones are represented by 0.1. Each input vector consists of nine real numbers.

3.2.1 The T-C Problem

The T-C problem is a fairly simple pattern recognition problem. It will not severely tax the computational resources of our computer, and the network converges quickly to a solution, making this problem ideal as a first example. We wish to train a network to distinguish between the letters T and C, independent of the angle of rotation of these letters. We shall restrict the rotation angles to multiples of 90 degrees, resulting in four possible inputs for each letter, as shown in Figure 3.2.

The neural network for this problem appears in Figure 3.3. We shall use only a single output unit. We choose to represent the letter "T" by an output value of 0.1, and the letter "C" by an output value of 0.9. An alternate approach would be to have two output units. Then an output vector of {0.9, 0.1} could represent the letter "T," and {0.1, 0.9} could represent the letter "C."

Notice that we do not use zero and one in the input or output vectors.

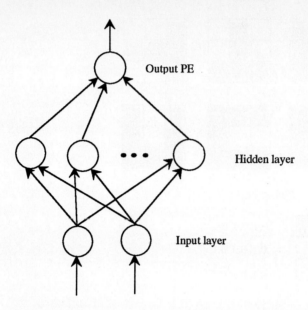

Figure 3.3 This figure shows a standard, three-layer BPN that we can use to solve the T-C problem. We only show one hidden layer in this figure, although we could add more. The number of units on the hidden layer can vary and has effects on the performance of the network. For this example, we assume all units have sigmoid outputs.

Recall that the sigmoid function asymptotically approaches the limits of zero and one for infinite arguments. If we insisted that the actual network outputs attained the values of zero and one, we could be iterating the weights forever, and they would grow to an extremely large value (positive or negative). To avoid this problem, we let 0.1 represent the binary zero state, and 0.9 the binary one state. As an alternative, we could use the identity output function (on the output layer only), then zero and one would be acceptable as desired output values. Nevertheless, we shall stick with the sigmoid function here.

Let's step through one cycle of the training algorithm of a BPN. Then we will put all of the steps together in a function that we can call with appropriate arguments. First, we define the ioPairs vectors. I will write each input vector in a matrix form, followed by the appropriate output vector. We shall also define the quantity ioPairsTC for convenience later on.

```
ioPairsTC =
ioPairs = {{{0.9,0.9,0.9,
          0.9,0.1,0.1,
          0.9,0.9,0.9},{0.1}},
         {{0.9,0.9,0.9,
          0.1,0.9,0.1,
          0.1,0.9,0.1},{0.9}},
         {{0.9,0.9,0.9,
          0.9,0.1,0.9,
          0.9,0.1,0.9},{0.1}},
         {{0.1,0.1,0.9,
          0.9,0.9,0.9,
          0.1,0.1,0.9},{0.9}},
         {{0.9,0.9,0.9,
          0.1,0.1,0.9,
          0.9,0.9,0.9},{0.1}},
         {{0.1,0.9,0.1,
          0.1,0.9,0.1,
          0.9,0.9,0.9},{0.9}},
         {{0.9,0.1,0.9,
          0.9,0.1,0.9,
          0.9,0.9,0.9},{0.1}},
         {{0.9,0.1,0.1,
          0.9,0.9,0.9,
          0.9,0.1,0.1},{0.9}} };
```

Next we shall establish the number of input units

```
inNumber = 9
```

9

the number of hidden units

```
hidNumber = 3
```

3

and the number of output-layer units

```
outNumber = 1
```

1

We need to initialize the matrices that will hold the weight values for the units on each layer. For the BPN, we use typically small, random real numbers.

```
hidWts = Table[Table[Random[Real,{-0.1,0.1}],
        {inNumber}],{hidNumber}]
```

```
{{-0.0339828, 0.00385251, -0.0174868, -0.0257278, -0.0029669,
  0.0580986, 0.0879445, 0.079082, -0.0360604},
 {-0.0250644, 0.0615698, -0.0770543, 0.0152563, -0.03313,
  -0.0941993, -0.00596479, -0.0440699, -0.05413},
 {-0.0214526, 0.0939241, 0.0398202, -0.026531, 0.0867308,
  0.0580687, -0.0883566, 0.0569707, 0.0859322}}
```

```
outWts = Table[Table[Random[Real,{-0.1,0.1}],
         {hidNumber}],{outNumber}]
```

```
{{-0.0671577, 0.0939334, -0.00400093}}
```

Finally, we pick a value for the learning-rate parameter:

```
eta = 0.5
```

```
0.5
```

We are now ready to begin forward propagation of an input vector through the network. During training, we will select input vectors at random from the ioPairs vector.

```
ioP=ioPairs[[Random[Integer,{1,Length[ioPairs]}]]]
```

```
{{0.1, 0.9, 0.1, 0.1, 0.9, 0.1, 0.9, 0.9, 0.9}, {0.9}}
```

Then extract the input and desired-output portions

```
inputs=ioP[[1]]
```

```
{0.1, 0.9, 0.1, 0.1, 0.9, 0.1, 0.9, 0.9, 0.9}
```

`outDesired=ioP[[2]]`

{0.9}

To compute the output of the hidden-layer units, take the dot product of the inputs and the hidden-layer weights and apply the sigmoid function to each element of the resulting vector.

`hidOuts = sigmoid[hidWts.inputs]`

{0.529156, 0.478449, 0.553957}

We can compute the output-layer outputs with a similar statement:

`outputs = sigmoid[outWts.hidOuts]`

{0.501797}

Forward propagation is now complete. Calculation of the deltas is next, starting with the output layer. We will employ an auxiliary variable to hold the difference between the desired and actual output.

`outErrors = outDesired-outputs`

{0.398203}

Then the output delta is

`outDelta= outErrors (outputs (1-outputs))`

{0.0995494}

The hidden-layer delta is a bit more complicated. The factor `Transpose[outWts]` `. outDelta` calculates the sum of products of the output weights and output deltas in Eq. (3.12).

`hidDelta=(hidOuts (1-hidOuts)) Transpose[outWts].outDelta`

{-0.00166569, 0.00233341, -0.0000984131}

To determine the new weights, we update according to Eqs. (3.13) and (3.14). We must take the outer product of the deltas on each layer and the inputs to the layer.

```
outWts += eta Outer[Times,outDelta,hidOuts]
```

```
{{-0.0408191, 0.117748, 0.0235721}}
```

```
hidWts += eta Outer[Times,hidDelta,inputs]
```

```
{{-0.0340661, 0.00310295, -0.0175701, -0.0258111, -0.00371646,
    0.0580153, 0.087195, 0.0783325, -0.0368099},
 {-0.0249478, 0.0626198, -0.0769376, 0.015373, -0.03208,
    -0.0940826, -0.00491475, -0.0430199, -0.0530799},
 {-0.0214575, 0.0938798, 0.0398153, -0.0265359, 0.0866865,
    0.0580638, -0.0884009, 0.0569265, 0.0858879}}
```

We are now finished with the first training vector. To continue, we would select a new input vector and repeat the above steps. To monitor our progress, we can watch the value of outErrors until it, or its square, reaches some acceptable level; or we can specify a certain number of iterations, which will be our approach here.

Notice that all of the processing for the BPN training algorithm comprises only six lines of *Mathematica* code. Let's put those lines together in a function, shown in Listing 3.1, that implements the simple BPN. Notice that we are constructing a table (vector) of error values as a part of the function. If you were programming this function in a high-level computer language, such as C, you would likely use a loop construct, such as a **for** or **while** loop in the main body of the code. Since we know exactly how many elements there will be in the final table (numIters), the Table function is more appropriate. If we were to iterate training until a certain error value was reached, we would also use a For construct, and Append the error to a preexisting array.

The function returns three important pieces of information: the new values for the hidden-layer weights, the new values for the output-layer weights, and the list of errors generated as training occurred. We shall use these values to assess how well the training went after we call the function. Let's run a short test of 10 iterations.

```
bpnStandard[inNumber_, hidNumber_, outNumber_,ioPairs_, eta_, numIters_] :=
  Module[{errors,hidWts,outWts,ioP,inputs,outDesired,hidOuts,
          outputs, outErrors,outDelta,hidDelta},
    hidWts = Table[Table[Random[Real,{-0.1,0.1}],{inNumber}],{hidNumber}];
    outWts = Table[Table[Random[Real,{-0.1,0.1}],{hidNumber}],{outNumber}];
    errors = Table[
          (* select ioPair *)
      ioP=ioPairs[[Random[Integer,{1,Length[ioPairs]}]]];
      inputs=ioP[[1]];
      outDesired=ioP[[2]];
          (* forward pass *)
      hidOuts = sigmoid[hidWts.inputs];
      outputs = sigmoid[outWts.hidOuts];
          (* determine errors and deltas *)
      outErrors = outDesired-outputs;
      outDelta= outErrors (outputs (1-outputs));
      hidDelta=(hidOuts (1-hidOuts)) Transpose[outWts].outDelta;
          (* update weights *)
      outWts += eta Outer[Times,outDelta,hidOuts];
      hidWts += eta Outer[Times,hidDelta,inputs];
          (* add squared error to Table *)
      outErrors.outErrors,{numIters}];  (* end of Table *)
    Return[{hidWts,outWts,errors}];
    ];                           (* end of Module *)
```

Listing 3.1

```
outs={0,0,0}; (* place holder for returned values *)
outs=bpnStandard[9,3,1,ioPairsTC,0.5,10];
```

Examine the results. First, the hidden-unit weight values:

```
outs[[1]]
```

```
{{0.0100008, 0.0554054, 0.0299096, 0.0309324, -0.0318445,
  0.0242747, 0.0837774, 0.0710365, 0.0341162},
 {0.0739625, -0.0485557, 0.0695227, -0.0686431, -0.0373425,
  0.0408982, 0.0913859, 0.00508364, -0.0908467},
 {0.0350314, 0.037319, -0.00618832, 0.0978313, -0.0689194,
  0.0794352, 0.0327677, 0.012315, -0.0586869}}
```

Next, the output-unit weights:

```
outs[[2]]
```

```
{{0.021414, 0.032426, -0.0746567}}
```

Finally, the list of errors:

```
outs[[3]]
```

```
{0.162749, 0.166452, 0.157103, 0.148467, 0.179714, 0.148903,
 0.179508, 0.149288, 0.178831, 0.170143}
```

We will generally be interested in a plot of the error values. We can get one as follows:

```
ListPlot[outs[[3]],PlotJoined->True];
```

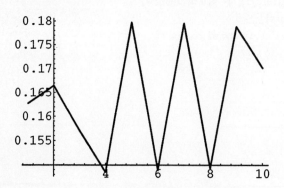

Rather than do individual calculations to assess how far along we are in the training process, we can define another function to take the weight vectors and the ioPairTC vector and calculate the individual errors for each input. That function is called bpnTest. You will find the listing for it in the appendix. The arguments of the function are the hidden-layer weights, the output-layer weights, and the ioPairs vector.

```
bpnTest[outs[[1]],outs[[2]],ioPairsTC];
```

```
Input 1 = {0.9, 0.9, 0.9, 0.9, 0.1, 0.1, 0.9, 0.9, 0.9}
 Output 1 = {0.475994} desired = {0.1} Error = {-0.375994}
Input 2 = {0.9, 0.9, 0.9, 0.1, 0.9, 0.1, 0.1, 0.9, 0.1}
 Output 2 = {0.477661} desired = {0.9} Error = {0.422339}
Input 3 = {0.9, 0.9, 0.9, 0.9, 0.1, 0.9, 0.9, 0.1, 0.9}
 Output 3 = {0.476084} desired = {0.1} Error = {-0.376084}
Input 4 = {0.1, 0.1, 0.9, 0.9, 0.9, 0.9, 0.1, 0.1, 0.9}
 Output 4 = {0.477411} desired = {0.9} Error = {0.422589}
Input 5 = {0.9, 0.9, 0.9, 0.1, 0.1, 0.9, 0.9, 0.9, 0.9}
 Output 5 = {0.476176} desired = {0.1} Error = {-0.376176}
Input 6 = {0.1, 0.9, 0.1, 0.1, 0.9, 0.1, 0.9, 0.9, 0.9}
 Output 6 = {0.476818} desired = {0.9} Error = {0.423182}
Input 7 = {0.9, 0.1, 0.9, 0.9, 0.1, 0.9, 0.9, 0.9, 0.9}
 Output 7 = {0.475935} desired = {0.1} Error = {-0.375935}
Input 8 = {0.9, 0.1, 0.1, 0.9, 0.9, 0.9, 0.9, 0.1, 0.1}
 Output 8 = {0.476766} desired = {0.9} Error = {0.423234}
```

```
Mean Squared Error = {{0.160101}}
```

All of the output values are clustered near the central region of the sigmoid function. The network has not been trained sufficiently to allow it to distinguish between the two classes of input vectors. Let's try again, this time increasing the number of iterations.

```
outs={0,0,0}  (* place holder for returned values *)
outs=bpnStandard[9,3,1,ioPairsTC,0.5,200];
```

```
ListPlot[outs[[3]],PlotJoined->True];
```

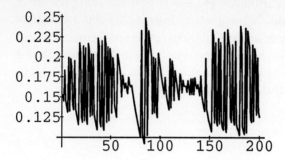

```
bpnTest[outs[[1]],outs[[2]],ioPairsTC];
```

```
Input 1 = {0.9, 0.9, 0.9, 0.9, 0.1, 0.1, 0.9, 0.9, 0.9}
 Output 1 = {0.551113} desired = {0.1} Error = {-0.451113}
Input 2 = {0.9, 0.9, 0.9, 0.1, 0.9, 0.1, 0.1, 0.9, 0.1}
 Output 2 = {0.554287} desired = {0.9} Error = {0.345713}
Input 3 = {0.9, 0.9, 0.9, 0.9, 0.1, 0.9, 0.9, 0.1, 0.9}
 Output 3 = {0.552132} desired = {0.1} Error = {-0.452132}
Input 4 = {0.1, 0.1, 0.9, 0.9, 0.9, 0.9, 0.1, 0.1, 0.9}
 Output 4 = {0.55632} desired = {0.9} Error = {0.34368}
Input 5 = {0.9, 0.9, 0.9, 0.1, 0.1, 0.9, 0.9, 0.9, 0.9}
 Output 5 = {0.552388} desired = {0.1} Error = {-0.452388}
Input 6 = {0.1, 0.9, 0.1, 0.1, 0.9, 0.1, 0.9, 0.9, 0.9}
 Output 6 = {0.553846} desired = {0.9} Error = {0.346154}
Input 7 = {0.9, 0.1, 0.9, 0.9, 0.1, 0.9, 0.9, 0.9, 0.9}
 Output 7 = {0.551687} desired = {0.1} Error = {-0.451687}
Input 8 = {0.9, 0.1, 0.1, 0.9, 0.9, 0.9, 0.9, 0.1, 0.1}
 Output 8 = {0.552483} desired = {0.9} Error = {0.347517}
```

```
Mean Squared Error = {{0.161853}}
```

We are not getting very far very fast. Let's try again.

```
outs={0,0,0}; (* place holder for returned values *)
outs=bpnStandard[9,3,1,ioPairsTC,0.5,700];
```

That calculation took quite a long time on my computer. Let's see where
we are.

```
bpnTest[outs[[1]],outs[[2]],ioPairsTC];
```

```
Input 1 = {0.9, 0.9, 0.9, 0.9, 0.1, 0.1, 0.9, 0.9, 0.9}
 Output 1 = {0.278072} desired = {0.1} Error = {-0.178072}
Input 2 = {0.9, 0.9, 0.9, 0.1, 0.9, 0.1, 0.1, 0.9, 0.1}
 Output 2 = {0.684431} desired = {0.9} Error = {0.215569}
Input 3 = {0.9, 0.9, 0.9, 0.9, 0.1, 0.9, 0.9, 0.1, 0.9}
 Output 3 = {0.286354} desired = {0.1} Error = {-0.186354}
Input 4 = {0.1, 0.1, 0.9, 0.9, 0.9, 0.9, 0.1, 0.1, 0.9}
 Output 4 = {0.677043} desired = {0.9} Error = {0.222957}
Input 5 = {0.9, 0.9, 0.9, 0.1, 0.1, 0.9, 0.9, 0.9, 0.9}
 Output 5 = {0.283591} desired = {0.1} Error = {-0.183591}
Input 6 = {0.1, 0.9, 0.1, 0.1, 0.9, 0.1, 0.9, 0.9, 0.9}
 Output 6 = {0.684752} desired = {0.9} Error = {0.215248}
Input 7 = {0.9, 0.1, 0.9, 0.9, 0.1, 0.9, 0.9, 0.9, 0.9}
 Output 7 = {0.276314} desired = {0.1} Error = {-0.176314}
Input 8 = {0.9, 0.1, 0.1, 0.9, 0.9, 0.9, 0.9, 0.1, 0.1}
 Output 8 = {0.695672} desired = {0.9} Error = {0.204328}

Mean Squared Error = 0.0394364
```

It looks like the categories are beginning to separate. We should see a decrease in the error values.

```
ListPlot[outs[[3]],PlotJoined->True];
```

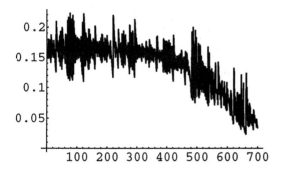

This plot is about what we might expect. If we went back and performed more iterations, we should do even better. By now, however, you should be asking if there are any ways in which we might speed up the convergence of the network. The answer, of course, is yes. The first thing we can do is try a few variations of the learning rate parameter to see if it has any effect on the convergence. In Section 3.3 we shall look at some other methods that have been proposed to speed convergence of the algorithm.

```
outs=bpnStandard[9,3,1,ioPairsTC,0.9,500];
ListPlot[outs[[3]],PlotJoined->True];
```

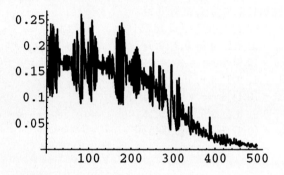

The larger value of learning rate resulted in a faster convergence. If larger is better, let's keep going.

```
outs=bpnStandard[9,3,1,ioPairsTC,1.3,500];
ListPlot[outs[[3]],PlotJoined->True];
```

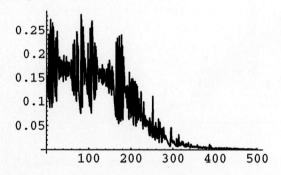

```
outs=bpnStandard[9,3,1,ioPairsTC,2.0,350];
ListPlot[outs[[3]],PlotJoined->True];
```

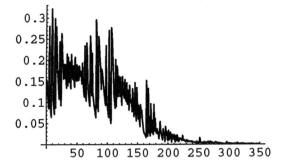

```
outs=bpnStandard[9,3,1,ioPairsTC,3.0,250];
ListPlot[outs[[3]],PlotJoined->True];
```

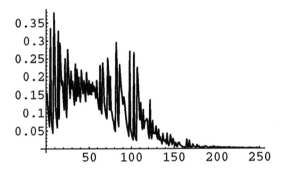

```
outs=bpnStandard[9,3,1,ioPairsTC,4.0,200];
ListPlot[outs[[3]],PlotJoined->True];
```

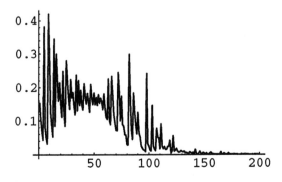

```
outs=bpnStandard[9,3,1,ioPairsTC,5.0,150];
ListPlot[outs[[3]],PlotJoined->True];
```

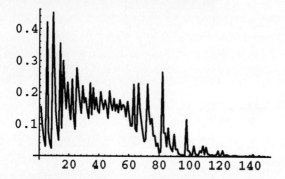

```
outs=bpnStandard[9,3,1,ioPairsTC,10,150];
ListPlot[outs[[3]],PlotJoined->True];
```

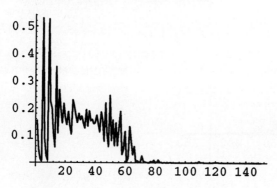

```
outs=bpnStandard[9,3,1,ioPairsTC,30,150];
ListPlot[outs[[3]],PlotJoined->True];
```

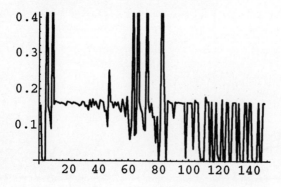

What is amazing about this example is the magnitude of the learning rate that you can use and still have a network that converges. It looks like somewhere between 10 and 30, convergence breaks down. In no way should you infer that such large learning rates are appropriate for other networks. Typically, most real networks require a very small ($\ll 1$) learning rate for convergence. Because it does take a fair amount of time for each run, and we are limited to small networks here, I suggest that you conduct parametric studies of this type using compiled code.

When you execute this network yourself, you might find that the network fails to converge with a learning rate as low as 2.5, for example. Alternatively, you may find that you can use learning rates in excess of 40. Given the combination of starting location (determined by the initial weights) and the learning rate, the network may find a local minimum in the weight space causing learning to cease before the overall error reaches a value low enough for each of the exemplars.

This phenomenon occurs sometimes when trying to solve real problems with neural networks; the network may fail to converge after a large number of training passes. If you get this result, you can try changing the weight initialization, or adjusting the learning rate. It may also be that there is not enough information in the set of exemplars to allow the network to learn properly, or you may have too few or too many units in the hidden layer. Experience is the best teacher in these cases.

3.2.2 The XOR Problem and the BPN

We have discussed aspects of the XOR problem in Chapters 1 and 2. In this section we will begin to examine how a BPN responds to the XOR problem. In comparison to the T-C problem, the XOR problem is quite hard. In fact, we will not actually see a solution to this problem until after we add a mechanism to speed convergence of the BPN, which we shall do in Section 3.3. The ioPairs array for the XOR problem appears below.

```
ioPairsXOR = { {{0.1,0.1},{0.1}}, {{0.1,0.9},{0.9}},
               {{0.9,0.1},{0.9}}, {{0.9,0.9},{0.1}} };
```

Let's begin by using the Timing function to see how long iterations take using the standard BPN model. My computer is a Macintosh IIsi with a math coprocessor, and the time required will be different depending on your computer.

```
Timing[outs=bpnStandard[2,3,1,ioPairsXOR,0.5,100];]
```

{36.15 Second, Null}

Let's see if anything has happened.

```
ListPlot[outs[[3]], PlotJoined->True];
```

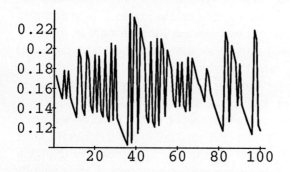

Not much has. Let's increase the learning rate significantly to see if that helps.

```
Timing[outs=bpnStandard[2,3,1,ioPairsXOR,5.0,100];]
```

{46.85 Second, Null}

```
ListPlot[outs[[3]], PlotJoined->True];
```

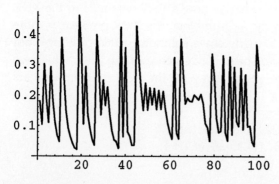

Once again there has not been any learning. Let's try more passes through the data.

```
Timing[outs=bpnStandard[2,3,1,ioPairsXOR,5.0,1500];]
```

```
{710.6 Second, Null}
```

```
ListPlot[outs[[3]], PlotJoined->True];
```

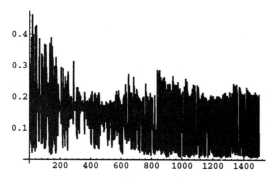

Let's look at the outputs explicitly to see what is happening.

```
bpnTest[outs[[1]],outs[[2]],ioPairsXOR];
```

```
Input 1 = {0.1, 0.1}
 Output 1 = {0.217616} desired = {0.1} Error = {-0.117616}
Input 2 = {0.1, 0.9}
 Output 2 = {0.753512} desired = {0.9} Error = {0.146488}
Input 3 = {0.9, 0.1}
 Output 3 = {0.795341} desired = {0.9} Error = {0.104659}
Input 4 = {0.9, 0.9}
 Output 4 = {0.554083} desired = {0.1} Error = {-0.454083}
```

```
Mean Squared Error = 0.0631092
```

The network seems to be learning three of the four points. Perhaps more iterations will do the trick. Based on the last results, this next calculation should take about 16 minutes on my computer.

```
outs=bpnStandard[2,3,1,ioPairsXOR,5.0,2000];
```

```
ListPlot[outs[[3]], PlotJoined->True];
```

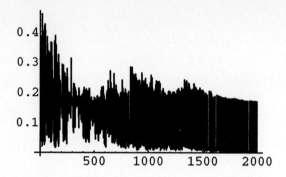

```
bpnTest[outs[[1]],outs[[2]],ioPairsXOR];
```

```
Input 1 = {0.1, 0.1}
 Output 1 = {0.137168} desired = {0.1} Error = {-0.0371683}
Input 2 = {0.1, 0.9}
 Output 2 = {0.864222} desired = {0.9} Error = {0.0357782}
Input 3 = {0.9, 0.1}
 Output 3 = {0.861855} desired = {0.9} Error = {0.0381451}
Input 4 = {0.9, 0.9}
 Output 4 = {0.51232} desired = {0.1} Error = {-0.41232}
```

```
Mean Squared Error = 0.0435311
```

Well, we are not much better off than we were before. Perhaps we have found another local minimum, where the network will never learn the fourth training vector.

One variation that we have not yet tried is in the number of hidden-layer units. In a sense, adding hidden-layer units adds "degrees of free-dom" that can help the network converge to a better solution, much like adding higher orders to the polynomial fit to a curve. You must use some restraint, however, since there is a trade-off between faster convergence in terms of the number of iterations required, and the time per iteration. Moreover, if you add too many hidden-layer units, you could end up worse off than when you started. Let's evaluate the case of doubling the number of hidden units to six.

```
outs={0,0,0};
Timing[outs=bpnStandard[2,6,1,ioPairsXOR,5.0,100];]
```

{66.2667 Second, Null}

The time required is about 50% more than the case with three hidden units. Let's see if we get as good a solution as before with only two thirds the number of iterations.

```
outs={0,0,0};
Timing[outs=bpnStandard[2,6,1,ioPairsXOR,5.0,1000];]
```

{660. Second, Null}

```
ListPlot[outs[[3]], PlotJoined->True];
```

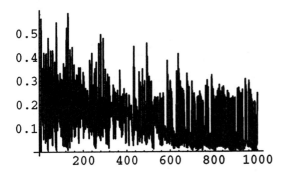

We are at about the same place as we were at the end of 1500 iterations using three hidden units. Moreover it has taken us just as much time to get to this point as it did to run 1500 iterations with three hidden units. While it may be true that learning requires fewer iterations with a larger number of hidden units, the actual amount of CPU time may, in fact, be as much, or even greater. Of course, if the network will not converge at all, adding hidden units may be the way to get it to converge. The point I am trying to make here is that the number of iterations required for convergence is not necessarily the best measure of learning speed. We shall need to keep this fact in mind when we examine other methods of increasing learning speed in Section 3.3. I should also point out that in most real-world problems where the number of inputs is large (say 10s or 100s) the number of hidden-layer units is typically *less* than the number of inputs, unlike our simple example here.

3.2.3 Adding a Bias Unit

Let's add the bias units to our BPN code. These units provide an extra degree of freedom that may help the network converge to a solution in fewer iterations. The trade-off, of course, is that there are more connections to process. The code appears in Listing 3.2.

Adding space for the bias terms in the weight matrices is no big problem; we just increase the column dimension by one. Two other modifications involve adding an additional input value of 1.0 to each input vector:

`inputs=Append[ioP[[1]],1.0]`

and forcing the last hidden output to be 1.0:

`outInputs = Append[hidOuts,1.0]`

These two changes are indicated in the code by the comment

`(* bias mod *)`

A third modification appears in the statement that updates the hidden-unit weights. Because of the way we calculate the weight deltas, the equations for the weight updates would automatically try to calculate new weights on connections from the input layer to the bias unit on the hidden layer; however, there are no such connections. Therefore, we must eliminate the last weight delta vector before updating the hidden weights. The statement:

`Drop[Outer[Times,hidDelta,inputs],-1]`

performs this task.

I have also added some optional print statements, an automatic call to the bpnTest routine, and an automatic plot of the errors. Notice that there are now four returned items: the lists of the hidden weights, output weights, output errors, and a graphics object representing the plot of the errors. Let's try the T-C problem again, since it will require less time than the XOR problem. The bpnTest function has an option that will allow it to handle the bias terms correctly. We can set that option before running the network.

```
outs={0,0,0,0};
SetOptions[bpnTest,bias->True];
Timing[outs=bpnBias[9,3,1,ioPairsTC,4.0,200];]
```

```
New hidden-layer weight matrix:
{{-0.375183, -0.235498, -0.41385, -0.31976, -0.00324652, -0.377699,
    -0.279365, -0.250795, -0.256884, -0.321761},
  {-0.917095, -0.198925, -0.708324, -0.150139, 2.98298, -0.267209,
    -0.797281, -0.137803, -0.708624, 0.637737},
  {-0.594783, -0.273314, -0.648397, -0.165679, 2.2331, -0.315633,
    -0.615488, -0.213412, -0.559986, 0.500099}}
```

```
bpnBias[inNumber_, hidNumber_, outNumber_,ioPairs_, eta_, numIters_] :=
  Module[{errors,hidWts,outWts,ioP,inputs,outDesired,hidOuts,
            outputs, outErrors,outDelta,hidDelta},
    hidWts = Table[Table[Random[Real,{-0.1,0.1}],{inNumber+1}],{hidNumber}];
    outWts = Table[Table[Random[Real,{-0.1,0.1}],{hidNumber+1}], {outNumber}];
    errorList = Table[
          (* select ioPair *)
      ioP=ioPairs[[Random[Integer,{1,Length[ioPairs]}]]];
      inputs=Append[ioP[[1]],1.0]; (* bias mod *)
      outDesired=ioP[[2]];
              (* forward pass *)
      hidOuts = sigmoid[hidWts.inputs];
      outInputs = Append[hidOuts,1.0];  (* bias mod *)
      outputs = sigmoid[outWts.outInputs];
              (* determine errors and deltas *)
      outErrors = outDesired-outputs;
      outDelta= outErrors (outputs (1-outputs));
      hidDelta=(outInputs (1-outInputs)) * Transpose[outWts].outDelta;
              (* update weights *)
      outWts += eta Outer[Times,outDelta,outInputs];
      hidWts += eta Drop[Outer[Times,hidDelta,inputs],-1];  (* bias mod *)
              (* add squared error to Table *)
      outErrors.outErrors,{numIters}];  (* end of Table *)
      Print["New hidden-layer weight matrix: "];
    Print[]; Print[hidWts];Print[];
    Print["New output-layer weight matrix: "];
    Print[]; Print[outWts];Print[];
    bpnTest[hidWts,outWts,ioPairs];   (* check how close we are *)
    errorPlot = ListPlot[errorList, PlotJoined->True];
    Return[{hidWts,outWts,errorList,errorPlot}];
      ];                              (* end of Module *)
```

Listing 3.2

```
New output-layer weight matrix:
{{0.384772, 3.2809, 2.42758, -2.38318}}
Input 1 = {0.9, 0.9, 0.9, 0.9, 0.1, 0.1, 0.9, 0.9, 0.9, 1.}
 Output 1 = {0.143134} desired = {0.1} Error = {-0.0431341}
Input 2 = {0.9, 0.9, 0.9, 0.1, 0.9, 0.1, 0.1, 0.9, 0.1, 1.}
 Output 2 = {0.876863} desired = {0.9} Error = {0.023137}
Input 3 = {0.9, 0.9, 0.9, 0.9, 0.1, 0.9, 0.9, 0.1, 0.9, 1.}
 Output 3 = {0.137324} desired = {0.1} Error = {-0.0373242}
Input 4 = {0.1, 0.1, 0.9, 0.9, 0.9, 0.9, 0.1, 0.1, 0.9, 1.}
 Output 4 = {0.883766} desired = {0.9} Error = {0.0162339}
Input 5 = {0.9, 0.9, 0.9, 0.1, 0.1, 0.9, 0.9, 0.9, 0.9, 1.}
 Output 5 = {0.136798} desired = {0.1} Error = {-0.0367985}
Input 6 = {0.1, 0.9, 0.1, 0.1, 0.9, 0.1, 0.9, 0.9, 0.9, 1.}
 Output 6 = {0.886159} desired = {0.9} Error = {0.0138414}
Input 7 = {0.9, 0.1, 0.9, 0.9, 0.1, 0.9, 0.9, 0.9, 0.9, 1.}
 Output 7 = {0.14003} desired = {0.1} Error = {-0.0400298}
Input 8 = {0.9, 0.1, 0.1, 0.9, 0.9, 0.9, 0.9, 0.1, 0.1, 1.}
 Output 8 = {0.869965} desired = {0.9} Error = {0.0300346}
Mean Squared Error = 0.00101283
```

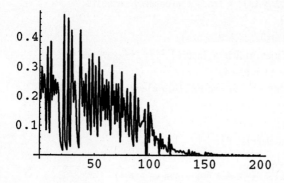

```
{152.967 Second, Null}
```

This result appears to be similar to that obtained without the bias term. Nevertheless, the bias term is often incorporated as a part of a standard BPN.

3.3 BPN Variations

If a BPN as small as that which we used for the XOR problem takes such a long time to converge, you might imagine that networks for more realistic problems might be incredibly time consuming. I recently did a problem with a BPN having only about 45,000 connections (a small network compared to some). The network took over two weeks to converge to a solution (using a 80386-class computer). Needless to say, it is difficult to justify waiting for two weeks to find out if you have a solution. If you have access to a supercomputer, the time may be reduced significantly, but the overall cost may rise. The problem is the BPN algorithm: It requires a large amount of computation for each iteration. Surely there must be a way to speed the convergence of these networks.

The quest for the BPN holy grail has taken researchers down many and varied paths. A recent conference proceedings contained upwards of fifty papers, each claiming to have found a method to speed convergence of the backpropagation algorithm. In this section we shall look at a few of those methods. The methods that we shall examine are not necessarily the best or fastest. My purpose here is not to identify the best method, but to illustrate how easily experimentation can be accommodated within the *Mathematica* environment. As a matter of fact, we have already employed some variations of what you might call the original BPN method.

For both the T-C and XOR problems, we used 0.1 and 0.9 instead of 0 and 1, for the components of both the input and output vectors. The argument that we gave was that the sigmoid function could never reach 0 or 1 and, therefore, we needed to back off from those limits. This argument is appropriate to explain why 0.1 and 0.9 are used as desired output values; it is not adequate to explain why we used them as input values instead of 0 and 1. To answer the latter question, let's look at one of the ioPairs for the T-C problem, and recall how the weight-update values are calculated on the hidden layer.

```
(* This is the "T" vector *)
```

```
{{0.9,0.9,0.9,
  0.1,0.9,0.1,
  0.1,0.9,0.1},{0.9}}
```

If we had used zeros and ones in the input vector instead of 0.1 and 0.9 the above would appear as follows:

```
{{1,1,1,
  0,1,0,
  0,1,0},{0.9}}
```

To update weights on the hidden layer, the equation is

```
hidWts += eta Outer[Times,hidDelta,inputs]
```

Each delta value for a given weight is multiplied by the corresponding input value. If that input value is zero, then there will be no change to that weight. If there is no change, there is no learning. Learning would only take place with inputs that are one. Thus, convergence should take a larger number of iterations, because some weights do not change during a given iteration. By using 0.1 and 0.9 as inputs, we ensure that weight changes will be nonzero. This simple technique is not actually a variation of the algorithm, however, so we will now turn our attention to some techniques that are.

3.3.1 Momentum

As a first example of a modification of the algorithm, we shall look at the addition of a term called **momentum** to the weight-update equations. This term will have a significant effect on the learning speed, in terms of the number of iterations required.

The idea behind momentum in a neural network is straightforward: Once you start adjusting weights in a certain direction, keep them moving generally in that direction. In more practical terms, after you adjust the weights during one training iteration, save the value of that adjustment; when calculating the adjustment for the next iteration, add a fraction of the previous change to the new one. In terms of an equation (in this case, for the hidden-layer weights):

$$w_{ji}(t+1) = w_{ji} + \eta \delta_{pj} x_{pi} + \alpha \Delta w_{ji}(t) \qquad (3.15)$$

where α is called the momentum term, typically a positive number less than one, and

$$\Delta w_{ji}(t) = w_{ji}(t) - w_{ji}(t-1)$$

The function bpnMomentum incorporates this momentum term as a parameter alpha in the function call. The following is a template of the function. A complete listing appears in the appendix.

```
bpnMomentum[inNumber,hidNumber,
  outNumber,ioPairs,eta,alpha,numIters]
```

To implement the function, we must keep track of the weight changes from one iteration to the next. To do that we introduce the following matrices into the code:

```
hidLastDelta = Table[Table[0,{inNumber}],{hidNumber}];
outLastDelta = Table[Table[0,{hidNumber}],{outNumber}];
```

We add a fraction, `alpha`, of these values to the weight changes before updating the weights:

```
outLastDelta= eta Outer[Times,outDelta,hidOuts]+
                    alpha outLastDelta;
outWts += outLastDelta;

hidLastDelta = eta Outer[Times,hidDelta,inputs]+
                    alpha hidLastDelta;
hidWts += hidLastDelta;
```

Let's try the T-C problem using this new network. We shall repeat an example that we ran in the previous section, this time including a momentum factor of 0.5.

```
outs={0,0,0,0};
Timing[outs=bpnMomentum[9,3,1,ioPairsTC,0.9,0.5,150];]
```

Mean Squared Error = 0.000846143

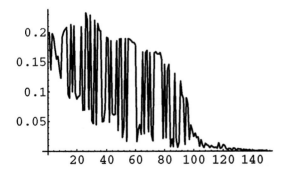

```
{102.15 Second, Null}
```

This result represents a significant improvement in convergence of the network. Let's try the network on the XOR problem to see if we obtain similar results.

```
outs={0,0,0,0};
Timing[outs=bpnMomentum[2,3,1,ioPairsXOR,2.0,0.9,1500];]
```

```
Mean Squared Error = 0.0709606
```

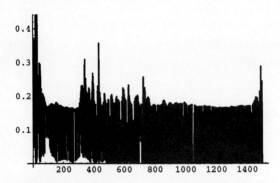

```
{786.083 Second, Null}
```

The network seems to be acting as it did before when it was learning only three of the four patterns. Perhaps we have found a local minimum and the network will never learn the fourth pattern. Alternately, more iterations may result in a complete solution.

In the spirit of experimentation, let's add another modification to the program. We can arbitrarily set a maximum acceptable error for any one pattern to some number, say 0.1. Then, we can add a conditional statement to the program so that, if the error for an input pattern is less than this acceptable value, no weight updates occur during that iteration. That way, the network is not overlearning one pattern at the expense of the others. I have included this modification in a program called bpnMomentumSmart (not that the other programs are not smart, but I am running out of names).

```
outs={0,0,0,0};
Timing[outs=bpnMomentumSmart[2,3,1,ioPairsXOR,2.0,0.9,1500];]
```

Mean Squared Error = 0.00434073

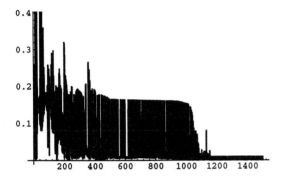

{575.25 Second, Null}

Not only did the network converge, but the time required to run 1500 iterations was significantly less in this case than it was for the unmodified program.

3.3.2 Competitive Weight Updates

In this section we shall examine a modification of the BPN that uses a competitive algorithm to update weight values. Recall that, according to Eqs. (3.13) and (3.14), weight changes are proportional to the delta terms (hidDelta and outDelta in our code); thus, we might reason that the unit with the largest value of delta should adjust its weights by the largest amount. All other units on the layer should adjust their weights in the direction opposite to that *winning* unit. In other words, after we calculate the delta values on a layer, we search for the unit with the largest delta (actually we need to look for the largest magnitude). That unit is declared the winner of the competition, and the delta value for all units on the layer becomes a function of that unit's delta.

For the hidden layer, the delta value is given by Eq. (3.12):

$$\delta_{pj}^h = f_j^{h'}(\text{net}_{pj}^h) \sum_{k=1}^{M} \delta_{pk}^o w_{kj}^o$$

Let

$$\varepsilon_{pj}^h = \begin{cases} \max_m(\delta_{pm}^h) & j = \text{ winning unit} \\ -\frac{1}{4}\max_m(\delta_{pm}^h) & \text{otherwise} \end{cases} \qquad (3.16)$$

Then Eq. (3.14) becomes

$$w_{ji}^h(t+1) = w_{ji}^h(t) + \eta \varepsilon_{pj}^h x_{pi}$$

with a similar equation for the output layer. Let's build these changes into a standard BPN program without momentum.

The algorithm proceeds as in the case of the standard algorithm until we calculate the delta values for each layer. After that calculation, we determine the epsilon values. We shall look at the code for the output layer here; the code for the hidden layer is analogous. First we search the delta values to find the one with the largest absolute value and save its position:

```
outPos = First[Flatten[Position[Abs[outDelta],Max[Abs[outDelta]]]]];
```

Since the Position function returns a list of lists, we must extract the actual number as shown, using First and Flatten. We need to remember the delta value at this position:

```
outEps = outDelta[[outPos]]
```

All outDelta values are changed to -(1/4) outEps

```
outDelta=Table[-1/4 outEps,{Length[outDelta]}]
```

except for the one at position outPos:

```
outDelta[[outPos]] = outEps
```

We can now perform the same calculation for the hidden layer and update the weights as usual. The new program is called bpnCompete, and a complete listing appears in the appendix.

Let's try the new algorithm on the T-C problem with one output. Recall from Section 3.2 that without momentum, the error was still fairly high, though it was diminishing after about 400 iterations.

```
outs={0,0,0,0};
outs = bpnCompete[9,3,1,ioPairsTC,5.0,150];
```

```
Mean Squared Error = 0.000880959
```

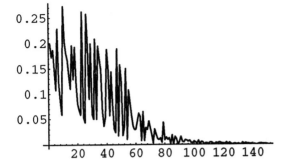

This result looks somewhat better than with the standard algorithm. You might want to experiment with this algorithm further to determine quantitatively if it is better than standard backpropagation.

There are dozens — perhaps hundreds — of other modifications that we could explore. Our intent, however, is not to examine all possibilities in an attempt to find the best one, but rather to learn how to use *Mathematica* as a tool to facilitate that exploration. With that philosophy in mind, let's move on to the discussion of a different network architecture called the functional link network.

3.4 The Functional Link Network

The XOR problem is a difficult one, and it is prototypical of problems whose classes are not linearly separable. By using hidden layers and units with nonlinear output functions, we can overcome this difficulty. The price we pay is the added computational complexity associated with the backpropagation algorithm.

In Chapter 1, we showed a way of transforming the XOR problem into one where the classes were linearly separable. In essence, we increased the dimensionality of the input space by adding a third input made up of the product of the original two inputs. This method allowed us to construct a solution with a single output unit and no hidden units. In this section we shall describe the **functional link network** (FLN) that uses the concept of **functional links** to increase the dimensionality of the input space.

3.4.1 FLN Architecture

In a typical feed-forward network, input units distribute input patterns unchanged to units on succeeding layers. In the FLN, input units pass their data through a functional link before distributing the data to other units. The purpose of the functional link is to produce multiple data elements from each individual input element by using the input elements as the arguments to certain functions, or by multiplying certain data elements together. The first method is called the **functional-expansion model**, and the second is called the **tensor model**, or **outer product model**.

The XOR example from Chapter 1 typifies the tensor model. In the tensor model, you increase the dimension of the input vector by multiplying components together using combinations of two inputs, then three, etc. You can keep the size of the resulting vector somewhat under control by eliminating redundant products and products whose components are uncorrelated over the set of input vectors.

Figure 3.4 illustrates the concept of the functional-expansion model. You can also combine the two methods into a hybrid model where functions of data elements are multiplied by functions of other data elements.

The choice and number of functions to use is problematical, as is whether to use the functional-expansion or tensor models. Experience is bound to yield insight in this area, and I do not wish to make any predictions about what might work. A major advantage of the network is that you can generally eliminate the hidden layer. Let's look at some examples in the next section.

3.4.2 FLN Examples

We shall look at an example of each type of FLN in this section. First, let's apply the tensor model to the XOR problem. Then we shall apply the functional-expansion model to a more complicated problem.

Tensor Model of the XOR Problem   Let's recall the ioPairs vectors for this problem:

```
ioPairsXOR = { { {0.1,0.1},{0.1} },
          { {0.1,0.9},{0.9} },
          { {0.9,0.1},{0.9} },
          { {0.9,0.9},{0.1} }  };
```

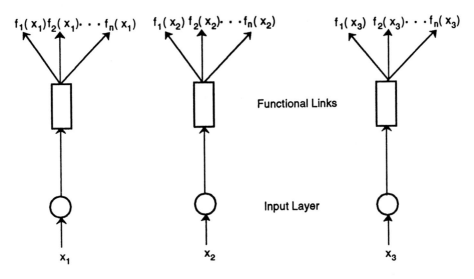

Figure 3.4 This figure illustrates the functional-expansion model for a three-input FLN. Each input passes through a functional link that generates n functions of the input value. These $3n$ values are passed to the next layer of the network. Note that each unit on the next layer would receive all $3n$ data elements from the functional links.

If we enhance the ioPairs vectors by adding to each input the product of the original two inputs, we will have the appropriate inputs to the network. Then, we need not write our code to be specific to the model or the problem: The same code can apply to either the tensor or functional-expansion model. The new ioPairs is:

```
ioPairsXORFLN = { { {0.1,0.1,0.1},{0.1} },
          { {0.1,0.9,0.1},{0.9} },
          { {0.9,0.1,0.1},{0.9} },
          { {0.9,0.9,0.9},{0.1} } };
```

Notice that $0.1 \times 0.9 = 0.1$, since this calculation represents 0×1.

Let's construct a program, called fln, to implement the network. We can construct the program itself by modifying the bpnMomentum code. Since there are no hidden units, we can eliminate all of the "hid" variables. Inputs to the output units become inputs rather than hidOuts. We shall use a linear unit as the output unit, so we do not need the sigmoid function, and the equation for outDelta will change since the derivative of the linear output function is unity. The argument list for fln is the same as that for the bpnMomentum function, with the exception that there are no hidden units. The function template is

```
fln[inNumber,outNumber,ioPairs,eta,alpha,numIters]
```

The function returns an array with four components: the new weight matrix, the list of errors generated during the iterations, the graphic object representing the plot of the errors, and the output vector generated by the call to flnTest, which is a modified version of bpnTest. See the appendix for the listings of these functions.

Let's try the fln function with only a few iterations.

```
outs={0,0,0,0};
Timing[outs=fln[3,1,ioPairsXORFLN,0.5,0.5,100];]
```

Mean Squared Error = 0.0019762

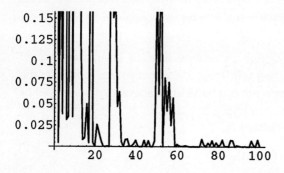

```
{22.2167 Second, Null}
```

That result is not too bad, considering the small number of passes through the data. Let's try again with a few more passes.

```
outs={0,0,0,0};
Timing[outs=fln[3,1,ioPairsXORFLN,0.5,0.5,500];]
```

Mean Squared Error = 0.0019765

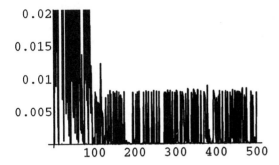

{78.5667 Second, Null}

The mean squared error for this run is not bad, although there appears to be one point that has a significantly larger error than the others. Since the output function is linear for this network, let's try using zeros and ones in the ioPairs vectors.

```
ioPairsXOR01FLN = { { {0,0,0},{0} },
          { {0,1,0},{1} },
          { {1,0,0},{1} },
          { {1,1,1},{0} } };
```

```
outs={0,0,0,0};
Timing[outs=fln[3,1,ioPairsXOR01FLN,0.5,0.5,500];]
```

Mean Squared Error = $5.18305 \; 10^{-22}$

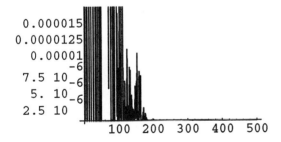

{83.2167 Second, Null}

The result of the change in desired output values is dramatic. The FLN performs quite well on the XOR problem as you can see, although it is somewhat sensitive to the learning rate parameter. You can see this fact for yourself if you experiment with larger values of **eta**.

The Functional-Expansion Model   In this section we shall teach an FLN a continuous function of one variable. That is, the input will be a single value, and the output will be some function of the input value. Moreover, we shall use only a finite number of input points to enable us to investigate how well the network learns to interpolate when we give it input values that were not used during the training procedure.

Let's choose a nontrivial, but well-behaved function. In this context, "well-behaved" means that there are no wild oscillations in the function that would require us to use an inordinate number of sample points for our training set. Here is the function, plotted between $x = 1$ and $x = 3$.

```
functionPlot=Plot[0.3x Sin[Pi x], {x,1,3}];
```

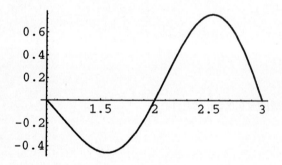

We build an **ioPairs** matrix by sampling the function at intervals of $0.1x$:

```
ioPairsFunct = Table[{{i},{0.3i Sin[Pi i]//N}}, {i,1,3,0.1}]
```

{{{1}, {0}}, {{1.1}, {-0.101976}}, {{1.2}, {-0.211603}},
  {{1.3}, {-0.315517}}, {{1.4}, {-0.399444}}, {{1.5}, {-0.45}},
  {{1.6}, {-0.456507}}, {{1.7}, {-0.412599}}, {{1.8}, {-0.317404}},

$$-20$$
  {{1.9}, {-0.17614}}, {{2.}, {6.50521 10   }}, {{2.1}, {0.194681}},
  {{2.2}, {0.387938}}, {{2.3}, {0.558222}}, {{2.4}, {0.684761}},
  {{2.5}, {0.75}}, {{2.6}, {0.741824}}, {{2.7}, {0.655304}},

$$-18$$
  {{2.8}, {0.49374}}, {{2.9}, {0.268845}}, {{3.}, {2.78098 10   }}}}

We can plot these values if we flatten the array and then partition it into pairs of coordinates.

```
functionListPlot = ListPlot[Partition[Flatten[ioPairsFunct],2]];
```

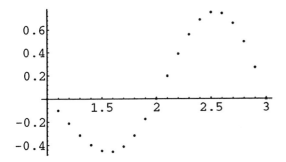

We must decide on the number and identity of the functions for the functional link. We shall use the following six functions in this example: x, $\sin(px)$, $\cos(px)$, $\sin(2px)$, $\cos(2px)$, and $\sin(4px)$. In order to simulate the functional link, we can replace the first element of each ioPairs vector with a list of these functions already evaluated. Because we will use it more than once, let's define a function that will produce the appropriate list of functions.

```
functionList[y_] := {y, Sin[Pi y]//N, Cos[Pi y]//N,
              Sin[2 Pi y]//N, Cos[2 Pi y]//N,
              Sin[4 Pi y]//N}
```

We generate the new ioPairs vectors by replacing the first element of each ioPair by the appropriate list of functions.

```
ioPairsFunctFLN = Map[ReplacePart[#,functionList[#[[1,1]]],1]&,ioPairsFunct];
```

Each ioPair input vector should now have six components, as the following example shows.

```
ioPairsFunctFLN[[1]]
```

```
{{2, 0, 1., 0, 1., 0}, {1.41421}}
```

We can now try the FLN on this data.

```
outs={0,0,0,0};
Timing[outs=fln[6,1,ioPairsFunctFLN,0.005,0.50,1050];]
```

Mean Squared Error = 0.00104127

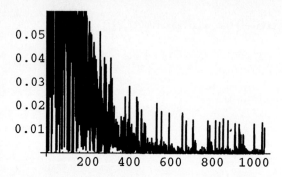

{193.183 Second, Null}

The agreement with the actual function appears to be fairly good. More-over, we have only executed 50 passes through the data set. These results are sufficient to illustrate the concepts, so I shall not perform any more executions of this network here.

By working on the data a bit, we can plot the output in order to compare it to the correct answers. First, look at the list of output values:

outs[[4]]

{{0.0118456}, {-0.13436}, {-0.255246}, {-0.347552}, {-0.406662}, {-0.432413}, {-0.429038}, {-0.39617}, {-0.32316}, {-0.197473}, {-0.0204939}, {0.186378}, {0.39137}, {0.565842}, {0.688298}, {0.741125}, {0.712402}, {0.605634}, {0.445142}, {0.266315}, {0.097578}}

We need to substitute these values into the **ioPairsFunct** array in place of the correct answers. To do this, we can use the **MapThread** function as follows:

ioPairsOut = MapThread[ReplacePart[#,#2,2]&,{ioPairsFunct,outs[[4]]}]

{{{1}, {0.0118456}}, {{1.1}, {-0.13436}}, {{1.2}, {-0.255246}}, {{1.3}, {-0.347552}}, {{1.4}, {-0.406662}}, {{1.5}, {-0.432413}}, {{1.6}, {-0.429038}}, {{1.7}, {-0.39617}}, {{1.8}, {-0.32316}}, {{1.9}, {-0.197473}}, {{2.}, {-0.0204939}}, {{2.1}, {0.186378}}, {{2.2}, {0.39137}}, {{2.3}, {0.565842}}, {{2.4}, {0.688298}}, {{2.5}, {0.741125}}, {{2.6}, {0.712402}}, {{2.7}, {0.605634}}, {{2.8}, {0.445142}}, {{2.9}, {0.266315}}, {{3.}, {0.097578}}}

Now we can flatten and partition this array and plot it.

```
outListPlot = ListPlot[Partition[Flatten[ioPairsOut],2]];
```

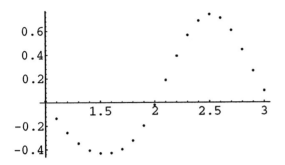

To see where we are, we can plot the output along with the original function.

```
Show[{functionPlot,outListPlot}];
```

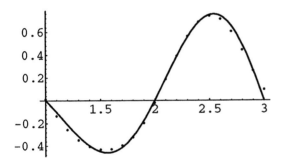

The results are not bad, and presumably could be improved with further training of the network. Let's see how well this network interpolates. We can construct a new **ioPairs** array using points in between those used for training.

```
ioPairsTest=Table[{{i},{0.3i Sin[Pi i]//N}},{i,1.1,3,0.1}]
```

{{{1.1}, {-0.101976}}, {{1.2}, {-0.211603}}, {{1.3}, {-0.315517}},
 {{1.4}, {-0.399444}}, {{1.5}, {-0.45}}, {{1.6}, {-0.456507}},
 {{1.7}, {-0.412599}}, {{1.8}, {-0.317404}}, {{1.9}, {-0.17614}},

$$-20$$

{{2.}, {6.50521 10   }}, {{2.1}, {0.194681}}, {{2.2}, {0.387938}},
{{2.3}, {0.558222}}, {{2.4}, {0.684761}}, {{2.5}, {0.75}},
{{2.6}, {0.741824}}, {{2.7}, {0.655304}}, {{2.8}, {0.49374}},

$$-18$$

{{2.9}, {0.268845}}, {{3.}, {2.78098 10   }}}}

Expand the input vectors as before.

```
ioPairsTestFLN = Map[ReplacePart[#,functionList[#[[1,1]]],1]&,ioPairsTest];
```

Test these new vectors using the weights from the previous run. The code for the function **flnTest** appears in the appendix.

```
outputValues=flnTest[outs[[1]],ioPairsTestFLN];
```

```
Output 1 = {-0.13436} desired = {-0.101976} Error = {0.0323845}
Output 2 = {-0.255246} desired = {-0.211603} Error = {0.0436432}
Output 3 = {-0.347552} desired = {-0.315517} Error = {0.0320357}
Output 4 = {-0.406662} desired = {-0.399444} Error = {0.00721808}
Output 5 = {-0.432413} desired = {-0.45} Error = {-0.0175867}
Output 6 = {-0.429038} desired = {-0.456507} Error = {-0.0274695}
Output 7 = {-0.39617} desired = {-0.412599} Error = {-0.0164282}
Output 8 = {-0.32316} desired = {-0.317404} Error = {0.00575561}
Output 9 = {-0.197473} desired = {-0.17614} Error = {0.0213337}
                                                    -20
Output 10 = {-0.0204939} desired = {6.50521 10    } Error = {0.0204939}
Output 11 = {0.186378} desired = {0.194681} Error = {0.00830251}
Output 12 = {0.39137} desired = {0.387938} Error = {-0.00343193}
Output 13 = {0.565842} desired = {0.558222} Error = {-0.00762052}
Output 14 = {0.688298} desired = {0.684761} Error = {-0.0035372}
Output 15 = {0.741125} desired = {0.75} Error = {0.00887472}
Output 16 = {0.712402} desired = {0.741824} Error = {0.0294223}
Output 17 = {0.605634} desired = {0.655304} Error = {0.04967}
Output 18 = {0.445142} desired = {0.49374} Error = {0.0485978}
Output 19 = {0.266315} desired = {0.268845} Error = {0.00253004}
                                                    -18
Output 20 = {0.097578} desired = {2.78098 10    } Error = {-0.097578}
Mean Squared Error = 0.00108632
```

These results are as good as the training set, indicating that the network can interpolate well. Can it extrapolate, however? Let's find out by constructing a new *ioPairs* array using the same function, but outside the range of the original data.

```
ioPairsTest2=Table[{{i},{0.3i Sin[Pi i]//N}},{i,3,5,0.1}]
```

{{{3}, {0}}, {{3.1}, {-0.287386}}, {{3.2}, {-0.564274}},
  {{3.3}, {-0.800927}}, {{3.4}, {-0.970078}}, {{3.5}, {-1.05}},
  {{3.6}, {-1.02714}}, {{3.7}, {-0.898009}}, {{3.8}, {-0.670075}},
  {{3.9}, {-0.36155}}, {{4.}, {-4.94396 10^{-17}}}, {{4.1}, {0.380091}},
  {{4.2}, {0.740609}}, {{4.3}, {1.04363}}, {{4.4}, {1.25539}},
  {{4.5}, {1.35}}, {{4.6}, {1.31246}}, {{4.7}, {1.14071}},

  {{4.8}, {0.846411}}, {{4.9}, {0.454255}}, {{5.}, {1.16281 10^{-17}}}}}

```
ioPairsTest2FLN = Map[ReplacePart[#,functionList[#[[1,1]]],1]&,ioPairsTest2];
```

```
outputValues2=flnTest[outs[[1]],ioPairsTest2FLN];
```

```
Output 1 = {0.097578} desired = {0} Error = {-0.097578}
Output 2 = {-0.0486277} desired = {-0.287386} Error = {-0.238758}
Output 3 = {-0.169513} desired = {-0.564274} Error = {-0.39476}
Output 4 = {-0.26182} desired = {-0.800927} Error = {-0.539107}
Output 5 = {-0.320929} desired = {-0.970078} Error = {-0.649148}
Output 6 = {-0.346681} desired = {-1.05} Error = {-0.703319}
Output 7 = {-0.343305} desired = {-1.02714} Error = {-0.683836}
Output 8 = {-0.310438} desired = {-0.898009} Error = {-0.587571}
Output 9 = {-0.237427} desired = {-0.670075} Error = {-0.432648}
Output 10 = {-0.111741} desired = {-0.36155} Error = {-0.249809}
Output 11 = {0.0652385} desired = {-4.94396 10$^{-18}$} Error = {-0.0652385}
Output 12 = {0.272111} desired = {0.380091} Error = {0.10798}
Output 13 = {0.477103} desired = {0.740609} Error = {0.263507}
Output 14 = {0.651575} desired = {1.04363} Error = {0.392057}
Output 15 = {0.77403} desired = {1.25539} Error = {0.481364}
Output 16 = {0.826858} desired = {1.35} Error = {0.523142}
Output 17 = {0.798134} desired = {1.31246} Error = {0.514324}
Output 18 = {0.691366} desired = {1.14071} Error = {0.449348}
Output 19 = {0.530874} desired = {0.846411} Error = {0.315536}
Output 20 = {0.352047} desired = {0.454255} Error = {0.102208}
```

```
                                     -17
     Output 21 = {0.18331} desired = {1.16281 10   } Error = {-0.18331}
     Mean Squared Error = 0.183144
```

As you might have guessed, these results are not so good. As a general rule, you should not expect a neural network to be able to respond properly to data that is outside of the domain used during the training process.

Summary

In this chapter we have explored a very powerful and robust learning methodology known as the generalized delta rule. This rule, which is the learning algorithm for the backpropagation network, is a multi-unit, multi-layer version of the delta rule discussed in Chapter 2. We also used the backpropagation network as a starting point for experimentation with modifications in an attempt to speed the convergence of the network to a solution for specific problems. Using *Mathematica* we can quickly make alterations in the code to accommodate our ideas. The functional link network, introduced in the final section, often allows us to find a solution to a problem without the need of a hidden layer of units. By expanding the dimension of the input space by combining inputs or mapping inputs onto a set of functions, the hidden layer may become unnecessary.

Chapter 4

Probability and Neural Networks

In the previous chapters, we have studied several types of neural networks, and in all cases the calculations that we performed were deterministic. In this chapter, we add elements of probability and stochastic processing to some neural-network models. The Hopfield network, which is the topic of Section 4.1, is a deterministic network. I introduce it here because there are analogies between the Hopfield network and physical systems having the properties of magnetic materials. In the next two sections, we shall look at some of the properties of magnetic materials and see how we can use these properties to extend the basic Hopfield model to include stochastic processes.

Next, we will examine a standard probabilistic technique for pattern classification, called Bayesian classification. We shall see that by making suitable changes in the basic feed-forward neural network architecture (such as that of the BPN) we can implement a Bayesian classifier in a neural network. The probabilistic neural network (PNN), based on this approach, is the subject of the final section in this chapter.

4.1 The Discrete Hopfield Network

Unlike the networks presented so far in this book, the Hopfield network has only a single layer of processing elements. Furthermore, the connectivity scheme has each unit connected to all other units on the layer. Figure 4.1 shows the architecture.

The Hopfield network is classified as an **associative memory**. Given pairs of vectors, such as $(x_1, y_1), (x_2, y_2)$, etc., an input of one of the x vectors should result in the output of the corresponding y vector. Moreover, a corrupted, or noisy, version of one of the input vectors should also recall the corresponding output vector. In the case of the Hopfield network, the y vectors are identical to the x vectors, making the network an **autoassociative memory**. The network stores x vectors so that later, if an incomplete, or noisy vector is used as an input, the network will find the stored vector closest in some sense to the input vector.

We use the adjective *discrete* to indicate that the output values of the Hopfield units take on discrete, rather than continuous, values. In this case, we shall restrict the outputs to the values of ± 1.

The output function is straightforward: If the net input is negative, the output value is -1; if the net input is positive, the output value is $+1$; and if the net input is zero, the output does not change. Let's call

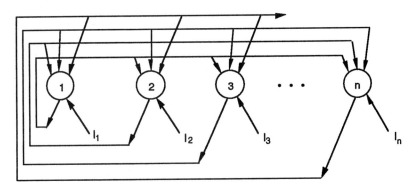

Figure 4.1 This figure shows the basic structure of the Hopfield network. Each of the n units is connected by a weighted connection to all other units. There is no feedback from a unit to itself. The I values are external inputs.

that output function psi, and define it as follows:

```
psi[inValue_,netIn_] := If[netIn>0,1,
                   If[netIn<0,-1,inValue]]
```

It will simplify things later if we also define a function that takes input vectors and net-input vectors as arguments and maps them onto the psi function. We shall call this new function phi.

```
phi[inVector_List,netInVector_List] :=
    MapThread[psi[#,#2]&,{inVector,netInVector}]
```

The net-input value to each unit can be found in the usual way by finding the scalar product of the input vector and the weight vector. What remains is to determine the appropriate weight vector for the given pairs of vectors that we wish to store in the network.

To determine the weights we can use a training method known as **Hebb's rule** (see Chapter 1). Hebb's rule was initially derived in an attempt to explain how learning takes place in real, biological systems. Simply put, it states that if two connected neurons are firing simultaneously, the strength of the connection between them will increase. A typical way to express this rule mathematically is

$$\Delta w_{ij} \propto x_i x_j$$

where x_i and x_j are the firing rates, or outputs of neurons i and j.

In a practical sense, such a simple formulation can lead to extremely large weight values, given that the units stay on long enough. Rather than try to come up with a more realistic model, we can just limit the weight value to the product of the outputs. In other words, let $w_{ij} = x_i x_j$.

If there is more than one vector in the training set, we can sum the contributions to each weight from the individual vectors. We write the equation for the entire weight matrix in the general case as

$$\mathbf{w} = \frac{1}{n} \sum_{i=1}^{L} \mathbf{x}_i \mathbf{x}_i^t \tag{4.1}$$

where L is the number of vectors in the training set, and n is the number of units in the network.

We can also associate with the Hopfield network a quantity called an **energy function**. The energy function has the form

$$E = -\frac{1}{2} \mathbf{x}^t \mathbf{w} \mathbf{x} \tag{4.2}$$

where the x vector is the current output vector of the network. This equation can also be written as

$$E = -\frac{1}{2} \sum_{i,j=1}^{n} x_i w_{ij} x_j \tag{4.3}$$

For future use, let's define the energy function using *Mathematica*.

```
energyHop[x_,w_] := -0.5 x . w . x;
```

Let's try a small Hopfield network, say one with 10 units, and three random training patterns. First the training patterns. We can use the Random function to generate binary vectors, then convert to bipolar vectors by multiplying each component by 2 and subtracting 1.

```
trainPats = 2 Table[Table[Random[Integer,{0,1}],{10}],{3}]-1
```

```
{{1, 1, 1, -1, -1, -1, -1, 1, 1, -1},
 {-1, -1, 1, -1, -1, 1, 1, -1, -1, 1},
 {-1, -1, 1, -1, 1, 1, 1, 1, 1, 1}}
```

To generate the weight matrix, we need to find the outer product of each training vector with itself, and add the contributions from each.

```
wts = Apply[Plus,Map[Outer[Times,#,#]&,trainPats]];
MatrixForm[wts]
```

3	3	-1	1	-1	-3	-3	1	1	-3
3	3	-1	1	-1	-3	-3	1	1	-3
-1	-1	3	-3	-1	1	1	1	1	1
1	1	-3	3	1	-1	-1	-1	-1	-1
-1	-1	-1	1	3	1	1	1	1	1
-3	-3	1	-1	1	3	3	-1	-1	3
-3	-3	1	-1	1	3	3	-1	-1	3
1	1	1	-1	1	-1	-1	3	3	-1
1	1	1	-1	1	-1	-1	3	3	-1
-3	-3	1	-1	1	3	3	-1	-1	3

As expected, the matrix is square and diagonal. Also notice that the diagonal elements are all equal. To be consistent with the Hopfield architecture as we described it above, we should set all of the diagonal elements to zero. It will not affect the results if we leave them as they are, however, so let's not do any more manipulations with the matrix.

Calculating the energy of the network for each of the training patterns gives the following:

```
eTrainPats = Map[energyHop[#,wts]&,trainPats]
```

```
{-60., -66., -60.}
```

These values represent minima on a hypersurface as a function of the vector that is the first argument to the energyHop function, in direct analogy to the error surfaces of the Adaline and BPN. Input vectors that are close to one of the training patterns should have an energy less negative than that of the training patterns (in this context, *close* refers to **Hamming distance**, or the number of bits that are different between the two vectors). Moreover, as the processing in the network proceeds, we might expect that the output vector will evolve toward the nearest local-minimum state. We also might expect that once the network settles into one of the local minimum, further processing will result in no changes to the output (more on this issue shortly); in other words, the network reaches a fixed point. Let's try with an initial input vector that differs by two bits, the first and the ninth, from the first training pattern:

```
input1 = {-1, 1, 1, -1, -1, -1, -1, 1, -1, -1};
```

The energy of the system with this input vector is

`energyHop[input1,wts]`

-20.

which is less negative than −60 as we expected. Before we proceed to propagate this vector through the network, we must confront an issue relating to the way in which that propagation occurs. There are two ways that we might proceed. The first is to calculate the net-input for all of the units in parallel, then calculate the new output vector and the new energy. We refer to this method as **synchronous updating**. The second method, called **asynchronous updating**, is to calculate the new output for one unit at a time, that unit generally being chosen at random, then propagating this new output value around to the other units before another unit is chosen. Although the asynchronous method is probably more indicative of the way real brains operate, we shall stick with the synchronous method here because it will make the code easier.

The calculation proceeds as follows:

`netInput1 = wts . input1`

{8, 8, 4, −4, −8, −8, −8, 4, 4, −8}

`output1 = phi[input1,netInput1]`

{1, 1, 1, −1, −1, −1, −1, 1, 1, −1}

`energyHop[output1,wts]`

−60.

Notice that the output is identical to the original training pattern, and the energy is at the corresponding local minimum. Further propagation through the network should result in no changes. Let's see if that statement is true. The new input vector is now `output1`.

`netInput12 = wts . output1`

{16, 16, 4, −4, −8, −16, −16, 12, 12, −16}

`output12 = phi[output1,netInput12]`

{1, 1, 1, -1, -1, -1, -1, 1, 1, -1}

energyHop[output12,wts]

-60.

which confirms the earlier statements.
Let's try a second example. For the next input vector, choose the
following:

input2 = {1, 1, 1, 1, 1, -1, 1, -1, 1, -1}

{1, 1, 1, 1, 1, -1, 1, -1, 1, -1}

Examine this input vector closely, and, before you continue reading, try to
guess to which of the three training patterns the network will converge.

netInput2 = wts . input2

{8, 8, -4, 4, 0, -8, -8, 4, 4, -8}

output2 = phi[input2,netInput2]

{1, 1, -1, 1, 1, -1, -1, 1, 1, -1}

energyHop[output2,wts]

-66.

Let's continue processing to see if things change.

netInput21 = wts . output2

{18, 18, -10, 10, 2, -18, -18, 10, 10, -18}

output21 = phi[output2,netInput21]

{1, 1, -1, 1, 1, -1, -1, 1, 1, -1}

energyHop[output21,wts]

-66.

```
makeHopfieldWts[trainingPats_,printWts_:True] :=
   Module[{wtVector},
   wtVector =
     Apply[Plus,Map[Outer[Times,#,#]&,trainingPats]];
   If[printWts,
       Print[];
       Print[MatrixForm[wtVector]];
       Print[];,Continue
       ]; (* end of If *)
   Return[wtVector];
   ] (* end of Module *)
```

Listing 4.1

There were no changes, so the network must be at a stable equilibrium point. This energy is equal to that of training pattern two, but the output vector is the negative, or complement, of that training pattern.

This example illustrates a peculiarity of this network (and some others that we shall discuss in Chapter 6): If you store a training vector, you also store its complement. Moreover, as you try to store an increasingly large number of training patterns, the network will experience a phenomenon known as **crosstalk**. Crosstalk manifests itself as the appearance of stable configurations that have no relationship to any of the training vectors. We call these states **spurious stable states**, and their existence limits the number of training patterns that we can store in a network of any given size. Usually, the limit is about $0.14n$, where n is the number of units in the network.

The code for the discrete Hopfield network appears below. First, you must make the appropriate weight matrix from the training set. The function makeHopfieldWts in Listing 4.1 performs this computation and returns the weight matrix.

After calculating the weight vector, we pass it and the input vector to the function discreteHopfield shown in Listing 4.2. The network will iterate until there are no further changes in the output vector.

```
discreteHopfield[wtVector_,inVector_,printAll_:True] :=
   Module[{done, energy, newEnergy, netInput,
             newInput, output},
   done = False;
   newInput = inVector;
   energy = energyHop[inVector,wtVector];
   If[printAll,
      Print[ ];Print["Input vector = ",inVector];
      Print[ ];
      Print["Energy = ",energy];
      Print[ ],Continue
      ];   (* end of If *)
   While[!done,
      netInput = wtVector . newInput;
      output = phi[newInput,netInput];
      newEnergy = energyHop[output,wtVector];
      If[printAll,
          Print[ ];Print["Output vector = ",output];
          Print[ ];
          Print["Energy = ",newEnergy];
          Print[ ],Continue
          ];   (* end of If *)
      If[energy==newEnergy,
         done=True,
         energy=newEnergy;newInput=output,
         Continue
         ];   (* end of If *)
      ]; (* end of While *)
   If[!printAll,
      Print[ ];Print["Output vector = ",output];
      Print[ ];
      Print["Energy = ",newEnergy];
      Print[ ];
      ]; (* end of If *)
   ]; (* end of Module *)
```

Listing 4.2

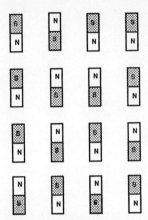

Figure 4.2 You can think of a magnetic material as comprising individual atomic magnets resulting from a quantum-mechanical property known as spin. In the presence of an external magnetic field, the spin can be in one of two directions, each of which results in a different orientation of the north and south poles of the individual atomic magnets.

4.2 Stochastic Methods for Neural Networks

In this section, we shall examine briefly several concepts from physics that have direct analogs for neural networks. Energy, temperature, atomic spin, entropy, and magnetic interactions are useful concepts, as is the process known as annealing. In particular, you should keep in mind the details of the Hopfield network as you read through this material.

4.2.1 Some Ideas About Magnetism and Statistical Physics

Let's talk about some simple physical concepts before we attempt to apply any of this physics to neural networks. First, consider Figure 4.2, which shows a simplified representation of a magnetic material.

We can begin to construct a physical model for this magnetic system by assigning a value to a variable, s_i, for each atom. The value is $+1$ if the spin is up (North pole is up in Figure 4.2), and -1 if the spin is down. Such a model is known as an **Ising model**.

The individual atomic magnets are acted upon by the constant external field, h, and the fields arising from the other magnets in the system. Each magnet, m_i, exerts an influence on the other magnets, m_j, in proportion to its own magnetic field, h_i. The proportionality constant is called the **exchange interaction strength,** w_{ij}. Moreover, this interaction is symmetric, so that $w_{ij} = w_{ji}$. Then the total magnetic field influencing the ith magnet is

$$h_i = \sum_{i \neq j} w_{ij} s_j + h \qquad (4.4)$$

We can associate a certain potential energy with these interactions. The potential energy of this system is

$$E = -\frac{1}{2} \sum_{\substack{i,j \\ i \neq j}} w_{ij} s_i s_j - h \sum_i s_i \qquad (4.5)$$

The factor of one half in the first term on the right accounts for the fact that each i and j index is counted twice in the summation.

At very low temperatures, individual magnets tend to line up in the direction of the local field, h_i. Thus, the spin becomes either positive or negative one depending on the sign of the local field. At higher temperatures, thermal effects tend to disrupt the orderliness of this arrangement.

Consider the physical model that we just examined above in relationship to the Hopfield network. The spins, s_i, are analogous to the unit outputs, the local magnetic fields, h_i, are analogous to the net inputs, and the potential energy of the system is analogous to the energy of the network (in the absense of any external field). The exchange interaction strengths form a symmetric matrix analogous to the weight matrix of the Hopfield network.

Incidentally, if all of the exchange interaction strengths are positive, we refer to the material as a **ferromagnet**. Random strengths result in a substance known as a **spin glass**. Since weights in a Hopfield network are more likely to appear to be random than all positive, the analogy is often made between the Hopfield network and spin glasses.

Thermal effects enter the picture because the random motions caused by thermal energy can cause a magnet to flip to a different state. Since there are a large number of atomic magnets in any system, you would not likely notice that the magnetization state of the material was changing, provided the temperature remained constant. However, if the temperature were high enough, these thermal motions could completely randomize the individual spin directions, resulting in a material that had no net magnetization.

As individual spins flipped, the total energy of the system would change slightly. On the average, however, the energy would remain at a constant value, provided the temperature does not change. Nevertheless, at any given instant, the total energy may differ from this average. In statistical physics, the probability, P_r, that a system in thermal equilibrium at a given temperature has an energy E_r, is proportional to a quantity known as the **Boltzmann factor**, $e^{-\beta E_r}$. In other words

$$P_r = Ce^{-\beta E_r} \tag{4.6}$$

where C is the proportionality constant, and β is a factor proportional to the inverse of the temperature of the system. In a physical system, this factor would take the form

$$\beta = \frac{1}{k_B T}$$

where k_B is called **Boltzmann's constant,** and T is the absolute temperature.

The porportionality constant, C, is related to a quantity known as the **partition function**. The partition function, Z, is the sum of all of the possible Boltzmann factors for the system, that is

$$Z = \frac{1}{C} = \sum_r e^{-\beta E_r}$$

where the sum is taken over all possible energy states of the system.

4.2.2 Statistical Mechanics and Neural Networks

We can now apply the results of the previous section to neural networks. Each unit in the Hopfield network has an output of either positive one or negative one. Thus, we can think of these units as the analogues of the magnets in the physical system described in the previous section, where the output of the units correspond to the values of the magnetic spin.

The weight values in the network correspond to the internal magnetic fields at each of the individual magnets. We shall consider a physical system with no external magnetic field. By doing so, Eq. (4.5) for the energy of the system of magnets corresponds directly with Eq. (4.3) for the energy of the Hopfield network.

In a neural network, such as the Hopfield network, we can impart a stochastic nature to the system by means of a fictitious temperature, whereby the unit outputs are made to fluctuate due to fictitious thermal motions. Moreover, if we assume a condition of thermal equilibrium, we can use the Boltzmann distribution to describe the effect of these fluctuations. The net effect is that the outputs of the network units are no longer completely determined by the net-input values to those units. Instead, there is the possibility that a unit will be *bumped* into a higher energy state due to random thermal fluctuations within the system. Remember that the ideas of temperature and thermal fluctuations in a neural network are strictly mathematical constructs.

To build such a network we must be able to calculate the probability that any given unit will undergo a change of state due to a random thermal fluctuation. To accomplish this task, we shall limit our consideration to a single unit and correspondingly change the unit-update strategy from a synchronous update to a random, asynchronous update procedure.

Let's focus our attention on the kth unit, whose output we denote x_k. We shall call the energy of the system with $x_k = +1$, $E_{(+1)}$, and the energy with $x_k = -1$, $E_{(-1)}$. According to the Boltzmann distribution, the probability that the system will be in the state with $x_k = +1$ is

$$P_{(+1)} = \frac{e^{-\beta E_{(+1)}}}{e^{-\beta E_{(+1)}} + e^{-\beta E_{(-1)}}}$$

or

$$P_{(+1)} = \frac{1}{1 + e^{-\beta(E_{(-1)} - E_{(+1)})}}$$

The energy difference is given by

$$E_{(-1)} - E_{(+1)} = \sum_{\substack{j=1 \\ j \neq k}}^{n} w_{kj} x_j = \text{net}_k$$

so that

$$P_{(+1)} = \frac{1}{1 + e^{-\text{net}_k/T}} \tag{4.7}$$

where we have absorbed the Boltzmann constant into the fictitious temperature. This equation gives the probability that a unit has an output of $+1$, regardless of the value of the net input. Notice that the probability curve has a sigmoidal shape, identical to the output function that we have used in other networks. Let's define the function for use later on.

```
prob[n_,T_] := 1/(1+E^(-n/T));
```

We can plot the probability function for several values of the temperature parameter. Notice that as the temperature decreases, the system behaves more and more like a deterministic system, until, at $T = 0$, the system is completely deterministic.

```
Plot[{prob[n,0.01],prob[n,.5],prob[n,5]},{n,-5,5},
    AxesLabel->{"net","P"}];
```

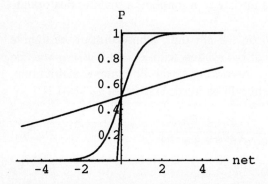

To determine the output of any unit, we must first calculate the net input. Then, depending on the temperature, calculate the probability that the unit will have a +1 output. We then compare this probability to a randomly generated number between zero and one. If this random number is less than or equal to the probability, then we set the unit output equal to +1, regardless of the net input. If the random number is greater than the probability, then the normal rules for the Hopfield network apply in determining the output.

By now, you may reasonably question why we would go to all this trouble when the deterministic Hopfield network seems to work just fine. The answer lies in the fact that this network, like others — in particular the BPN — potentially can settle into a local minimum energy state, or a spurious energy minimum, rather than one that corresponds to one of the items stored in the network's weight matrix. Adding a stochastic element to the unit outputs helps the network avoid such errors. The procedure we employ is similar to the annealing process used in materials processing, and hence we call it **simulated annealing**.

4.2.3 Simulated Annealing

Let's consider the example of a silicon boule being grown in a furnace to be used as a substrate for integrated-circuit devices. It is highly desirable that the crystal structure be a perfect, regular crystal lattice at ambient temperature. Once the silicon boule is formed, it must be cooled slowly to ensure that the crystal lattice forms properly. Rapid cooling can result in many imperfections within the crystal structure, or in a substance that is glasslike, with no regular crystalline structure at all. Both of these configurations have a higher energy than the crystal with the perfect lattice structure.

An annealing process must be used to find the global energy minimum. The temperature of the boule must be lowered gradually, giving atoms within the structure time to rearrange themselves into the proper configuration. At each temperature, sufficient time must be allowed so that the material reaches an equilibrium. To understand how this annealing process helps the crystal avoid a local minimum, we shall employ an intuitive argument used by Hinton and Sejnowski in their discussion of simulated annealing[1]. Consider the simple energy landscape shown in Figure 4.3.

The ball-bearing, which begins with an energy of E_s, has insufficient energy initially to roll up the other side of the hill and down into the global minimum. If we shake the whole system, we might give the ball enough of a push to get it up the hill. The harder we shake, the more likely it is that the ball will be given enough energy to get over that hill. On the other hand, vigorous shaking might also push the ball from the valley with the global minimum back over to the local minimum side.

If we give the system a gentle shaking, then once the ball gets to the global minimum side, it is less likely to acquire sufficient energy to get back across to the local minimum side. However, because of the gentle shaking, it might take a very long time before the ball gets just the right push to get it over to the global minimum side in the first place.

Annealing represents a compromise between hard shaking and gentle shaking. At high temperatures, the large thermal energy corresponds to vigorous shaking. Low temperatures correspond to gentle shaking. To anneal an object, we raise the temperature then gradually lower it back

---

[1]Learning and relearning in Boltzmann machines. In David E. Rumelhart and James L. McClelland, editors, *Parallel Distributed Processing: Explorations in the Microstructure of Cognition*. MIT Press: Cambridge, MA, pages 282-317, 1986.

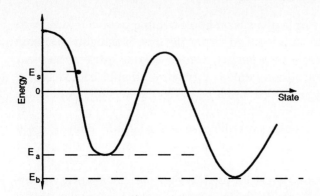

Figure 4.3 This figure shows a simple energy landscape with two minima, a local minimum, E_a, and a global minimum, E_b. The system begins with some energy, E_s. We can draw an analogy to a ball bearing rolling down a hill. The bearing rolls down the hill toward the local minimum, E_a, but has insufficient energy to roll up the other side and down into the global minimum.

to ambient temperature, allowing the object to reach equilibrium at each stop along the way. The technique of gradually lowering the temperature is the best way to ensure that a local minimum can be avoided without having to spend an infinite amount of time waiting for a transition out of a local minimum.

To anneal a neural network, raise the fictitious temperature to some value above zero and apply the stochastic processing prescription described above. You must continue allowing the units to change until equilibrium is reached. You could measure the properties of the network to determine when it has reached equilibrium, or you could simply guess at how long it might take to reach equilibrium. The latter procedure has the advantage of requiring less computations, and a little trial and error should give you a feel for making a reasonable choice.

Once the network has reached equilibrium at one temperature, then lower the temperature slightly and allow the network to reach equilibrium at the new temperature. Continue reducing the temperature in this manner until you reach a suitably low temperature. Once again, when to stop is a matter of personal experience for a given problem.

The annealing process is often described in terms of an **annealing schedule.** An annealing schedule is a list of pairs of numbers, for which each pair comprises a temperature and the number of sweeps at that temperature. A **sweep** is the number of times each unit has an opportunity to change while the network is at a particular temperature. An example of an annealing schedule is: $((10, 5), (8, 10), (4, 20), (1, 20), (0.1, 50))$.

You can imagine that executing such an annealing schedule would take a considerable number of computations for a network of any size, and you would be correct. To *ensure* that the network reaches the global minimum energy, the temperature needs to be reduced very slowly. Often we can live with an imperfect annealing schedule that may get us close to the global minimum, but will get us there in our lifetime.

4.2.4 The Stochastic Hopfield Network

The following function implements the stochastic output function for the Hopfield network:

```
probPsi[inValue_,netIn_,temp_] :=
  If[Random[]<=prob[netIn,temp],1,psi[inValue,netIn]];
```

We shall adopt the asynchronous processing model for this network rather than the synchronous one that we used earlier. We must, therefore, have two loops: one that specifies how many sweeps at a given temperature, and one that specifies how many unit-updates per sweep, depending on the number of units in the network. Moreover, we must run through this double loop for each temperature specified in the annealing schedule. After updating each unit, we must remember to replace the new value into the appropriate slot in the input vector.

If `numUnits` is the number of units in the network, and `numSweeps` is the number of sweeps, then the code for processing each temperature step in the annealing schedule would look like Listing 4.3. Notice that there is no guarantee that every unit will be updated `numSweeps` times.

The function `stochasticHopfield` in Listing 4.4 incorporates the above code and computes the output vectors for a given number of sweeps at a particular temperature. As we did with the discrete Hopfield network, let's compute a random set of input vectors to test this network.

```
trainPats = 2 Table[Table[Random[Integer,{0,1}],{10}],{3}]-1
```

```
{{-1, -1, 1, -1, -1, 1, -1, 1, 1, -1},
 {1, -1, -1, 1, 1, 1, 1, 1, 1, 1},
 {-1, -1, 1, -1, -1, 1, -1, -1, 1, -1}}
```

```
For[i=1;i<=numSweeps;i++;
  For[j=1;j<=numUnits;j++;
            (* select unit *)
    indx = Random[Integer,{1,numUnits}];
            (* net input to unit *)
    net=inVector . weights[[indx]];
            (* undate input vector *)
    inVector[[indx]]=probPsi[inVector[[indx]],net,temp];
  ]; (* end For j *)
]; (* end For i *)
```

Listing 4.3

```
wts = Apply[Plus,Map[Outer[Times,#,#]&,trainPats]];
MatrixForm[wts]
```

3	1	-3	3	3	-1	3	1	-1	3
1	3	-1	1	1	-3	1	-1	-3	1
-3	-1	3	-3	-3	1	-3	-1	1	-3
3	1	-3	3	3	-1	3	1	-1	3
3	1	-3	3	3	-1	3	1	-1	3
-1	-3	1	-1	-1	3	-1	1	3	-1
3	1	-3	3	3	-1	3	1	-1	3
1	-1	-1	1	1	1	1	3	1	1
-1	-3	1	-1	-1	3	-1	1	3	-1
3	1	-3	3	3	-1	3	1	-1	3

We shall use the following as an initial input vector:

```
input1 = {-1, 1, 1, -1, -1, -1, -1, 1, -1, -1};
```

With an arbitrary selection of temperature of 5, and the number of sweeps set at 10, we can run the network through its paces:

```
stochasticHopfield[input1,wts,10,8];
```

```
i= 1
New input vector =
{-1, 1, 1, -1, -1, 1, -1, 1, -1, -1}
```

```
stochasticHopfield[inVector_,weights_,numSweeps_,temp_]:=
  Module[ {input, net, indx, numUnits, indxList, output},
    numUnits=Length[inVector];
    indxList=Table[0,{numUnits}];
    input=inVector;
    For[i=1,i<=numSweeps,i++,
    Print["i= ",i];
      For[j=1,j<=numUnits,j++,
            (* select unit *)
        indx = Random[Integer,{1,numUnits}];
          (* net input to unit *)
        net=input . weights[[indx]];
          (* undate input vector *)
        output=probPsi[input[[indx]],net,temp];
        input[[indx]]=output;
        indxList[[indx]]+=1;
      ]; (* end For numUnits *)
    Print[ ];Print["New input vector = "];Print[input];
    ];   (* end For numSweeps *)
  Print[ ];Print["Number of times each unit was updated:"];
  Print[ ];Print[indxList];
  ];   (* end of Module *)
```

Listing 4.4


```
i= 2
New input vector =
{-1, -1, 1, -1, -1, 1, -1, -1, 1, -1}
i= 3
New input vector =
{-1, 1, 1, -1, -1, 1, -1, 1, 1, -1}
i= 4
New input vector =
{-1, 1, 1, -1, -1, 1, -1, -1, 1, -1}
i= 5
New input vector =
```

```
{-1, -1, 1, -1, -1, 1, -1, 1, 1, -1}
i= 6
New input vector =
{-1, -1, 1, -1, -1, 1, -1, 1, 1, -1}
i= 7
New input vector =
{-1, -1, 1, -1, -1, 1, -1, 1, 1, -1}
i= 8
New input vector =
{-1, -1, 1, -1, -1, 1, -1, 1, 1, -1}
i= 9
New input vector =
{-1, -1, 1, -1, -1, 1, -1, 1, 1, -1}
i= 10
New input vector =
{-1, 1, 1, -1, -1, 1, -1, 1, 1, -1}
Number of times each unit was updated:
{11, 11, 11, 8, 9, 14, 8, 11, 11, 6}
```

You should notice that the results tend to cluster around one of the training vectors, but that there is some variation due to the finite temperature. When you run this code on your computer, you will see different results due to the random nature of the process.

Remember, this function executes the network only at a single temperature. To anneal this network properly, we should begin at a temperature considerably higher than 5, perform more sweeps, then reduce the temperature according to some annealing schedule. You can use the above code as a basis for a complete function that performs the entire annealing process.

4.2.5 Boltzmann Machine Architecture

The Hopfield network is not the only one that can be annealed in the manner of the previous section. A network called the **Boltzmann Machine** performs an annealing during the learning process as well as during the postlearning production process. Figures 4.4 and 4.5 illustrate two variations of the Boltzmann machine architecture. Because the learning procedure for the Boltzmann machine is so time consuming, we shall not attempt to simulate it here.

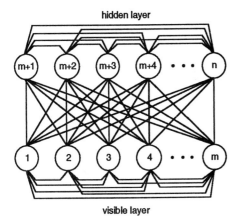

hidden layer

visible layer

Figure 4.4 In the Boltzmann-completion architecture, there are two layers of units: visible and hidden. The network is fully interconnected between layers and among units on each layer. The connections are bidirectional and the weights are symmetric, $w_{ij} = w_{ji}$. All of the units are updated according to the stochastic method that we described for the Hopfield network. The function of the Boltzmann-completion network is to learn a set of input patterns and then to be able to supply missing parts of the patterns when a partial, or noisy, input pattern is processed.

4.3 Bayesian Pattern Classification

In this section we look at the theory of Bayesian pattern classification. This look will be necessarily brief and we will consider only those points needed for the implementation of the probabilistic neural network in the next section.

4.3.1 Conditional Probability and Bayes' Theorem

To begin the discussion, let's consider a simple problem involving choosing an object at random from a number of possible objects. To simplify the problem further, let's assume we have a red marble, a white marble and a blue marble in a box and we are going to choose one blindly. What is the probability that the chosen marble will be blue? Clearly, the answer is 1/3. Denote this probability as $P(B)$. Similarly, the probability of choosing the white marble is 1/3 — or, is it?

Suppose we actually choose the blue marble from the box. Now

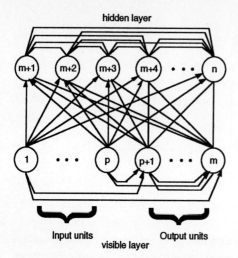

Figure 4.5 For the Boltzmann-input/output network, the visible units are separated into input and output units. There are no connections among input units, and the connections from input units to other units in the network are unidirectional. All other connections are bi-directional, as in the Boltzmann-completion network. This network functions as a heteroassociative memory. During the recall process, the input-vector units are clamped permanently and are not updated during the annealing process. All hidden units and output units are updated according to the simulated-annealing procedure described above for the Hopfield network.

what is the probability that our next choice will be the white marble. The answer depends on what we do with the blue marble that we have already chosen. If we replace the blue marble in the box before we make a second choice, then the probability of choosing the white marble is $P(W) = 1/3$, because the two events of choosing are totally independent of one another. $P(B)$ and $P(W)$ are called **a priori probabilities**. They are the probabilities we would assign to the selection of a blue or white marble initially, without any other information.

Let's look at the different ways that we can choose two objects, one after the other, without replacing the first object in the box after it has been chosen.

```
outcomes=Map[Drop[#,-1]&,Permutations[{R, W, B}]]
```

```
{{R, W}, {R, B}, {W, R}, {W, B}, {B, R}, {B, W}}
```

There are only two possiblilities, having chosen the blue marble first: red or white. Then the probability of choosing the white marble with our next choice is 0.5. In other words, the probability changes based on the results of the first choice. We shall call this new result the **conditional probability** of choosing the white marble, given that we have already chosen the blue marble and have not replaced it in the box. The symbol that we give to this probability is $P(W2|B)$. Similarly, the conditional probability of choosing the blue marble given that we have already chosen the white one is denoted $P(B2|W)$. Notice, however, that there are two out of six ways in which the white marble may be chosen second. Thus, $P(W2) = 1/3$.

We can also define the joint probability of choosing, for example, a blue and a white marble as the result of two successive choices. We call that value $P(B \cap W2)$.

We already know that $P(W) = 1/3$, and $P(B) = 1/3$; also, $P(R) = 1/3$:

```
P[R]=1./3;
P[W]=1./3;
P[B]=1./3;
```

The conditional probabilities are:

```
P[W2|B]=P[W2|R]=P[R2|B]=P[R2|W]=P[B2|W]=P[B2|R]=0.5;
```

We can also calculate joint probabilities, such as $P(B \cap W2)$. From the list of results, there is only a one out of six possibility of obtaining a blue marble, followed by a white one. Thus:

```
P[BandW2]=1./6;
```

Assume that we conduct n independent tests where we select two marbles in the manner described above. Let n_B be the total number of times a blue marble was selected first. Furthermore, let $n_{B \cap W2}$ be the number of times the two choices resulted in a blue and a white marble, in that order. We can write the ratio of these two quantities as

$$\frac{n_{B \cap W2}}{n_B} = \frac{n_{B \cap W2}/n}{n_B/n}$$

The numerator is the frequency of a blue then a white marble being selected, and the denominator is the frequency of the blue marble being

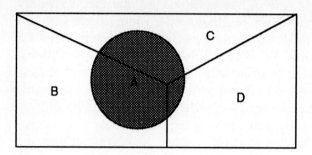

Figure 4.6 This figure shows a region of two-dimensional space broken up into three categories, or classes: B, C, and D. Each point in a given region belongs to the same class. The
circular region, A, is superimposed on the space.

selected first. The ratio, then, represents the ratio of the frequency of selecting a white and a blue marble given that a blue marble was selected
first. As the number of trials increases, the frequencies approach the true
probabilities of occurrence. Then the ratio becomes the conditional probability of W given B. In other words, we *define* the conditional probability
as follows

$$P(W2|B) = \frac{P(B \cap W2)}{P(B)}$$

You can see that this relationship holds for the above example:

P[BandW2]/P[B]

0.5

Moving on to a slightly more complicated example, consider the situation shown in Figure 4.6. We can think of the two-dimensional space
in that figure as possible outcomes, or events.

We can write the set A as follows: $A = (A \cap B) \cup (A \cap C) \cup (A \cap D)$.
If we select a point at random from the space, what is the probability of
that point being in the region A? The answer is

$$P(A) = P(A \cap B) + P(A \cap C) + P(A \cap D) \tag{4.8}$$

If we use the definition of conditional probability, the equation becomes

$$P(A) = P(A|B)P(B) + P(A|C)P(C) + P(A|D)P(D) \tag{4.9}$$

We are now in a position to ask the following question: Given that the selected point is in region A, what is the probability that it is also in region B? According to the definition of conditional probability, the answer is

$$P(B|A) = \frac{P(A \cap B)}{P(A)}$$

We can use Eq. (4.9) for the denominator, resulting in

$$P(B|A) = \frac{P(A \cap B)}{P(A|B)P(B) + P(A|C)P(C) + P(A|D)P(D)}$$

Bayes' theorem is a generalization of this last result. Let $B_1, B_2, \ldots B_n$, partition a region of space, S. Further, let A be an event associated with one of the points of S. Then the probability that event A is in region B_i is

$$P(B_i|A) = \frac{P(A \cap B_i)}{\sum_j P(A|B_j)P(B_j)} = \frac{P(A|B_i)P(B_i)}{P(A)} \qquad (4.10)$$

Bayes' theorem shows us how to convert the *a priori* probability, $P(B_i)$, into an *a posteriori* **probability**, $P(B_i|A)$, based on obtaining first the result A. Now that we have Bayes' theorem, let's move on to its application to decision theory.

4.3.2 Bayesian Strategies for Pattern Classification

Pattern classification is another name for decision making based on information. Consider a simple example where you must decide whether a particular pattern belongs to one of two classes, A or B. The pattern may, in fact, be a picture comprising many picture elements, or **pixels,** or it may be a series of facts or measurements about the pattern. The only restriction we impose is that these measurements all be reducible to numerical form. In other words, we can describe the set of measurements by a vector, $\mathbf{x} = (x_1, x_2, \ldots, x_n)^t$. Each component of the vector represents some feature of the pattern. Based on the value of $\mathbf{x}$, we must decide into which class to put the pattern.

If we know the conditional probabilities, $P(A|\mathbf{x})$ and $P(B|\mathbf{x})$, then our best guess will be to choose class A if $P(A|\mathbf{x}) > P(B|\mathbf{x})$, and class B if $P(A|\mathbf{x}) < P(B|\mathbf{x})$. This example illustrates the **Bayes' decision rule.** Using the notation $d(\mathbf{x})$ for the decision as a function of $\mathbf{x}$, we can use Bayes' theorem to write an equation for the result

$$d(\mathbf{x}) = \left\{ \begin{array}{ll} A & P(\mathbf{x}|A)P(A) > P(\mathbf{x}|B)P(B) \\ B & P(\mathbf{x}|A)P(A) < P(\mathbf{x}|B)P(B) \end{array} \right. \tag{4.11}$$

The boundary between the two decisions is known as the decision surface or decision boundary; it is defined by the equation

$$P(\mathbf{x}|A) = KP(\mathbf{x}|B)$$

where

$$K = \frac{P(B)}{P(A)}$$

In a typical problem, we would have several examples of the measurement results from each class. In order to be able to classify some previously unseen pattern, we must use these exemplars to estimate the decision boundary. To do this estimation, we must either know, or be able to approximate, the underlying probability distribution functions, $P(\mathbf{x}|A)$ and $P(\mathbf{x}|B)$.

A common way of estimating the probability distribution functions is to construct some standard distribution function centered at each exemplar point and sum the results. A Gaussian function is a common choice, although it is by no means a required choice. Let's look at a simple example to see how this process works.

Figure 4.7 shows a two-dimensional space having points in two classes, evenly distributed within the regions shown. In this case, each $\mathbf{x}$ vector has only two dimensions. If the ith exemplar from category A is x_{Ai}, then the estimate of the probability distribution function for class A is

$$P(\mathbf{x}|A) = \frac{1}{(2\pi)^{p/2}\sigma^p n} \sum_{i=1}^{n} \exp\left[\frac{(\mathbf{x} - \mathbf{x}_{Ai}) \cdot (\mathbf{x} - \mathbf{x}_{Ai})}{2\sigma^2}\right]$$

where n is the number of exemplars, p is the dimension of the space, and σ is an adjustable parameter that determines the width of the individual Gaussians.

The examplars for categories A and B are:

```
exemplarsA={ {2.5, 1.5}, {2.5, 2.5},
             {3.5, 1.5}, {3.5, 2.5} };

exemplarsB={ {2.5, -1.5}, {2.5, -2.5},
             {3.5, -1.5}, {3.5, -2.5} };
```

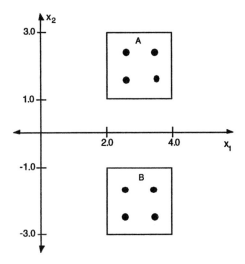

Figure 4.7 This figure shows a plane with two categories of points, A and B. The points are uniformly distributed within each region. The examplar points are indicated by the black dots.

The two-dimensional Gaussian function has the form:

```
gauss2[x_,y_] :=
(1/((2.0 Pi) sigma^2)) E^(-{(x-xa),(y-ya)}.
                  {(x-xa),(y-ya)}/(2sigma^2))
```

To approximate the distribution function for one of the classes, we must sum four of these functions, each with different values of xa and ya. There are several ways to accomplish this task. The particular method that I show here is not the most elegant, but will serve to illustrate the calculation explicitly. First, let's transform the exemplarsA array into an array of rules.

```
Clear[xa,ya];
ruleSetA = Map[{xa->#[[1]],ya->#[[2]]}&,exemplarsA]
```

```
{{xa -> 2.5, ya -> 1.5}, {xa -> 2.5, ya -> 2.5},
 {xa -> 3.5, ya -> 1.5}, {xa -> 3.5, ya -> 2.5}}
```

Then create a list of functions, each with the appropriate replacements for xa and ya.

```
gaussList={};
For[i=1,i<=Length[exemplarsA],i++,
    AppendTo[gaussList,gauss2[x,y]/.ruleSetA[[i]]];
    ];
    gaussList
```

$$\left\{\frac{0.5}{E^{((-2.5 + x)^2 + (-1.5 + y)^2)/(2\ \text{sigma}^2)}\ \text{Pi}\ \text{sigma}^2},\right.$$

$$\frac{0.5}{E^{((-2.5 + x)^2 + (-2.5 + y)^2)/(2\ \text{sigma}^2)}\ \text{Pi}\ \text{sigma}^2},$$

$$\frac{0.5}{E^{((-3.5 + x)^2 + (-1.5 + y)^2)/(2\ \text{sigma}^2)}\ \text{Pi}\ \text{sigma}^2},$$

$$\left.\frac{0.5}{E^{((-3.5 + x)^2 + (-2.5 + y)^2)/(2\ \text{sigma}^2)}\ \text{Pi}\ \text{sigma}^2}\right\}$$

Sum these functions, then divide by the number of exemplars.

```
ClearAll[classA];
classA[x_,y_] :=
        Apply[Plus,gaussList]/Length[exemplarsA]
```

Now let's plot the result.

```
Plot3D[classA[x,y]/.sigma->0.1,{x,0,5},{y,0,4},
        PlotPoints->25,PlotRange->All];
```

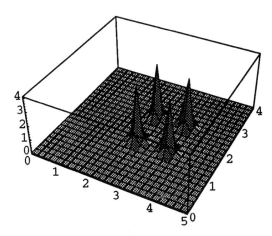

With a sigma of 0.1, the classA function represents the exemplars well, but does not approximate the desired distribution over the entire class. By adjusting the value of sigma, we can make the distribution more reasonable.

```
Plot3D[classA[x,y]/.sigma->0.45,{x,0,5},{y,0,4},
    PlotPoints->25,PlotRange->All];
```

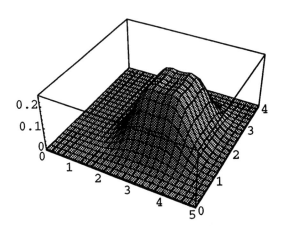

To continue with this example, you should repeat the above development to construct a function classB. These functions can then be used in the Bayes' decision rule, Eq. (4.11), to classify any point in the plane. Notice

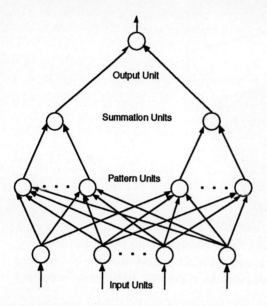

Figure 4.8 This figure shows the connectivity of a PNN designed to classify input vectors into one of two classes. The input values are fully connected to the layer of pattern units. Pattern units that correspond to a single class are connected to one summation unit. Both summation units are connected to the output unit. Details of the processing performed by these units are in the text.

that points that are very far from either class will still be classified in one of the two classes. You can fix this problem be requiring some threshold value for either class function to validate the classification. Let's move on now to the implementation of this methodology in a neural network.

4.4 The Probabilistic Neural Network

The **probabilistic neural network** (PNN) is a feed-forward neural network that implements a Bayesian decision strategy for classifying input vectors. The basic architecture appears in Figure 4.8.

The input units distribute their values unchanged to the units of the second layer. We shall assume that the input vectors have all been normalized to unity.

Each unit in the second layer is called a **pattern unit**. There is one pattern unit for each exemplar in the training set. The weight vector for each pattern unit is a copy of the corresponding exemplar, and is also normalized. Moreover, training is accomplished by adding pattern units with the appropriate weight vectors in place.

In the pattern units, we take the dot product of the input vector and the weight vector, as is typically done in feed-forward networks. We then apply a nonlinear output function, although we depart from the sigmoid function commonly used. Instead of the sigmoid, we use the gaussian function, $\exp\{(\text{net} - 1)/\sigma^2\}$, where $\text{net} = \mathbf{x} \cdot \mathbf{w}$ is the net input to the unit, $\mathbf{x}$ is the input vector, $\mathbf{w}$ is the weight vector and σ is a smoothing parameter.

Since both $\mathbf{x}$ and $\mathbf{w}$ are normalized, the value of net is restricted to the range $-1 \leq \text{net} \leq -1$. Let's define the output function and plot it between these limits.

```
gaussOut[x_] := E^( (x-1)/sigma^2)
```

```
Plot[gaussOut[x]/.sigma->.7,{x,-1,1},PlotRange->All];
```

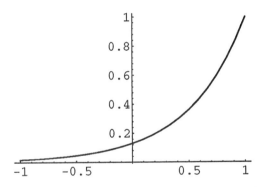

This Gaussian output function is equivalent to the exponential term in the Gaussian distribution function that we used in the previous section, provided both the input and weight vectors are normalized. You can verify this statement with a simple calculation.

By summing the outputs of all of the pattern units belonging to a single class, we have in effect computed the *a posteriori* probability distribution function for that class, evaluated at the input point. In other words, if the class is A and the input vector is $\mathbf{x}$, then the combination of the pattern units and the summation unit for class A computes

$$F_a(\mathbf{x}) = (2\pi)^{p/2}\sigma^p n_A P(\mathbf{x}|A)$$

where n_A is the number of examplars in class A. The decision boundary occurs at $P(\mathbf{x}|A) = KP(\mathbf{x}|B)$, or in terms of the f functions

$$\frac{f_A(\mathbf{x})}{n_A} = K\frac{f_B(\mathbf{x})}{n_B}$$

or

$$f_A(\mathbf{x}) - Cf_B(\mathbf{x}) = 0$$

where

$$C = \frac{P(B)n_A}{P(A)n_B}$$

This result suggests that we configure the output unit to have two inputs: one from each summation unit. The connection from class A will have a weight of one, and the connection from class B will have a weight of $-C$. The output unit computes the net input as usual. The output function can be the sign function: If the net input is positive, the output is $+1$, corresponding to class A; if the net input is negative, the output is -1, corresponding to class B.

You can make a final simplification if you can be sure that the number of exemplars from each class is taken in proportion to the corresponding *a priori* probability. In that case, $C = 1$ and the weight on the connection from class B is just -1.

Let's step through an example using the classes described in the previous section:

exemplarsA

{{2.5, 1.5}, {2.5, 2.5}, {3.5, 1.5}, {3.5, 2.5}}

exemplarsB

{{2.5, -1.5}, {2.5, -2.5}, {3.5, -1.5}, {3.5, -2.5}}

Since the input vectors must be normalized, we must define a function to accomplish that task.

```
normalize[x_List] := x/(Sqrt[x.x]//N)
```

Since each exemplar array has more than one vector in it, use the **Map** function to perform the normalization.

```
exemplarsAnorm = Map[normalize,exemplarsA]
```

{{0.857493, 0.514496}, {0.707107, 0.707107},
 {0.919145, 0.393919}, {0.813733, 0.581238}}

exemplarsBnorm = Map[normalize,exemplarsB]

{{0.857493, -0.514496}, {0.707107, -0.707107},
 {0.919145, -0.393919}, {0.813733, -0.581238}}

Before continuing on with the calculation, let's plot the original exemplars from class A along with the normalized points.

```
p1 = ListPlot[exemplarsA,PlotStyle->PointSize[0.05],
         PlotRange->{ {0,5},{0,4}},
         Prolog->{Line[{{2,1},{2,3}}],
              Line[{{2,3},{4,3}}],
              Line[{{4,3},{4,1}}],
              Line[{{4,1},{2,1}}]}];
```

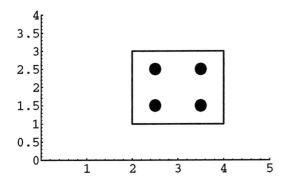

11 = ListPlot[exemplarsAnorm];

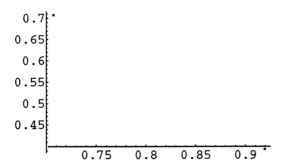

`Show[{p1,l1}];`

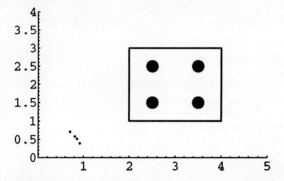

When you normalize vectors in the plane, all of the points project down to the unit circle. All points that lie along a line in a particular direction from the origin, when normalized, will fall on the same point on the unit circle. Thus, you would not be able to separate classes that are in different regions of the plane, but that lie along the same direction. When you want to use normalization of input vectors, make sure that the direction of the vector is the only relevant attribute, and that the vector's magnitude does not matter. With that point made, let's return to the calculation.

The weights on the pattern units are equal to the normalized exemplar vectors.

`weightsA = exemplarsAnorm;`
`weightsB = exemplarsBnorm;`

For input points, we shall use a table of random numbers, generally within the range of the two classes.

`inputs = Table[{Random[Real,{1,5}],`
`          Random[Real,{-4,4}]}, {10}]`

{{2.52819, −1.74313}, {1.27255, −0.78729},
 {3.03809, −0.768469}, {4.08654, 2.79729},
 {2.91019, −0.760464}, {2.27138, −3.95153}, {2.5855, 1.5419},
 {3.52378, −1.41451}, {2.65525, −1.11967},
 {1.25173, 0.721864}}

Seven of these vectors belong to class B and three (components 4, 7, and 10) belong to class A. Next, we must normalize these input vectors.

```
inputsNorm = Map[normalize,inputs]
```

{{0.823282, -0.567633}, {0.850408, -0.526124},
 {0.969467, -0.245222}, {0.82519, 0.564855},
 {0.967513, -0.252821}, {0.498348, -0.866977},
 {0.858867, 0.512198}, {0.928022, -0.372525},
 {0.921428, -0.388549}, {0.866273, 0.499571}}

Net inputs to the pattern units are the standard dot products. Since there is more than one input vector, we cannot simply dot inputsNorm with weightsA and weightsB.

```
patternAnet = inputsNorm . Transpose[weightsA]
```

{{0.413913, 0.180771, 0.533114, 0.340002},
 {0.45853, 0.229303, 0.574397, 0.386202},
 {0.705146, 0.512119, 0.794483, 0.646356},
 {0.99821, 0.98291, 0.980977, 0.9998},
 {0.69956, 0.505363, 0.789694, 0.640348},
 {-0.0187266, -0.260661, 0.116535 ,-0.0983982},
 {0.999996, 0.96949, 0.991188, 0.996598},
 {0.60411, 0.392796, 0.706242, 0.538637},
 {0.590211, 0.376802, 0.693869, 0.523957},
 {0.99985, 0.965798, 0.993021, 0.995285}}

```
patternBnet = inputsNorm . Transpose[weightsB]
```

{{0.998003, 0.983525, 0.980317, 0.999862},
 {0.999907, 0.973355, 0.988899, 0.997809},
 {0.957477, 0.858915, 0.987678, 0.93142},
 {0.416979, 0.184085, 0.535962, 0.34317},
 {0.959711, 0.862907, 0.988876, 0.934247},
 {0.873386, 0.965431, 0.799573, 0.909442},
 {0.472949, 0.245132, 0.587659, 0.40118},
 {0.987435, 0.919626, 0.999732, 0.971688},
 {0.990025, 0.926294, 0.999983, 0.975636},
 {0.485795, 0.259297, 0.599439, 0.414545}}

We determine the outputs of the pattern units by applying the gaussian output function. We must also select a value for sigma.

```
sigma = 0.45;
patternAout = gaussOut[patternAnet]
```

{{0.0553402, 0.0174996, 0.0996977, 0.0384172},
 {0.0689808, 0.0222389, 0.122243, 0.0482624},
 {0.23315, 0.0898791, 0.362439, 0.174402},
 {0.991201, 0.91907, 0.910335, 0.999014},
 {0.226807, 0.0869301, 0.353967, 0.169304},
 {0.00653392, 0.00197837, 0.0127428, 0.00440864},
 {0.999982, 0.860133, 0.957419, 0.983341},
 {0.141563, 0.0498599, 0.234417, 0.102455},
 {0.132172, 0.0460734, 0.220522, 0.0952902},
 {0.99926, 0.844593, 0.966123, 0.976985}}

```
patternBout = gaussOut[patternBnet]
```

{{0.990187, 0.921865, 0.907374, 0.999318},
 {0.999542, 0.876709, 0.946653, 0.989237},
 {0.810591, 0.498218, 0.940967, 0.71272},
 {0.0561845, 0.0177884, 0.10111, 0.0390229},
 {0.819584, 0.508137, 0.946548, 0.72274},
 {0.535124, 0.843063, 0.371664, 0.639417},
 {0.0740718, 0.0240471, 0.130517, 0.0519676},
 {0.939836, 0.672394, 0.998676, 0.869523},
 {0.951934, 0.694904, 0.999916, 0.886642},
 {0.078923, 0.0257894, 0.138335, 0.0555132}}

Now we must sum the outputs of the pattern units for each of the input vectors.

```
sumAout = Map[Apply[Plus,#]&,patternAout]
```

{0.210955, 0.261726, 0.859871, 3.81962, 0.837009, 0.0256637,
 3.80088, 0.528294, 0.494058, 3.78696}

```
sumBout = Map[Apply[Plus,#]&,patternBout]
```

{3.81874, 3.81214, 2.9625, 0.214106, 2.99701, 2.38927,
 0.280603, 3.48043, 3.5334, 0.298561}

The sign of the difference of each of these output values is the network output for the corresponding input vector.

```
pnnTwoClass[class1Exemplars_,class2Exemplars_,
                   testInputs_,sig_] :=
  Module[{weightsA,weightsB,inputsNorm,patternAout,
         patternBout,sumAout,sumBout},
     weightsA = Map[normalize,class1Exemplars];
     weightsB = Map[normalize,class2Exemplars];
     inputsNorm = Map[normalize,testInputs];
     sigma = sig;
     patternAout =
        gaussOut[inputsNorm . Transpose[weightsA]];
     patternBout =
        gaussOut[inputsNorm . Transpose[weightsB]];
     sumAout = Map[Apply[Plus,#]&,patternAout];
     sumBout = Map[Apply[Plus,#]&,patternBout];
     outputs = Sign[sumAout-sumBout];
     sigma=.;
     Return[outputs];
     ]
```

Listing 4.5

```
outputs = Sign[sumAout-sumBout]
```

{-1, -1, -1, 1, -1, -1, 1, -1, -1, 1}

These results are consistent with our analysis of the original ten input vectors. The function pnnTwoClass, shown in Listing 4.5, implements the two-class PNN.

Summary

In this chapter we have explored two different ways in which probabilistic concepts can be used to advantage in neural networks. The Ising model from statistical mechanics has a direct analog with the Hopfield neural network. Using concepts from statistical mechanics, in particular the concepts of temperature and stochastic processes, we can change the processing performed by neural-network units from deterministic to stochastic. In doing so, we can endow the network with the ability to escape from local minimum states. Bayesian pattern classification is a traditional methodology based on probabilistic concepts. By drawing on this technology as a basis, we were able to construct a probabilistic neural network which embodies the main features of Bayesian pattern classification.

Chapter 5

Optimization and Constraint Satisfaction

The subject of this chapter is a class of problems for which there may be many solutions, but for which one solution may be judged to be *better* than another. The classic example of this type of problem is the traveling salesperson problem: Given a list of cities and a known cost of traveling from one city to the next, what is the most efficient route such that all cities are visited, no cities are visited twice, and the total distance traveled, and hence cost, is kept to a minimum?

Conditions that we impose on the problem, such as the restriction that each city be visited only once, are called **strong constraints**. Any solution must satisfy all strong constraints. On the other hand, the desire to minimize the cost is a **weak constraint**, since not all possible solutions will be minimum-cost solutions. Let's look at some of the details, and then apply neural networks to the solution of this problem.

5.1 The Traveling Salesperson Problem (TSP)

If you choose a path at random through a given list of cities, you are likely to find that it is not the most efficient in terms of cost. One way to ensure efficiency is to compute the cost for all possible paths, and then to follow the one with the least cost. Unfortunately, such a computation may take an extremely long time. Given any n cities, there are $n!$ possible tours. If you consider the fact that, for a given tour, it does not matter where you begin, or in which direction you travel, then the total number of independent tours is $n!/2n$.

```
numTours[n_]:=n!/(2 n)
```

For a small number of cities, you would simply compute the cost of each tour, and choose the one with the minimum. Unfortunately, for a tour of more than a few cities, this exhaustive search can become quite time consuming. For five cities, the number of possible tours is

```
numTours[5]
```

12

We could easily compute the cost of these twelve tours and select the most efficient one. However, if there are ten cities on the tour, the number of different possibilities is

```
numTours[10]
```

181440

You can see that the computations involved will quickly overwhelm us for a tour of any size greater than a few cities. Let's examine some of the details of this problem by considering a specific case: a five-city tour.

We can express the cost of travel from one city to another using a matrix of values where each row refers to a starting city, and each column refers to a destination city. We assume that the cost of travel from one city to another is independent of the direction of travel, making the matrix symmetric. Moreover, all of the diagonal elements will be zero, since there will be no travel from one city to itself. We construct such a matrix as follows, choosing random values for the costs. First, we construct a lower triangular matrix.

```
costs =
 Table[If[i<=j,0,Random[Integer,{1,10}]],{i,5},{j,5}]
```

{{0, 0, 0, 0, 0}, {4, 0, 0, 0, 0}, {3, 9, 0, 0, 0},
  {8, 4, 6, 0, 0}, {3, 4, 8, 5, 0}}

```
MatrixForm[%]
```

```
0  0  0  0  0
4  0  0  0  0
3  9  0  0  0
8  4  6  0  0
3  4  8  5  0
```

By transposing the matrix and adding it to the original, we construct a symmetric matrix with all diagonal elements equal to zero.

```
costs = costs + Transpose[costs]
```

{{0, 4, 3, 8, 3}, {4, 0, 9, 4, 4}, {3, 9, 0, 6, 8},
  {8, 4, 6, 0, 5}, {3, 4, 8, 5, 0}}

```
MatrixForm[%]
```

```
0  4  3  8  3
4  0  9  4  4
3  9  0  6  8
8  4  6  0  5
3  4  8  5  0
```

To compute the cost of a particular tour, we add the appropriate elements, for example:

t1=costs[[1,2]]+costs[[2,3]]+costs[[3,4]]+costs[[4,5]]+costs[[5,1]]

27

Continuing the process for the remaining tours, we find:

t2=costs[[1,2]]+costs[[2,3]]+costs[[3,5]]+costs[[5,4]]+costs[[4,1]]

34

t3=costs[[1,2]]+costs[[2,4]]+costs[[4,5]]+costs[[5,3]]+costs[[3,1]]

24

and so on. The cheapest tour is tour nine, and the range goes from 20 to 34.

Remember that your results may be quite different. Nevertheless, you can see that any random selection is likely to result in a tour that is not optimum from a cost standpoint.

It is often the case with problems such as the TSP, that a good solution obtained quickly is more desirable than the best solution obtained after laborious calculation. In the example above, we might be quite satisfied with any solution whose cost is less than 25. In the next section we shall look at how to apply a neural network to this problem. We shall see that the network can provide a solution quickly (relative to an exhaustive search), but that the solution is not always the absolute best.

5.2 Neural Networks and the TSP

In this section we shall look at how to apply a Hopfield network to the solution of constraint satisfaction problems in general and to the TSP in particular. We use a different procedure for calculating the weights than we used for the associative memory application in Chapter 4. Although there are several different ways of determing weights for the TSP, we shall follow a method outlined by Page, Tagliarini, and Christ[1]. First, however, we shall need to modify the Hopfield network slightly so that the unit output values are continuous functions of the net input, rather than binary.

---

[1]Page, Ed, G. A. Tagliarini, and F. Christ. Optimization using neural networks. *IEEE Transactions on Computers*, Vol. 40, No. 12, pp. 1347-58, Dec. 1991.

5.2.1 The Continuous Hopfield Network

By allowing the output of the units in a Hopfield network to be a continuous function of the net-input value, the units will more closely resemble the biological neurons they emulate. Moreover, there exists an analogous electrical circuit, using nonlinear amplifiers, resistors, and capacitors, which suggests the possibility of building a continuous Hopfield memory circuit using VLSI technology.

To develop the continuous model, we shall define u_i to be the net input to the ith processing element. One possible biological analog of u_i is the summed action potentials at the axon hillock of a neuron. In the case of the neuron, the output of the cell would be a series of potential spikes whose mean frequency versus total action potential resembles the sigmoid curve that we introduced in previous chapters.

We use the following function as the output function,

```
g[lambda_,u_] := 0.5 (1+Tanh[lambda u])
```

where l is a constant called the **gain parameter**. Let's plot this function for several values of l. We can use the *Mathematica* package, Graphics`Legend` to help us distinguish the various graphs.

```
<<Graphics`Legend`
```

```
Plot[{g[0.2,u],g[0.5,u],g[1,u],g[5,u]},{u,-5,5},
  PlotStyle->{GrayLevel[0],Dashing[{0.01}],
  Dashing[{0.03}],Dashing[{0.05}]},
  PlotLegend->{"l=.2","l=.5","l=1","l=5"}];
```

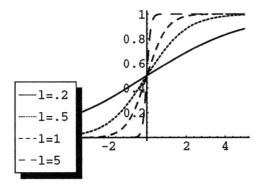

The function g[0.5,u] is identical to the sigmoid function.

`Plot[{g[0.5,u],sigmoid[u]},{u,-5,5}];`

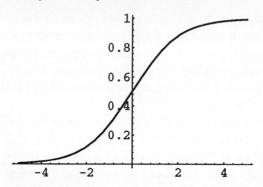

We shall denote $v_i = g[\lambda, u_i]$ as the output of the ith unit. In real neurons, there will be a time delay between the appearance of the outputs, v_j, of other cells, and the resulting net input, u_i, to a cell. This delay is caused by the resistance and capacitance of the cell membrane and the finite conductance of the synapse between the jth and ith cells. These ideas are incorporated into the circuit shown in Figure 5.1. At each connection, we place a resistor having a value $R_{ij} = 1/|T_{ij}|$, where T_{ij} represents the weight matrix. Inverting amplifiers simulate inhibitory signals. If the output of a particular element excites some other element, then the connection is made with the signal from the noninverting amplifier. If the connection is inhibitory, it is made from the inverting amplifier.

Each amplifier has an input resistance, ρ, and an input capacitance, C, as shown. Also shown are the external signals, I_i. In the case of an actual circuit, the external signals would supply a constant current to each amplifier.

The net-input current to each amplifier is the sum of the individual current contributions from other units, plus the external-input current, minus leakage across the input resistor, ρ. The contribution from each connecting unit is the voltage value across the resistor at the connection, divided by the connection resistance. For the connection from the jth unit to the ith, this contribution would be $(v_j - u_i)/R_{ij} = (v_j - u_i)T_{ij}$. The leakage current is u_i/ρ. If we make the definition

$$\frac{1}{R_i} = \frac{1}{\rho} + \sum_j \frac{1}{R_{ij}} \tag{5.1}$$

then we can write a differential equation describing the input voltage for each amplifier by considering the charging of the capacitor as a result of

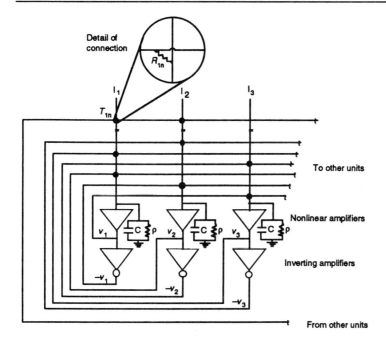

Figure 5.1 In this circuit diagram for the continuous Hopfield memory, amplifiers with a sigmoid output characteristic are the processing elements. The black circles at the intersection points of the lines represent connections between processing elements.

the total input current.

$$C\frac{du_i}{dt} = \sum_j T_{ij}v_j - \frac{u_i}{R_i} + I_i \tag{5.2}$$

These equations, one for each unit in the memory circuit, completely describe the time evolution of the system. Unfortunately, since these equations are a set of coupled differential equations, they cannot be solved in closed form. If each processing element is given an initial value, $u_i(0)$, these equations can be solved on a digital computer using the numerical techniques for initial value problems. Before we can proceed, however, we must determine the value of the weight matrix, T_{ij}, and the external inputs, I_i.

5.2.2 Calculating Weights and External Inputs for the TSP

Provided that the gain parameter is sufficiently high, we can write the energy function of the continuous Hopfield network as

$$E = -\frac{1}{2}\sum_{i=1}^{n}\sum_{j=1}^{n}T_{ij}v_iv_j - \sum_{i=1}^{n}I_iv_i \tag{5.3}$$

A solution to the TSP, or for that matter any constraint satisfaction problem, will minimize the value of the energy function. We can exploit this fact to determine the values for T_{ij} and I_i. In particular, we shall be interested in networks for which the outputs equilibrate at values near zero or one, even though each unit's output may assume any value in the range of zero to one.

In our Hopfield network for the TSP, each unit represents a hypothesis that we visit a particular city at a particular point in the sequence of the tour. Figure 5.2 illustrates the data representation.

The n-out-of-N Problem   Suppose for the moment that the only constraint in the problem is that n cities are visited out of a total of N. We can represent that constraint in the form of an equation as follows:

$$\sum_{i=1}^{N}v_i = n \tag{5.4}$$

where n is the number of cities, and $N = n^2$ is the number of units in the network. The energy function

$$E = \left(n - \sum_{i=1}^{N}v_i\right)^2 \tag{5.5}$$

is a minimum when n of the units have outputs of 1. Furthermore, if we add the term

$$\sum_{i=1}^{N}v_i(1-v_i) \tag{5.6}$$

then the energy function will be a minimum for $v_i \in \{0,1\}$, since this condition minimizes the new term. The new energy function is then

$$E = \left(n - \sum_{i=1}^{N}v_i\right)^2 + \sum_{i=1}^{N}v_i(1-v_i) \tag{5.7}$$

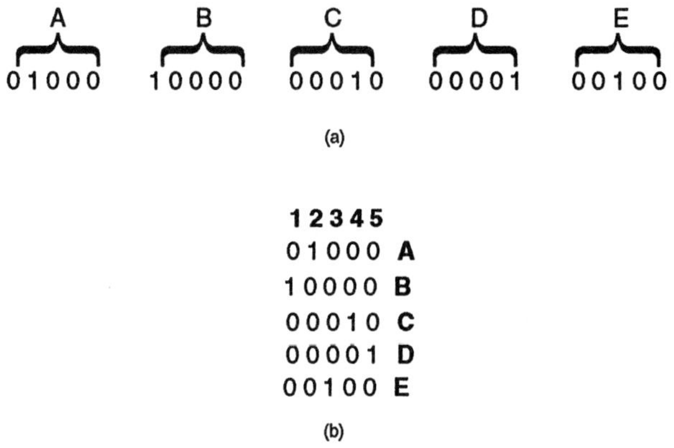

```
A        B        C        D        E
01000    10000    00010    00001    00100
```

(a)

```
12345
01000 A
10000 B
00010 C
00001 D
00100 E
```

(b)

Figure 5.2 (a) In this representation scheme for the output vectors in a five-city TSP problem, five units are associated with each of the five cities. The cities are labeled A through E. The position of the 1 within any group of five represents the location of that particular city in the sequence of the tour. For this example, the sequence is B–A–E–C–D with the return to B assumed. Notice that $N = n^2$ processing elements are required to represent the information for an n-city tour. (b) This figure shows an alternative way of looking at the units. The processing elements are arranged in a two-dimensional matrix configuration with each row representing a city and each column representing a position on the sequence of the tour.

If we expand Eq. (5.7) and ignore the n^2 term, we can rewrite the energy function as

$$E = -\frac{1}{2} \sum_{i=1}^{N} \sum_{\substack{i=1 \\ j \neq i}}^{N} (-2) v_i v_j - \sum_{i=1}^{N} v_i (2n - 1) \qquad (5.8)$$

which is identical to Eq. (5.3), provided we make the following definitions:

$$T_{ij} = \begin{cases} -2 & i \neq j \\ 0 & \text{otherwise} \end{cases} \qquad (5.9)$$

$$I_i = 2n - 1$$

for all i. Notice that each unit in the network exerts an inhibitory strength of -2 on all other units in the network. Moreover, the number of units to be on is strictly a function of the external inputs, I_i.

Before we continue on with the weight calculation for the TSP, let's apply the results so far to a simple problem where we have four units, and only two of them are to be on; it does not matter which two. We can calculate the weight matrix from Eq. (5.9).

```
testWts1 = Table[If[i!=j,-2,0],{i,4},{j,4}]
```

{{0, -2, -2, -2}, {-2, 0, -2, -2}, {-2, -2, 0, -2},
  {-2, -2, -2, 0}}

```
MatrixForm[%]
```

```
0    -2   -2   -2
-2    0   -2   -2
-2   -2    0   -2
-2   -2   -2    0
```

Since $n = 2$, the vector of external inputs is

```
testIn1 = Table[2*2-1,{4}]
```

{3, 3, 3, 3}

We must integrate the equations for each of the units, as specified in Eq. (5.2). In order to perform that integration, we first make the assumptions that $C = 1$, and that $R_i = R = 1$ for all units. Furthermore, we approximate the derivative by a difference equation:

$$\frac{du_i}{dt} \approx \frac{\Delta u_i}{\Delta t} = \frac{u_i(t+1) - u_i(t)}{\Delta t} \qquad (5.10)$$

Let's assign random starting values to the unit outputs,

```
ui = Table[Random[],{4}]
```

{0.114204, 0.332446, 0.551176, 0.708964}

and values for `lambda` and `deltat`; in addition we should initialize the `vi` array that we shall need later.

```
lambda=2;
deltat = 0.01;
vi = g[lambda,ui];
```

The current output values are given by the array vi.

```
vi
```

{0.612258, 0.790805, 0.900671, 0.944583}

We begin the calculation by selecting a unit at random.

```
indx = Random[Integer,{1,4}]
```

2

Then we calculate the new net-input value for that unit.

```
ui[[indx]] = ui[[indx]] +
        deltat (vi . testWts1[[indx]] -
        ui[[indx]] + testIn1[[indx]])
```

0.31662

Calculate the new output values.

```
vi[[indx]] = g[lambda,ui[[indx]]]
```

0.78014

```
vi
```

{0.612258, 0.78014, 0.900671, 0.944583}

To continue we would select another unit at random and perform the required updates until the network settled into a stable solution. Let's assemble the pieces into a function called nOutOfN to indicate the specific problem we are solving. See Listing 5.1. Let's try the code with our example problem.

```
nOutOfN[testWts1,testIn1,4,10,0.1,100,20,True];
```

```
initial ui = {0.405085, 0.677264, 0.0962308, 0.0902886}
initial vi = {0.999697, 0.999999, 0.872652, 0.85885}
iteration = 20
net inputs = {1.63788, 0.772332, -0.209322, -0.534506}
outputs =
{1., 1., 0.0149727, 0.0000227684}
```

```
nOutOfN[weights_,externIn_,numUnits_,lambda_,deltaT_,
numIters_,printFreq_,reset_:False]:=
   Module[{iter,l,dt,indx,ins},
     dt=deltaT;
     l=lambda;
     iter=numIters;
     ins=externIn;
           (* only reset if starting over *)
     If[reset,ui=Table[Random[],{numUnits}];
           vi = g[l,ui],Continue];  (* end of If *)
       Print["initial ui = ",N[ui,2]];Print[];
       Print["initial vi = ",N[vi,2]];
     For[iter=1,iter<=numIters,iter++,
       indx = Random[Integer,{1,numUnits}];
       ui[[indx]] = ui[[indx]]+
         dt (vi . weights[[indx]] - ui[[indx]] + ins[[indx]]);
       vi[[indx]] = g[l,ui[[indx]]];
       If[Mod[iter,printFreq]==0,
           Print[];Print["iteration = ",iter];
           Print["net inputs = "];
           Print[N[ui,2]];
           Print["outputs = "];
           Print[N[vi,2]];Print[];
           ];  (* end of If *)
       ];  (* end of For *)
     Print[ ];Print["iteration = ",--iter];
     Print["final outputs = "];
     Print[vi];
     ];  (* end of Module *)
```

Listing 5.1

```
iteration = 40
net inputs = {4.1303, 1.35895, -1.35663, -1.04605}
outputs =
                       -12           -10
{1., 1., 1.64622 10   , 8.20544 10   }
iteration = 60
net inputs = {4.64333, 5.11851, -2.13667, -2.62471}
outputs =
                       -19
{1., 1., 2.71051 10   , 0.}
iteration = 80
net inputs = {5.82843, 7.9581, -4.05164, -7.54687}
outputs =
{1., 1., 0., 0.}
iteration = 100
net inputs = {11.097, 16.4568, -5.11248, -12.7648}
outputs =
{1., 1., 0., 0.}
iteration = 100
final outputs =
{1., 1., 0., 0.}
```

You can see that the network quickly settles on an appropriate solution.

Adding Constraints   The TSP is a bit more complicated than a simple n-out-of-N problem. In a five-city problem, we would have $N = 25$ units. In a simple n-out-of-N problem, the network would converge on a solution with five cities — a 5-out-of-25 problem in this case — but there would be no guarantee that we would not violate some other hard constraint; for example, the constraint that we should visit each city only once. To illustrate how we can account for the additional constraints, recall the 2-of-4 problem that we did in the previous section, and add the additional constraint that of the two units selected, one must be from units one and two, and one must be from units three and four. Each of these constraints is a 1-out-of-2 problem.

These constraints translate to additional weight values of -2 between the units of each of the pairs of units. For example, units one and two would each exert an additional -2 inhibitory connection on the other unit. We add these weights to the original weights.

```
testWtsAdd = { {0,-2,0,0},{-2,0,0,0},{0,0,0,-2},{0,0,-2,0} }
```

{{0, -2, 0, 0}, {-2, 0, 0, 0}, {0, 0, 0, -2}, {0, 0, -2, 0}}

```
MatrixForm[testWtsAdd]
```

```
0    -2   0    0
-2   0    0    0
0    0    0    -2
0    0    -2   0
```

All four of the units receive an additional +1 initial input value, according to the second part of Eq. (5.9).

```
testInAdd = {1,1,1,1}
```

{1, 1, 1, 1}

```
MatrixForm[testWts2 = testWts1+testWtsAdd]
```

```
0    -4   -2   -2
-4   0    -2   -2
-2   -2   0    -4
-2   -2   -4   0
```

```
testIn2 = testIn1+testInAdd
```

{4, 4, 4, 4}

TSP Solutions   Let's rerun the network with the weights that we calculated in the previous section. First we shall make a few changes in the nOutOfN code to accommodate specifics of the TSP. The function tsp appears in Listing 5.2.

One particular item to note about the code is the way we calculate the initial u_i values. We know that the sum of the output values should be equal to Sqrt[numUnits] when the network has settled on a solution. We calculate an initial u_i so that the network starts out with the sum of its outputs equal to the proper number, but in addition, we add a little random noise to the u_i values to give the network a start. Let's run the code with the new weight and input values.

```
tsp[weights_,externIn_,numUnits_,lambda_,deltaT_,
numIters_,printFreq_,reset_:False]:=
    Module[{iter,l,dt,indx,ins,utemp},
      dt=deltaT;
      l=lambda;
      iter=numIters;
      ins=externIn;
            (* only reset if starting over *)
      If[reset,
        utemp = ArcTanh[(2.0/Sqrt[numUnits])-1]/l;
        ui=Table[utemp+Random[Real,{-utemp/10,utemp/10}],
               {numUnits}];  (* end of Table *)
            vi = g[l,ui],Continue];  (* end of If *)
        Print["initial ui = ",N[ui,2]];Print[];
        Print["initial vi = ",N[vi,2]];
      For[iter=1,iter<=numIters,iter++,
        indx = Random[Integer,{1,numUnits}];
        ui[[indx]] = ui[[indx]]+
            dt (vi . Transpose[weights[[indx]]] -
            ui[[indx]] + ins[[indx]]);
        vi[[indx]] = g[l,ui[[indx]]];
        If[Mod[iter,printFreq]==0,
            Print[];Print["iteration = ",iter];
            Print["net inputs = "];
            Print[N[ui,2]];
            Print["outputs = "];
            Print[N[vi,2]];Print[];
            ];  (* end of If *)
        ];  (* end of For *)
      Print[];Print["iteration = ",--iter];
      Print["final outputs = "];
      Print[MatrixForm[Partition[N[vi,2],Sqrt[numUnits]]]];
      ];  (* end of Module *)
```

Listing 5.2

```
tsp[testWts2,testIn2,4,10,0.1,100,20,True];

initial ui = {0.892655, 0.46726, 0.996994, 0.989973}
initial vi = {1., 0.999913, 1., 1.}


iteration = 20
net inputs = {1.12986, -0.700786, 0.3861, 0.25233}
outputs =
                        -7
{1., 8.18559 10   , 0.999557, 0.99361}
iteration = 40
net inputs = {3.20793, -1.61986, -1.13265, 1.23898}
outputs =
               -15              -10
{1., 8.5124 10   , 1.45196 10   , 1.}
iteration = 60
net inputs = {5.62494, -1.98185, -4.71511, 4.31185}
outputs =
                      -18
{1., 6.12574 10   , 0., 1.}
iteration = 80
net inputs = {6.38743, -4.41281, -13.8339, 8.1653}
outputs =
{1., 0., 0., 1.}
iteration = 100
net inputs = {8.14879, -9.36068, -23.5006, 17.8093}
outputs =
{1., 0., 0., 1.}
iteration = 100
final outputs =
{1., 0., 0., 1.}
```

Notice that the additional constraint has been satisfied by this solution: One solution is from the first two units, and one is from the final two units.

Think back to the data representation for the TSP given in Figure 5.2. In order to account for the fact that each city is visited only once, units in each row of Figure 5.2(b) would have to exert an inhibitory connection on all other units in the same row. This situation amounts to a 1-out-of-5 problem for each row. Similarly, since you can only visit one city at a time, units in each column would have to inhibit all other units in the column.

We can construct the weight matrix for the TSP starting with the original n-out-of-N. Because a five-city problem results in a weight matrix having $25^2 = 625$ elements, we would be better off here to consider a simple three-city problem. In that case, n=3 and N=9, and the weight matrix has only 81 elements. First, we construct the part of the weight matrix that accounts for the 3-out-of-9 constraint.

```
MatrixForm[tspWts1 = Table[If[i!=j,-2,0],{i,9},{j,9}]]
```

```
0    -2   -2   -2   -2   -2   -2   -2   -2
-2   0    -2   -2   -2   -2   -2   -2   -2
-2   -2   0    -2   -2   -2   -2   -2   -2
-2   -2   -2   0    -2   -2   -2   -2   -2
-2   -2   -2   -2   0    -2   -2   -2   -2
-2   -2   -2   -2   -2   0    -2   -2   -2
-2   -2   -2   -2   -2   -2   0    -2   -2
-2   -2   -2   -2   -2   -2   -2   0    -2
-2   -2   -2   -2   -2   -2   -2   -2   0
```

```
tspIn1 = Table[2*3-1,{9}]
```

```
{5, 5, 5, 5, 5, 5, 5, 5, 5}
```

We can add the next constraint — that we visit each city only once — with the following weights. Remember, each set of three units represents all three cities at a particular position on the tour; thus, we must select only one unit from units 1-3, one from 4-6, and one from 7-9. For example, among the first three units we would have inhibitory connections between the unit pairs, 1-2, 1-3, 2-1, 3-1, 2-3, and 3-2. The appropriate additions to the weight matrix and input values are as follows.

```
tspWts2 = { { 0,-2,-2, 0, 0, 0, 0, 0, 0},
            {-2, 0,-2, 0, 0, 0, 0, 0, 0},
            {-2,-2, 0, 0, 0, 0, 0, 0, 0},
            { 0, 0, 0, 0,-2,-2, 0, 0, 0},
            { 0, 0, 0,-2, 0,-2, 0, 0, 0},
            { 0, 0, 0,-2,-2, 0, 0, 0, 0},
            { 0, 0, 0, 0, 0, 0, 0,-2,-2},
            { 0, 0, 0, 0, 0, 0,-2, 0,-2},
            { 0, 0, 0, 0, 0, 0,-2,-2, 0} };
```

```
tspIn2 = Table[2*1-1,{9}];
```

To account for the fact that we can only visit one city at a time, we must inhibit the corresponding unit in each of the three groups; for example, units 1, 4, and 7. The corresponding weights and inputs are

```
tspWts3 = { { 0, 0, 0,-2, 0, 0,-2, 0, 0},
            { 0, 0, 0, 0,-2, 0, 0,-2, 0},
            { 0, 0, 0, 0, 0,-2, 0, 0,-2},
            {-2, 0, 0, 0, 0, 0,-2, 0, 0},
            { 0,-2, 0, 0, 0, 0, 0,-2, 0},
            { 0, 0,-2, 0, 0, 0, 0, 0,-2},
            {-2, 0, 0,-2, 0, 0, 0, 0, 0},
            { 0,-2, 0, 0,-2, 0, 0, 0, 0},
            { 0, 0,-2, 0, 0,-2, 0, 0, 0} };
tspIn3 = Table[2*1-1,{9}];
```

We must still account for the weak constraint: that constraint having to do with the distances between the cities. Assume that the distance between cities one and two is one unit, that between cities two and three is two units, and that between one and three is three units. At a given step on the tour, each unit corresponding to a certain city should inhibit the units at either the next step or the previous step that correspond to other cities, in proportion to the distance to that city. For example, unit four, which corresponds to city one, tour position two, should inhibit units eight (city two, position three) and nine (city three, position three), as well as units two (city two, position one) and three (city three, position one). Of course, since there is only one unique tour for the three-city problem, the results that we get will be trivial. Nevertheless, the network should settle on a solution that conforms to the strong constraints. The corresponding weight matrix for the distances is

```
tspWts4 = 0.2 { { 0, 0, 0, 0,-1,-3, 0,-1,-3},
                { 0, 0, 0,-1, 0,-2,-1, 0,-2},
                { 0, 0, 0,-3,-2, 0,-3,-2, 0},
                { 0,-1,-3, 0, 0, 0, 0, 0, 0},
                {-1, 0,-2, 0, 0, 0, 0, 0, 0},
                {-3,-2, 0, 0, 0, 0, 0, 0, 0},
                { 0,-1,-3, 0, 0, 0, 0, 0, 0},
                {-1, 0,-2, 0, 0, 0, 0, 0, 0},
                {-3,-2, 0, 0, 0, 0, 0, 0, 0} };
```

The final weight matrix is the sum of the four individual matrices, and likewise for the external inputs. I have included the factor of 0.2 in the above formula because the distance constraint is a weak constraint; thus its effect on the network should not be such as to overpower the other constraints. A factor of 0.2 may, in fact, be too small, but if you run the network without any multiplicative factor, you will sometimes get a solution with only two cities. This result is presumably because of the stronger inhibitory connections due to the distances between cities. Here is the weight matrix and the vector of external inputs:

```
MatrixForm[tspWts = tspWts1+tspWts2+tspWts3+tspWts4]
```

0	-4	-4	-4	-2.2	-2.6	-4	-2.2	-2.6
-4	0	-4	-2.2	-4	-2.4	-2.2	-4	-2.4
-4	-4	0	-2.6	-2.4	-4	-2.6	-2.4	-4
-4	-2.2	-2.6	0	-4	-4	-4	-2	-2
-2.2	-4	-2.4	-4	0	-4	-2	-4	-2
-2.6	-2.4	-4	-4	-4	0	-2	-2	-4
-4	-2.2	-2.6	-4	-2	-2	0	-4	-4
-2.2	-4	-2.4	-2	-4	-2	-4	0	-4
-2.6	-2.4	-4	-2	-2	-4	-4	-4	0

```
tspIn = tspIn1+tspIn2+tspIn3
```

{7, 7, 7, 7, 7, 7, 7, 7, 7}

Now let's run the network. For space considerations, I have suppressed printing of all but the initial values and final result.

```
tsp[tspWts,tspIn,9,50,0.002,800,200,True];
```

```
initial ui = {-0.0072, -0.0067, -0.0068, -0.0071, -0.007,
     -0.0075, -0.0066, -0.0075, -0.0074}
initial vi = {0.33, 0.34, 0.34, 0.33, 0.33, 0.32, 0.34, 0.32, 0.32}
iteration = 800
final outputs =
```

0.	1.	0.
1.	1.6 10^{-19}	0.
0.	0.	1.

The solution meets all of the strong constraints, as we might expect. Let's try again.

```
tsp[tspWts,tspIn,9,50,0.002,800,200,True];
```

```
initial ui = {-0.0073, -0.0065, -0.0067, -0.0069, -0.0071,
   -0.0071, -0.0063, -0.0066, -0.0075}
initial vi = {0.32, 0.34, 0.34, 0.33, 0.33, 0.33, 0.35, 0.34, 0.32}
```

```
iteration = 800
final outputs =
        -14         -9           -14
3.8 10      5.1 10       1.7 10

0.          1.          0.

1.          0.          1.
```

Notice in this example that the network found a solution that violated one of the strong constraints (although I had to run the program about a dozen times before this solution appeared). We can attempt to fix this problem by increasing the efficacy of the weights associated with those constraints; thus, we can recompute tspWts as follows:

```
MatrixForm[tspWts = tspWts1+ 2 tspWts2+ 2 tspWts3+tspWts4]
```

0	-6	-6	-6	-2.2	-2.6	-6	-2.2	-2.6
-6	0	-6	-2.2	-6	-2.4	-2.2	-6	-2.4
-6	-6	0	-2.6	-2.4	-6	-2.6	-2.4	-6
-6	-2.2	-2.6	0	-6	-6	-6	-2	-2
-2.2	-6	-2.4	-6	0	-6	-2	-6	-2
-2.6	-2.4	-6	-6	-6	0	-2	-2	-6
-6	-2.2	-2.6	-6	-2	-2	0	-6	-6
-2.2	-6	-2.4	-2	-6	-2	-6	0	-6
-2.6	-2.4	-6	-2	-2	-6	-6	-6	0

Let's try the network again.

```
tsp[tspWts,tspIn,9,50,0.002,800,200,True];
```

```
initial ui = {-0.0069, -0.0062, -0.0072, -0.0062, -0.0071,
   -0.007, -0.0063, -0.0076, -0.0064}
```

```
initial vi = {0.33, 0.35, 0.33, 0.35, 0.33, 0.33, 0.35, 0.32,
iteration = 800
final outputs =
0.   1.   0.
0.   0.   1.
1.   0.   0.
```

I ran this program numerous times and never saw a forbidden solution. That is not to say that you may never see one; nevertheless, the modification appears to have helped. I suggest that you construct a four-city problem on your own. The solutions will not be trivial in that case.

5.2.3 Constraints Expressed As Inequalities

So far, our constraints have required that a fixed number of units are "on." Suppose we have the condition that n or less units out of a group are "on." Consider, for example, the problem we did in Section 5.2.2 where we had four units, and one unit among units one and two, and one unit among units three and four, were to be "on." Suppose that we impose the constraint that two or less units are to be "on" among units three and four.

We can impose such a constraint within the context of an n-out-of-N problem through the addition of extra units which we shall call **slack units**. These units are added to the problem during its solution, but are ignored during the interpretation of the solution.

Let's set up the problem that we posed in the first paragraph: four units, with one of the first two on and less than or equal to two of the second two on. This problem requires that we add two slack units to the second group. For the first group, we set up a 1-out-of-2 problem, and for the second group, we set up a 2-out-of-4 problem.

The weight matrix for the first group is

```
group1Wts = { { 0,-2, 0, 0, 0, 0},
              {-2, 0, 0, 0, 0, 0},
              { 0, 0, 0, 0, 0, 0},
              { 0, 0, 0, 0, 0, 0},
              { 0, 0, 0, 0, 0, 0},
              { 0, 0, 0, 0, 0, 0} };
```

For the second group, the weight matrix is

```
group2Wts = { { 0, 0, 0, 0, 0, 0},
              { 0, 0, 0, 0, 0, 0},
              { 0, 0, 0,-2,-2,-2},
              { 0, 0,-2, 0,-2,-2},
              { 0, 0,-2,-2, 0,-2},
              { 0, 0,-2,-2,-2, 0} };
```

The total weight matrix is the sum of the above two matrices,

MatrixForm[groupWts = group1Wts+group2Wts]

```
0   -2   0    0    0    0
-2   0   0    0    0    0
0    0   0   -2   -2   -2
0    0  -2    0   -2   -2
0    0  -2   -2    0   -2
0    0  -2   -2   -2    0
```

The first group of two units gets an external input of 2*1-1=1, while the second group gets 2*2-1=3.

groupIn = {1,1,3,3,3,3}

{1, 1, 3, 3, 3, 3}

Let's run the network several times to see how the results are distributed. Once again I have suppressed all output but the initial values and final results.

nOutOfN[groupWts,groupIn,6,10,0.1,150,150,True]

```
initial ui = {0.53, 0.88, 0.94, 0.54, 0.024, 0.098}
initial vi = {1., 1., 1., 1., 0.62, 0.88}
iteration = 150
final outputs =
{0., 1., 1., 1., 0., 0.}
```

Notice that the first group of two has only one unit on, while the second group has two out of four on. Since the two that are on in the second group are units three and four, the actual solution that we are interested in is 0, 1, 1, 1, assuming that units five and six are the slack units. Let's try again.

```
nOutOfN[groupWts,groupIn,6,10,0.1,100,100,True]
```

```
initial ui = {0.27, 0.31, 0.3, 0.24, 0.77, 0.97}
initial vi = {1., 1., 1., 0.99, 1., 1.}
iteration = 100
final outputs =
{0., 1., 0., 0., 1., 1.}
```

In this solution, neither units three or four are on, but that condition still satisfies the constraint. The actual solution in this case is 0, 1, 0, 0. Let's try one more time.

```
nOutOfN[groupWts,groupIn,6,10,0.1,100,100,True]
```

```
initial ui = {0.28, 0.56, 0.68, 0.42, 0.7, 0.75}
initial vi = {1., 1., 1., 1., 1., 1.}
iteration = 100
final outputs =
{0., 1., 1., 0., 1., 0.}
```

The solution here would be 0, 1, 1, 0, which again satisfies all of the constraints.

Summary

Constraint satisfaction and optimization problems form a large class for which the traveling salesperson problem is the prototypical example. In this chapter we modified the Hopfield network to allow the units to take on continuous values. Then, using a procedure based on n-out-of-N units allowed to be in the "on" state, we showed how to calculate the weights for a Hopfield network that solves the TSP. This method is quite general and can be applied to many similar constraint-satisfaction problems.

Chapter 6

Feedback and Recurrent Networks

The title of this chapter implies the existence of neural networks whose outputs find their way back to become inputs, or in which data moves both forward and backward in the network. There are many varieties of these networks. One such network is the Hopfield network, which was the subject of Chapters 4 and 5. The Hopfield network is a derivative of a two-layer network called a **bidirectional associative memory** (BAM) (You could, alternatively, think of the BAM as a generalization of the Hopfield network.) The BAM is a recurrent network that implements an associative memory. We shall study the BAM first in this chapter.

Following the BAM, we shall look at two multilayer network architectures that have feedback paths within their structures. These networks are named after individuals: Elman and Jordan. With these architectures, we shall be able to develop neural networks that can learn a time sequence of input vectors.

6.1   The BAM

The BAM is similar to the Hopfield network in several ways. Like the Hopfield network, we can compute a weight matrix in advance, provided we know what we want to store. Moreover, you will notice a similarity in the way the weights are determined and in the way processing is done by the individual units in the BAM. This network implements a heteroassociative memory rather than an autoassociative memory, as was the case with the Hopfield network. For example, we might store pairs of vectors representing the names and corresponding phone numbers of our friends or customers. To see how we can accomplish this feat, let's look at the BAM architecture.

6.1.1   BAM Architecture and Processing

Figure 6.1 illustrates the architecture of the BAM. The BAM comprises two layers of units that are fully interconnected between the layers. The units may, or may not, have feedback connections to themselves.

To apply the BAM to a particular problem, we assemble a set of pairs of vectors where each pair comprises two pieces of information that we would like to associate with each other; for example, a name and a phone number. To store this information in the BAM, we must first represent each datum as a vector having components in $\{-1, +1\}$. We refer to these

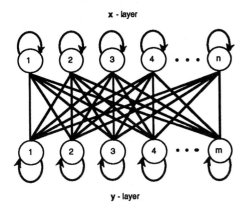

x - layer

y - layer

Figure 6.1 The BAM shown here has n units on the x layer, and m units on the y layer. For convenience, we shall call the x vector the input vector, and the y vector, the output vector. In this network all of the elements in either the x or y vectors must be members of the set $\{-1, +1\}$. All connections between units are bi-directional with weights at each end. Information passes back and forth from one layer to the other, through these connections. Feedback connections at each unit may not be present in all BAM architectures.

vectors as **bipolar vectors,** rather than binary vectors, whose components would be in the set $\{0, +1\}$. Then we construct weight matrices for the x- and y-layers in a manner similar to that used for the Hopfield network. Once the weight matrix has been constructed, the BAM can be used to recall information (for example, a phone number), when presented with some key information (a name corresponding to a particular phone number). If the desired information is only partially known in advance or is noisy (a misspelled name such as "Simth"), the BAM may be able to correct the error and provide the correct corresponding information (giving the proper spelling, "Smith," and the correct phone number). Since our examples here will all be fictitious, we shall make the assumption that the data-representation issue has been addressed elsewhere. Let's define some exemplars and examine BAM processing in some detail.

```
exemplars={ {{1,-1,-1,1,-1,1,1,-1,-1,1},{1,-1,-1,-1,-1,1}},
            {{1,1,1,-1,-1,-1,1,1,-1,-1},{1,1,1,1,-1,-1}} };
```

There are two vector pairs in this example. The first vector of each pair is the x-layer vector, and the second is the y-layer vector. There are 10 units on the x layer and six on the y layer, and hence, 10 connections to each y-layer unit and six to each x-layer unit.

There are two weight matrices: one on the connections from the x layer to the y layer, and one on the connections from the y layer to the x layer. To construct the first weight matrix (x layer to y layer), we compute the sum of the outer products of the vector pairs as follows

$$w = \sum_{i=1}^{L} y_i x_i^t \tag{6.1}$$

where L is the number of vector pairs in the training set. To calculate the second weight matrix (y layer to x layer), we simply transpose the matrix in Eq. (6.1). The following function will calculate the x-to-y weight matrix.

```
makeXtoYwts[exemplars_] :=
  Module[{temp},
    temp = Map[Outer[Times,#[[2]],#[[1]]]&,exemplars];
    Apply[Plus,temp]
  ]; (* end of Module *)
```

We can now calculate the two weight matrices.

```
MatrixForm[x2yWts=makeXtoYwts[exemplars]]
```

2	0	0	0	-2	0	2	0	-2	0
0	2	2	-2	0	-2	0	2	0	-2
0	2	2	-2	0	-2	0	2	0	-2
0	2	2	-2	0	-2	0	2	0	-2
-2	0	0	0	2	0	-2	0	2	0
0	-2	-2	2	0	2	0	-2	0	2

```
MatrixForm[y2xWts = Transpose[x2yWts]]
```

2	0	0	0	-2	0
0	2	2	2	0	-2
0	2	2	2	0	-2
0	-2	-2	-2	0	2
-2	0	0	0	2	0
0	-2	-2	-2	0	2
2	0	0	0	-2	0
0	2	2	2	0	-2
-2	0	0	0	2	0
0	-2	-2	-2	0	2

Unit outputs will be -1, or $+1$, depending on the value of the net input to the unit. We calculate net inputs in the usual manner of the dot product between the input vector and the weight vector for each unit. Then the output of the unit is given by

$$s_i(t+1) = \begin{cases} +1 & \text{net}_i^s > 0 \\ s_i(t) & \text{net}_i^s = 0 \\ -1 & \text{net}_i^s < 0 \end{cases} \qquad (6.2)$$

where s refers to a unit on either layer, and we use the discrete variable t to denote a particular timestep. Notice that if the net input is zero, the output does not change from what it was in the previous timestep.

The two functions, psi and phi, that we defined for the Hopfield network (see Section 4.1), also apply to the BAM. These functions implement the output function of the BAM units as specified in Eq. (6.2).

```
psi[inValue_,netIn_] := If[netIn>0,1,
                    If[netIn<0,-1,inValue]];
phi[inVector_List,netInVector_List] :=
    MapThread[psi[#,#2]&,{inVector,netInVector}];
```

The energy function for the BAM is also similar to that of the Hopfield network.

$$E = -\mathbf{y}^t \mathbf{w} \mathbf{x} \qquad (6.3)$$

```
energyBAM[xx_,w_,zz_] := - (xx . w . zz)
```

We can use this function to calculate the energy of the network with the exemplars.

```
energyBAM[exemplars[[1,2]],x2yWts,exemplars[[1,1]]]
```

-64

```
energyBAM[exemplars[[2,2]],x2yWts,exemplars[[2,1]]]
```

-64

To recall stored information from the BAM, we perform the following steps:

1. Apply an initial vector pair, $(\mathbf{x}_0, \mathbf{y}_0)$, to the processing elements of the BAM.

2. Propagate the information from the x layer to the y layer and update the values on the y-layer units. Although we shall consistently begin with the x-to-y propagation, you could begin in the other direction.

3. Propagate the updated y information back to the x layer and update the units there.

4. Repeat steps 2 and 3 until there is no further change in the units on each layer, or, equivalently, there is no further change in the energy of the system.

This algorithm is what gives the BAM its bi-directional nature. The terms *input* and *output* refer to different quantities, depending on the current direction of the propagation. For example, in going from y to x, the **y** vector is considered as the input to the network, and the **x** vector is the output. The opposite is true when propagating from x to y.

If all goes well, the final, stable state will recall one of the exemplars used to construct the weight matrix. Since in this example, we assume we know something about the desired **x** vector, but perhaps nothing about the associated **y** vector, we hope that the final output is the exemplar whose x_i vector is *closest* to the original input vector. There are many definitions of the word *close* that are used when discussing neural networks. In the case of the BAM, we use **Hamming distance** as the measure of closeness between two vectors. The Hamming distance between two vectors is the number of bits that differ between the two. The concept applies equally to bipolar or binary vectors.

The above scenario works well provided we have not overloaded the BAM with exemplars. If we try to put too much information in a given BAM, a phenomenon known as **crosstalk** occurs between exemplar patterns. Crosstalk occurs when exemplar patterns are too close to each other. The interaction between these patterns can result in the creation of **spurious stable states**. In that case, the BAM could stabilize on meaningless vectors. If we think of the BAM in terms of an energy surface in weight space, each exemplar pattern occupies a deep minimum well in the space. Spurious stable states correspond to energy minima that appear between the minima that correspond to the examplars.

```
bam[initialX_,initialY_,x2yWeights_,y2xWeights_,printAll_:False] :=
  Module[{done,newX,newY,energy1,energy2},
    done = False;
    newX = initialX;
    newY = initialY;
    While[done == False,
      newY = phi[newY,x2yWeights.newX];
      If[printAll,Print[];Print[];Print["y = ",newY]];
      energy1 = energyBAM[newY,x2yWeights,newX];
      If[printAll,Print["energy = ",energy1]];
      newX = phi[newX,y2xWeights . newY];
      If[printAll,Print[];Print["x = ",newX]];
      energy2 = energyBAM[newY,x2yWeights,newX];
      If[printAll,Print["energy = ",energy1]];
      If[energy1 == energy2,done=True,Continue];
    ]; (* end of While *)
    Print[];Print[];
    Print["final y = ",newY," energy= ",energy1];
    Print["final x = ",newX," energy= ",energy2];
  ]; (* end of Module *)
```

Listing 6.2

6.1.2 BAM Processing Examples

Let's use the exemplars and weights that we calculated in the previous section to exercise the BAM for a number of different initial vectors. First, let's assemble the necessary code into a procedure as shown in Listing 6.2. For our first example, we shall select an initial **x** vector that differs from the first x-vector exemplar by only one bit. The initial **y** vector will be equal to the second y-vector exemplar.

```
initX = {-1,-1,-1,1,-1,1,1,-1,-1,1};
initY = {1,1,1,1,-1,-1};
```

The energy of a BAM in this initial state is

```
energyBAM[initY,x2yWts,initX]
```

40

By setting printAll to True, we can watch the progression of events as the data propagate back and forth through the BAM.

```
bam[initX,initY,x2yWts,y2xWts,True]
```

```
y = {1, -1, -1, -1, -1, 1}
energy = -56
x = {1, -1, -1, 1, -1, 1, 1, -1, -1, 1}
energy = -56
y = {1, -1, -1, -1, -1, 1}
energy = -64
x = {1, -1, -1, 1, -1, 1, 1, -1, -1, 1}
energy = -64
final y = {1, -1, -1, -1, -1, 1}  energy= -64
final x = {1, -1, -1, 1, -1, 1, 1, -1, -1, 1}  energy= -64
```

Notice that we have recovered the first exemplar.

For our second example, we shall define the starting vectors as follows:

```
ClearAll[initX,initY];
initX = {-1,1,1,-1,1,1,1,-1,1,-1};
initY = {-1,1,-1,1,-1,-1};
```

```
energyBAM[initY,x2yWts,initX]
```

```
-8
```

The Hamming distances of the x_0 vector from the training vectors is $h(x_0, x_1) = 7$ and $h(x_0, x_2) = 5$. For the y_0 vector, the values are $h(y_0, y_1) = 4$ and $h(y_0, y_2) = 2$. Based on these results, we might expect that the BAM would settle on the second exemplar as a final solution. Let's see what happens.

```
bam[initX,initY,x2yWts,y2xWts,True]
```

```
y = {-1, 1, 1, 1, 1, -1}
energy = -24
x = {-1, 1, 1, -1, 1, -1, -1, 1, 1, -1}
energy = -24
y = {-1, 1, 1, 1, 1, -1}
energy = -64
```

```
x = {-1, 1, 1, -1, 1, -1, -1, 1, 1, -1}
energy = -64
final y = {-1, 1, 1, 1, 1, -1}  energy= -64
final x = {-1, 1, 1, -1, 1, -1, -1, 1, 1, -1}  energy= -64
```

Compare these results with the exemplars

exemplars

```
{{{1, -1, -1, 1, -1, 1, 1, -1, -1, 1}, {1, -1, -1, -1, -1, 1}},
  {{1, 1, 1, -1, -1, -1, 1, 1, -1, -1}, {1, 1, 1, 1, -1, -1}}}
```

You will notice that the final output vectors do not match any of the examplars. Furthermore, they are actually the complement of the first training set, $(x_{out}, y_{out}) = (x_1^c, y_1^c)$, where the c superscript refers to the complement. This example illustrates a basic property of the BAM: If you encode an exemplar, (x, y), you also encode its complement, (x^c, y^c).

Let's try a pair of random vectors to see if we always get an exemplar or a complement of an exemplar.

```
initX = 2 Table[Random[Integer,{0,1}],{10}]-1
```

```
{-1, -1, 1, 1, -1, -1, 1, -1, 1, 1}
```

```
initY = 2 Table[Random[Integer,{0,1}],{6}]-1
```

```
{-1, 1, 1, -1, 1, -1}
```

```
bam[initX,initY,x2yWts,y2xWts,False]
```

```
final y = {-1, -1, -1, -1, 1, 1}  energy= -64
final x = {-1, -1, -1, 1, 1, 1, -1, -1, 1, 1}  energy= -64
```

Right away, we have found a spurious stable state whose energy is equal to that of the exemplars' states. You can see that the problem of spurious stable states is not one to be dismissed casually.

6.2 Recognition of Time Sequences

Mapping networks, such as the backpropagation network, and associative memories, such as the BAM and Hopfield networks, generally deal with static or spatial patterns. The final output from these networks does not depend on any previous output. There are applications, however, for which a network that can accommodate a time-ordered sequence of patterns would be necessary. An example, currently unattainable by any neural network except a human one, would be learning the sequence of finger and arm movements necessary to play a piece on the piano.

One way of encoding such a sequence is with a type of neural network called an **avalanche**, in which a series of units are triggered in a time sequence. A second way of dealing with time in a neural network is to take the results of processing at one particular time step and feed that data back to the network inputs at the next time step. This latter method is the one that we shall explore in this section.

6.2.1 The Elman Network

The architecture of the **Elman network** appears in Figure 6.2. The network resembles a standard, feed-forward, layered network such as a BPN. In fact, the training of all of the feed-forward connection weights follows the standard generalized delta rule. The extra input units are called **context units**.

Let's apply this network to a simple problem in which we present two different sequences of numbers to the network. The first sequence is 1, 2, 3, 1, the second is 2, 1, 3, 2. We shall ask the network to supply the next number in the sequence as we present it with the first three numbers. In each sequence, the third number is the same, but the fourth number is different, which requires that the network "remembers" the context in which the "3" is presented. After the third input, we shall reset the network to begin on a new sequence.

This problem would likely confound a standard BPN. Such a network could easily learn to map a "1" to a "2," a "2" to a "3," and a "3" to a "1," as in the first sequence. However, when learning the second sequence, we ask the network to learn that a "2" maps to a "1" and that a "3" maps to a "2." In a standard BPN, where each input pattern is presented independently, there is no context to alert the network as to which of the two contradictory mappings is the appropriate one. For the BPN, this situation represents a **one-to-many mapping**, for which the BPN is ill-equipped to handle.

To solve this problem, we shall construct an Elman network with three input units, one for each of the possible values (1, 2, or 3) in the first three positions of the input sequences. For this example, we put four

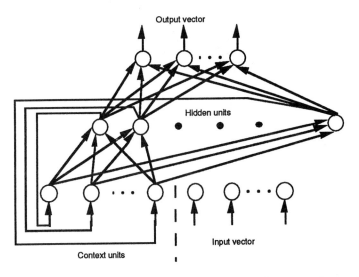

Figure 6.2 In this representation of the Elman network, outputs from each of the hidden-layer units at timestep t, become additional inputs to the network at timestep $t + 1$. At each timestep, information from all previous timesteps influences the output of the hidden layer and hence also influences the network output.

units on the hidden layer. Correspondingly, there will be four context units, for a total of seven units on the first layer. The output can be one of three numbers (1, 2, or 3), so we assign one unit to each of those values, making three units on the output layer.

We begin by constructing the input-output sequences.

```
ClearAll[ioPairsEl]
ioPairsEl =
          (*    inputs       outputs   *)
{    (*  1   2   3     1   2   3 *)
    {{ {0.9, 0.1, 0.1}, {0.1, 0.9, 0.1} },
      { {0.1, 0.9, 0.1}, {0.1, 0.1, 0.9} },
      { {0.1, 0.1, 0.9}, {0.9, 0.1, 0.1} }},
    {{ {0.1, 0.9, 0.1}, {0.9, 0.1, 0.1} },
      { {0.9, 0.1, 0.1}, {0.1, 0.1, 0.9} },
      { {0.1, 0.1, 0.9}, {0.1, 0.9, 0.1} }
    } };
```

The degree of nesting in the ioPairsEl list maintains separation between the sequences. For example:

`ioPairsEl[[1]]`

```
{{{0.9, 0.1, 0.1}, {0.1, 0.9, 0.1}},
  {{0.1, 0.9, 0.1}, {0.1, 0.1, 0.9}},
  {{0.1, 0.1, 0.9}, {0.9, 0.1, 0.1}}}
```

is the first sequence, comprising three `ioPair` vectors:

`ioPairsEl[[1,1]]`

```
{{0.9, 0.1, 0.1}, {0.1, 0.9, 0.1}}
```

Since the Elman network uses a standard backpropagation-of-errors during the learning process, we can begin the code development with the BPN code from Chapter 3. We shall need to make several modifications, but the basic algorithm remains intact.

First, we need to increase the size of the hidden-unit weight table. Instead of (`hidNumber` by `inNumber`), the dimension of the table will be (`hidNumber` by (`inNumber` +`hidNumber`)), where `hidNumber` is the number of hidden units, which is equal to the number of context units. Likewise, we must increase the vector that stores the previous delta values on the hidden-layer units (see Chapter 3).

```
hidWts = Table[Table[Random[Real,{-0.5,0.5}],
    {inNumber+hidNumber}],{hidNumber}];
hidLastDelta = Table[Table[0,{inNumber+hidNumber}],
    {hidNumber}];
```

Instead of calculating a `Table` of errors, as we did in the BPN code, we shall switch over to a `For` loop. The `numIters` parameter will be the number of times that we cycle through each sequence. We begin the actual processing by selecting a sequence at random.

```
ioSequence=ioPairs[[Random[Integer,{1,Length[ioPairs]}]]];
```

Then, since we are beginning a new sequence, we reset the outputs of the context units to a value of 0.5.

```
conUnits = Table[0.5,{hidNumber}];
```

Next we begin a second For loop to cycle through the individual patterns in the sequence. Using i as the index, we select the next pattern to be processed:

```
ioP = ioSequence[[i]];
```

then identify the input vector and desired output vector. In this case, however, we concatenate the context units to the sequence's input vector.

```
inputs=Join[conUnits,ioP[[1]] ];
outDesired=ioP[[2]];
```

The remainder of the processing in this inner loop is identical to the BPN processing. Before completing the loop, we must remember to set the context-unit outputs equal to the current outputs of the hidden-layer units.

```
conUnits = hidOuts;
```

Finally, we add the square of the current error value to the errorList.

```
AppendTo[errorList,outErrors.outErrors];
```

We then repeat the inner loop for as many patterns as there are in the sequence. When finished with a sequence, we select another, reset the context units to 0.5, and begin another inner loop. The entire program appears in Listing 6.3. We also must write a new test program to accommodate the sequences. Call the new test program, elmanTest. This program, which appears in Listing 6.4, is similar in intent to bpnTest, but has an additional parameter, conNumber, that explicitly defines the number of context units. Let's use this code to attempt our example problem. For space considerations I have suppressed some of the printout from the function. After this first run, I will also suppress the printout of the results of individual patterns, showing only the error plot.

```
ClearAll[elOut];
elOut = {};
Timing[elOut = elman[3,4,3,ioPairsEl,0.5,0.9,100];]

Sequence 1 input 1
inputs:
{0.5, 0.5, 0.5, 0.5, 0.9, 0.1, 0.1}
outputs:
```

```
elman[inNumber_,hidNumber_,outNumber_,ioPairs_,eta_,alpha_,numIters_] :=
  Module[{hidWts,outWts,ioP,inputs,hidOuts,outputs,outDesired,
          i,indx,hidLastDelta,outLastDelta,outDelta,errorList={},
          ioSequence, conUnits,hidDelta,outErrors},
  hidWts = Table[Table[Random[Real,{-0.5,0.5}],{inNumber+hidNumber}],{hidNumber}];
  outWts = Table[Table[Random[Real,{-0.5,0.5}],{hidNumber}],{outNumber}];
  hidLastDelta = Table[Table[0,{inNumber+hidNumber}],{hidNumber}];
  outLastDelta = Table[Table[0,{hidNumber}],{outNumber}];
  For[indx=1,indx<=numIters,indx++,  (* begin forward pass; select a sequence *)
    ioSequence=ioPairs[[Random[Integer,{1,Length[ioPairs]}]]];
    conUnits = Table[0.5,{hidNumber}];    (* reset conUnits *)
    For[i=1,i<=Length[ioSequence],i++,    (* process the sequence in order *)
    ioP = ioSequence[[i]];               (* pick out the next ioPair *)
    inputs=Join[conUnits,ioP[[1]] ];     (* join context and input units *)
      outDesired=ioP[[2]];
      hidOuts = sigmoid[hidWts.inputs];    (* hidden-layer outputs *)
      outputs = sigmoid[outWts.hidOuts];   (* output-layer outputs *)
      outErrors = outDesired-outputs;      (* calculate errors *)
      outDelta= outErrors (outputs (1-outputs));
      hidDelta=(hidOuts (1-hidOuts)) Transpose[outWts].outDelta;
      outLastDelta= eta Outer[Times,outDelta,hidOuts]+alpha outLastDelta;
      outWts += outLastDelta;              (* update weights *)
      hidLastDelta = eta Outer[Times,hidDelta,inputs]+alpha hidLastDelta;
      hidWts += hidLastDelta;
      conUnits = hidOuts;                  (* update context units *)
        (* put the sum of the squared errors on the list *)
      AppendTo[errorList,outErrors.outErrors];
      ]; (* end of For i *)
    ];    (* end of For indx *)
  Print["New hidden-layer weight matrix: "];
  Print[ ]; Print[hidWts];Print[ ];
  Print["New output-layer weight matrix: "];
  Print[ ]; Print[outWts];Print[ ];
  elmanTest[hidWts,outWts,ioPairs,hidNumber];   (* check how close we are *)
  errorPlot = ListPlot[errorList, PlotJoined->True];
  Return[{hidWts,outWts,errorList,errorPlot}];
  ]                     (* end of Module *)
```

Listing 6.3

```
elmanTest[hiddenWts_,outputWts_,ioPairVectors_,conNumber_,printAll_:False] :=.
  Module[{inputs,hidden,outputs,desired,errors,i,j,
           prntAll,conUnits,ioSequence,ioP},
    If[printAll,Print[];Print["ioPairs:"];Print[];Print[ioPairVectors]];
              (* loop through the sequences *)
      For[i=1,i<=Length[ioPairVectors],i++,
              (* select the next sequence *)
    ioSequence = ioPairVectors[[i]];
              (* reset the context units  *)
    conUnits = Table[0.5,{conNumber}];
              (* loop through the chosen sequence *)
      For[j=1,j<=Length[ioSequence],j++,
          ioP = ioSequence[[j]];
                (* join context and input units *)
        inputs=Join[conUnits,ioP[[1]] ];
        desired=ioP[[2]];
        hidden=sigmoid[hiddenWts.inputs];
        outputs=sigmoid[outputWts.hidden];
        errors= desired-outputs;
            (* update context units *)
        conUnits = hidden;
        Print[ ];
        Print["Sequence ",i, " input ",j];
        Print[ ];Print["inputs:"];Print[ ];
        Print[inputs];
        If[printAll,Print[ ];Print["hidden-layer outputs:"];
            Print[hidden];Print[];];
        Print["outputs:"];Print[ ];
        Print[outputs];Print[];
        Print["desired:"];Print[];Print[desired];Print[ ];
        Print["Mean squared error:"];
        Print[errors.errors/Length[errors]];
        Print[ ];
        ]; (* end of For j *)
      ];   (* end of For i *)
  ]                (* end of Module *)
```

Listing 6.4

{0.00991694, 0.848143, 0.342235}
desired:
{0.1, 0.9, 0.1}
Mean squared error:
0.0231606
Sequence 1 input 2
inputs:
{0.033297, 0.686708, 0.352224, 0.801336, 0.1, 0.9, 0.1}
outputs:
{0.164773, 0.095997, 0.676043}
desired:
{0.1, 0.1, 0.9}
Mean squared error:
0.0181227
Sequence 1 input 3
inputs:
{0.187346, 0.130752, 0.673253, 0.595115, 0.1, 0.1, 0.9}
outputs:
{0.549356, 0.366293, 0.105307}
desired:
{0.9, 0.1, 0.1}
Mean squared error:
0.0646305
Sequence 2 input 1
inputs:
{0.5, 0.5, 0.5, 0.5, 0.1, 0.9, 0.1}
outputs:
{0.83715, 0.00746378, 0.296124}
desired:
{0.9, 0.1, 0.1}
Mean squared error:
0.0169926
Sequence 2 input 2
inputs:
{0.720089, 0.0110963, 0.815086, 0.348975, 0.9, 0.1, 0.1}
outputs:
{0.0757287, 0.183033, 0.672605}
desired:
{0.1, 0.1, 0.9}

```
Mean squared error:
0.0197307
Sequence 2 input 3
inputs:
{0.152164, 0.214958, 0.591788, 0.733609, 0.1, 0.1, 0.9}
outputs:
{0.229314, 0.771018, 0.0831117}
desired:
{0.1, 0.9, 0.1}
Mean squared error:
0.0112145
```

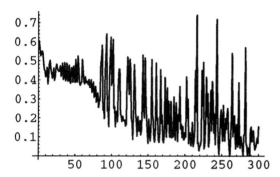

{393.383 Second, Null}

We do not need to require that the error drop to an extremely small value in this case. We can be satisfied if one node has an output that is significantly larger than the other nodes. Using this criterion, the network has learned all of the patterns after 100 passes. We also learn from this test that the program takes a while to run.

The wild oscillations in the error plot may be an indication that either the learning rate or the momentum, or both, is too large. You may want to experiment with different parameters to see if you can get better performance.

Before leaving this network, let's consider experimenting with the architecture a bit. Since we know that we would like only one unit in the output layer to be "on" for any given input pattern, we can use our knowledge of inhibitory connections, gained in Chapter 5, to facilitate this behavior. There are several ways in which you might implement inhibitory connections between units on the output layer. The following code represents one attempt.

```
outputs = outWts.hidOuts;
            (* modify by inhibitory connections *)
outputs = sigmoid[outputs -
            0.3 Apply[Plus,outputs] + .5 outputs];
```

The function elmanComp, which appears in the appendix, implements this code. You can see by the following example that we did not gain much, if anything, using the specific changed listed above. Nevertheless the idea holds promise, and you may want to see if you can improve on the above attempt.

```
ClearAll[elOut];
elOut = {};
elOut = elmanComp[3,4,3,ioPairsEl,0.5,0.9,100];
```

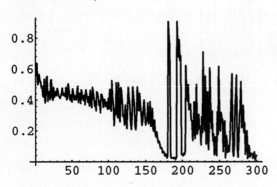

6.2.2 The Jordan Network

With a very straightforward modification of the Elman network architecture, we produce another type of feedback network called the **Jordan network**. Instead of taking the feedback from the hidden-layer units, we take it from the output-layer units. The architecture appears in Figure 6.3.

We shall use this network to learn sequences, but in a slightly different manner than we did with the Elman network. Assume that we have several sequences of output vectors that we would like to encode in this network. We can represent each sequence as a set of output vectors; for example, the ith sequence would be $\{x_{i1}, x_{i2}, \ldots, x_{in}\}$, where we

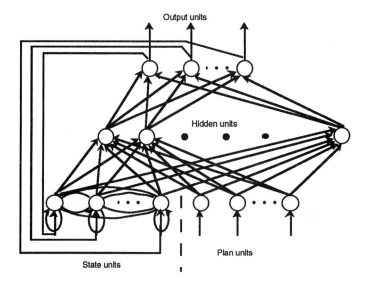

Figure 6.3 This figure illustrates the architecture of the Jordan network. Notice that units called state units receive their inputs from the output-layer units instead of the hidden-layer units as in the case of the Elman network. Notice also that there are connections between all of the state units as well as feedback from each state unit to itself. The function of the plan units and state units is described in the text.

have assumed that the sequence contains n vectors. Let's associate a unique **plan vector**, $\mathbf{p}_i$, with the ith sequence. This plan vector uniquely identifies the associated output sequence. When we apply the plan vector to the plan units of the Jordan network, we want the network to respond with the appropriate sequence of output vectors.

Because of the feedback connections from each state unit to itself, the output of the state units can be influenced by all previous states in the sequence, thus providing a context for the next output vector in the sequence. We shall assume that the connection between the output unit and its corresponding state unit carries a connection-weight value of one. In a more general network, these connection weights could be learned like other weights in the network. In general, the output of each state unit is some function of the corresponding output-unit value at the previous time step and the previous output of the state unit. For our examples we shall use the following formulation:

$$s_i(t) = \mu s_i(t-1) + o_i \tag{6.4}$$

Plan Unit	State Units		Output Units	
0	0	0	0	1
0	0	1	1	0
0	1	0	1	1
0	1	1	0	0
1	0	0	1	1
1	1	1	1	0
1	1	0	0	1
1	0	1	0	0

Table 6.1 This table shows the inputs and outputs for the counting example.

where s_i is the output of the ith state unit, o_i is the output of the ith output unit, and the value of μ determines the amount of influence of previous time steps. If μ is less than one, then the influence of previous time steps decreases exponentially as we look farther back in time. In the following examples, we shall not use the connections between the state units.

Let's apply the Jordan network to a simple example and discuss the processing within the context of that example. We shall call this example the counting example. For this first example, we shall assume that $\mu = 0$. Table 6.1 shows the various vectors in their proper sequence.

We require one plan unit that can take on a value of 0 or 1. The sequence corresponding to a plan unit of 0 counts upward from binary 1. The other sequence counts down from binary 11. Because $\mu = 0$, the state units take on values equal to the output units at the previous time step. The network will have two state units, two output units, and two hidden units, although the number of hidden units is not specified by the example. Although we are using binary units here, there is nothing that precludes the use of continuous-value units.

There are not many changes required to convert the elman function into a jordan function. First we need to add an additional parameter, mu, to the calling sequence.

```
jordan[inNumber_,hidNumber_,outNumber_,ioPairs_,
    eta_,alpha_,mu_,numIters_]
```

Then we need to alter the size of the hidden-unit weight matrix and last-delta matrix, changing `hidNumber` in `elman`, to `outNumber`.

```
hidWts = Table[Table[Random[Real,{-0.5,0.5}],
          {inNumber+outNumber}],{hidNumber}];
hidLastDelta = Table[Table[0,{inNumber+outNumber}],
                              {hidNumber}];
```

In addition, we initialize the `stateUnits` array to zeros (actually 0.1), in place of the `conUnits` array in elman which we initialized to 0.5.

```
stateUnits = Table[0.1,{outNumber}];
```

Update the value of the state units according to Eq. (6.4):

```
stateUnits = mu stateUnits + outputs;
```

We must also make corresponding changes to convert `elmanTest` into `jordanTest`. Both complete routines appear in the appendix.

Using the table for the counting problem we can construct the appropriate `ioPair` vector.

```
ioPairsJor = {
          {{{0.1}, {0.1, 0.9}},
            {{0.1}, {0.9, 0.1}},
            {{0.1}, {0.9, 0.9}},
            {{0.1}, {0.1, 0.1}}},
          {{{0.9}, {0.9, 0.9}},
            {{0.9}, {0.9, 0.1}},
            {{0.9}, {0.1, 0.9}},
            {{0.9}, {0.1, 0.1}}} };
```

Let's make a number of different runs using the Jordan network in various configurations. There are several modifications that we can try in order to assess the corresponding performance impact. You should be aware that the runs that follow generally show only a relatively few iterations. If you actually want to reduce the error to a value that we would consider appropriate for actual applications, you would likely have to run the network for a significantly longer time. We restrict the number of iterations here so that we can perform this experiment in a reasonable time. Note, however, that many of the runs are quite time consuming. We begin with the standard Jordan network as we have described it above.

For the first run, we set $\mu = 0$. As with the Elman-network output, I have edited out some information. For this first example I will leave intact the results from individual inputs.

```
Timing[jordan[1,2,2,ioPairsJor,0.5,0.9,0,200];]
```

Sequence 1 input 1
inputs:
{0.1, 0.1, 0.1}
outputs:
{0.497832, 0.84752}
desired:
{0.1, 0.9}
Mean squared error:
0.0805123
Sequence 1 input 2
inputs:
{0.497832, 0.84752, 0.1}
outputs:
{0.48581, 0.112169}
desired:
{0.9, 0.1}
Mean squared error:
0.0858507
Sequence 1 input 3
inputs:
{0.48581, 0.112169, 0.1}
outputs:
{0.498776, 0.898134}
desired:
{0.9, 0.9}
Mean squared error:
0.080492
Sequence 1 input 4
inputs:
{0.498776, 0.898134, 0.1}
outputs:
{0.485458, 0.102813}
desired:
{0.1, 0.1}

```
Mean squared error:
0.074293
Sequence 2 input 1
inputs:
{0.1, 0.1, 0.9}
outputs:
{0.500204, 0.886611}
desired:
{0.9, 0.9}
Mean squared error:
0.0800082
Sequence 2 input 2
inputs:
{0.500204, 0.886611, 0.9}
outputs:
{0.486778, 0.124524}
desired:
{0.9, 0.1}
Mean squared error:
0.0856769
Sequence 2 input 3
inputs:
{0.486778, 0.124524, 0.9}
outputs:
{0.500819, 0.9171}
desired:
{0.1, 0.9}
Mean squared error:
0.0804742
Sequence 2 input 4
inputs:
{0.500819, 0.9171, 0.9}
outputs:
{0.486519, 0.117791}
desired:
{0.1, 0.1}
Mean squared error:
0.0748567
```

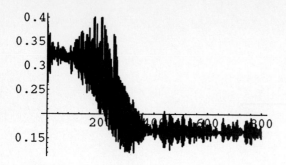

{581.1 Second, Null}

If we consider all output values above 0.5 to be "1," and all below 0.5 to be "0," then this network appears to be on the verge of performing well, although it seems to be stalled. Adjustments in the parameters may help, but we shall not undertake such a study here. Instead, let's redo the example with a nonzero value of μ.

```
Timing[jordan[1,2,2,ioPairsJor,0.5,0.9,0.1,200];]
```

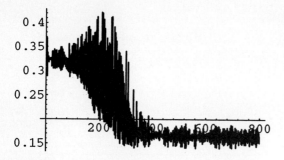

{715.517 Second, Null}

The results here seem to be fairly close to those for $\mu = 0$. Let's see if increasing the number of hidden units helps.

```
Timing[jordan[1,4,2,ioPairsJor,0.5,0.9,0.1,100];]
```

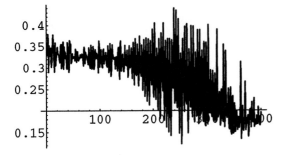

{486.333 Second, Null}

It does not look like we accomplished very much with that change, though more passes through the data may help. Let's try something different. Instead of setting the stateUnits equal to the actual output units during training, we can set them equal to the desired outputs. The function jordan2 implements this variation. For this test I have set the μ factor back to zero.

Timing[jordan2[1,4,2,ioPairsJor,0.5,0.9,0,100];]

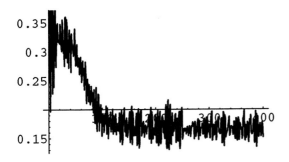

{497.133 Second, Null}

The error dropped much faster for this run than it did for the previous runs. Using the desired outputs as state vectors appears to have helped. Let's make another change for purely aesthetic reasons. If you look at the code, you will see that we are capturing the sum of the squares of the errors as each pattern is presented to the network. When we print the

results, we show the mean squared error, averaged over all of the output
units. The function *jordan2a* plots the average mean squared error; that
is, the squared error averaged over the output units, then averaged over
all of the patterns in a sequence.

```
Timing[jordan2a[1,4,2,ioPairsJor,0.5,0.9,0,100];]
```

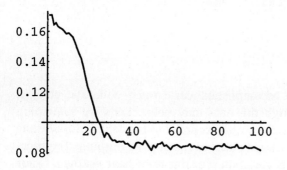

```
{484.75 Second, Null}
```

We can also try a different representation of the plan vector. The following uses a two-element plan vector for the counter problem.

```
ioPairsJor2 = {
              {{{0.1, 0.9}, {0.1, 0.9}},
                {{0.1, 0.9}, {0.9, 0.1}},
                {{0.1, 0.9}, {0.9, 0.9}},
                {{0.1, 0.9}, {0.1, 0.1}}},
              {{{0.9, 0.1}, {0.9, 0.9}},
                {{0.9, 0.1}, {0.9, 0.1}},
                {{0.9, 0.1}, {0.1, 0.9}},
                {{0.9, 0.1}, {0.1, 0.1}}}
              };
```

```
Timing[jordan2a[2,4,2,ioPairsJor2,0.5,0.9,0,100];]
```

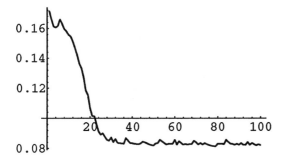

{274.05 Second, Null}

Although we are not seeing much difference here from run to run, such changes often result in performance improvements. One final modification represents a somewhat radical change from the way we have been doing the generalized delta rule algorithm.

The Tanh[u] function has the same general shape as the sigmoid function, but the limits are +1 and −1, rather than 0 and 1. We can use Tanh in place of the sigmoid function and at the same time change the representation of the vectors.

Plot[Tanh[u],{u,-4,4}];

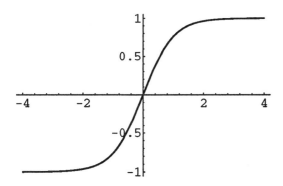

For the desired-output vectors, we use -0.9 to represent binary 0, and 0.9 to represent binary 1. The corresponding iopair vectors for the counter problem appear as follows:

```
ioPairsJor3 = {
            {{{-1}, {-0.9, 0.9}},
             {{-1}, { 0.9,-0.9}},
             {{-1}, { 0.9, 0.9}},
             {{-1}, {-0.9,-0.9}} },
            {{{1}, { 0.9, 0.9}},
             {{1}, { 0.9,-0.9}},
             {{1}, {-0.9, 0.9}},
             {{1}, {-0.9,-0.9}} }  };
```

To accomplish this modification of the Jordan network we must make several changes in the code. First, of course, we must change the calculation of the hidden- and output-layer output values to incorporate the Tanh function.

```
hidOuts = Tanh[hidWts.inputs];
outputs = Tanh[outWts.hidOuts];
```

If you recall from Chapter 3, the calculation of the weight updates involved the derivative of the output function. For the sigmoid, the derivative turned out to be outputs(1-outputs), for the output layer, with a similar expression for the hidden layer. In the case of the Tanh[u] output function, the derivative is Sech[u]^2 = 1 - Tahn[u]^2 which for the output layer would be (1-output^2). We must modify two expressions in the function to reflect these differences.

```
outDelta= outErrors (outputs (1-outputs));
```

becomes

```
outDelta= outErrors (1-outputs^2);
```

and

```
hidDelta=(hidOuts (1-hidOuts)) Transpose[outWts].outDelta;
```

becomes

```
hidDelta=(1-hidOuts^2) Transpose[outWts].outDelta;
```

We call the new function jordan2aTanh. We must also modify the test function. Both functions appear in the appendix. Let's try the new function.

```
jordan2aTanh[1,4,2,ioPairsJor3,0.1,0.9,0,100];
```

Sequence 1 input 1
inputs:
{-0.9, -0.9, -1}
outputs:
{-0.905053, 0.900023}
desired:
{-0.9, 0.9}
Mean squared error:
0.0000127663
Sequence 1 input 2
inputs:
{-0.9, 0.9, -1}
outputs:
{0.903497, -0.897313}
desired:
{0.9, -0.9}
Mean squared error:
$$9.72306\ 10^{-6}$$
Sequence 1 input 3
inputs:
{0.9, -0.9, -1}
outputs:
{0.910307, 0.885798}
desired:
{0.9, 0.9}
Mean squared error:
0.000153967
Sequence 1 input 4
inputs:
{0.9, 0.9, -1}
outputs:
{-0.893995, -0.959445}
desired:
{-0.9, -0.9}
Mean squared error:
0.00178488

Sequence 2 input 1
inputs:
{-0.9, -0.9, 1}
outputs:
{0.893995, 0.959445}
desired:
{0.9, 0.9}
Mean squared error:
0.00178488
Sequence 2 input 2
inputs:
{0.9, 0.9, 1}
outputs:
{0.905053, -0.900023}
desired:
{0.9, -0.9}
Mean squared error:
0.0000127663
Sequence 2 input 3
inputs:
{0.9, -0.9, 1}
outputs:
{-0.903497, 0.897313}
desired:
{-0.9, 0.9}
Mean squared error:
            -6
9.72306 10
Sequence 2 input 4
inputs:
{-0.9, 0.9, 1}
outputs:
{-0.910307, -0.885798}
desired:
{-0.9, -0.9}
Mean squared error:
0.000153967

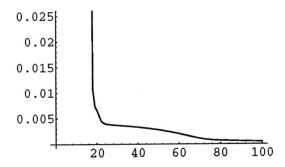

This version appears to work extremely well; notice that far fewer than 100 cycles would have been sufficient. You should be aware, however, of two minor additional changes: First, note that the learning rate is only 0.1 instead of 0.5 for previous runs. Second, if you examine the code, you will see that I initialized the state units to -0.9 instead of 0.1. I know that it is not advisable to change more than one item at a time when running these experiments, but I have done so here in the interest of space.

   I have presented a large number of variations to further illustrate the kind of experimentation that is often necessary to get a network to perform adequately. Feel free to continue to experiment.

Summary

In this chapter we studied several networks that include feedback connections as a part of their architecture. The BAM is a general form of a network that reduces to the Hopfield network if we think of both layers of BAM units as the same layer. The Elman and Jordan networks incorporate feedback from hidden and output units respectively back to the input layer. These networks can learn sequences of input patterns using a backpropagation algorithm. Both networks are fertile ground for experimentation with feedback structures.

Chapter 7

Adaptive Resonance Theory

One of the nice features of human memory is its ability to learn many new things without necessarily forgetting things learned in the past. A frequently cited example is the ability to recognize your parents even if you have not seen them for some time and have learned many new faces in the interim. Some popular neural networks, the backpropagation network in particular, cannot learn new information incrementally without forgetting old information, unless it is retrained with the old information along with the new.

Another characteristic of most neural networks is that if we present to them a previously unseen input pattern, there is generally no built-in mechanism for the network to be able to recognize the novelty of the input. The neural network doesn't know that it doesn't know the input pattern. On the other hand, suppose that an input pattern is simply a distorted or noisy version of one already learned by the network. If a network treats this pattern as a totally new pattern, then it may be overworking itself to learn what it has already learned in a slightly different form.

We have been describing a situation called the **stability-plasticity dilemma**. We can restate this dilemma as a series of questions: How can a learning system remain adaptive (plastic) in response to significant input, yet remain stable in response to irrelevant input? How does the system know to switch between its plastic and its stable modes? How can the system retain previously-learned information while continuing to learn new information?

Adaptive resonance theory (ART) attempts to address the stability-plasticity dilemma. A key to solving the stability-plasticity dilemma is the addition of a feedback mechanism between the layers of the ART network. This feedback mechanism facilitates the learning of new information without destroying old information, automatic switching between stable and plastic modes, and stabilization of the encoding of the classes done by the nodes. We shall discuss two classes of neural-network architectures that result from this approach. We refer to these network architectures as ART1 and ART2. ART1 and ART2 differ in the nature of their input patterns. ART1 networks require that the input vectors be binary. ART2 networks are suitable for processing analog, or grey-scale, patterns.

ART gets its name from the particular way in which learning and recall interplay in the network. In physics, resonance occurs when a small amplitude vibration of the proper frequency causes a large amplitude vibration in an electrical or mechanical system. In an ART network, information in the form of processing-element outputs, reverberates back and forth between layers of the network. If the proper patterns develop, a stable oscillation ensues, which is the neural-network equivalent of resonance. During this resonant period, learning, or adaptation, can occur. Before the network has achieved a resonant state, no learning takes place.

An ART network can achieve a resonant state in one of two ways. If the network has previously learned to recognize an input vector, then it will achieve a resonant state quickly when that input vector is presented again. During the resonance period, the adaptation process will reinforce the memory of the stored pattern. If the network does not immediately recognize the input vector, it will rapidly search through its stored patterns looking for a match. If no match is found, the network will enter a resonant state whereupon the new pattern will be stored for the first time. Thus, the network responds quickly to previously-learned data, yet remains able to learn when we present novel data.

Among other details, which we shall develop in this chapter, ART networks utilize the concept of competition between units. We have already seen an example of competition in the constraint satisfaction problem which we discussed in Chapter 5. Recall that, in that problem, only a certain few units were allowed to be on for any given solution, according to the constraints of the problem. We implemented these constraints among the units by means of equally strong inhibitory connections between all units subject to a particular constraint. Thus, if a particular unit in a set were to have a larger output than the others, it would tend to inhibit the others more strongly than it was inhibited by the others. This situation represents a form of competition among units for the "privilege" of being on. Units with large outputs tend to inhibit those with smaller outputs driving their outputs to zero while they themselves increase their output as a result of diminished inhibition from others.

7.1 ART1

As mentioned in the introduction to this chapter, ART1 networks require binary input vectors. This limitation is not necessarily a severe handicap, since many problems lend themselves reasonably well to a binary representation. In this section we shall examine some of the details of the ART1 architecture and processing. The treatment of those topics here will not be as complete as it is in *Neural Networks*, however, due to space considerations. On the other hand, Section 7.1.3 shows a detailed calculation using *Mathematica* to illustrate the performance of ART1.

7.1.1 ART1 Architecture

The basic features of the ART architecture appear in Figure 7.1. The two major subsystems are the **attentional subsystem** and the **orienting subsystem**. Patterns of activity that develop over the units in the two layers of the attentional subsystem are called **short term memory** (STM) traces because they exist only in association with a single application of an input vector. The weights associated with the bottom-up and top-down connections between F_1 and F_2 are called **long term memory** (LTM) traces because they encode information that remains a part of the network for an extended period.

We shall delay any consideration of the mathematics governing the ART1 network and describe the processing in the form of an algorithm. Furthermore, we shall ignore, for the moment, the gain control system; we will revisit that topic later in this section.

The following algorithm is brief, and omits many details of ART1 processing, but it does illustrate conceptually how the network responds to inputs.

1. Apply a binary input vector to the F_1 layer units.

2. Determine the output of the F_1-layer units and propagate that output up to the F_2 layer.

3. Allow the F_2 units to compete based on their net-input value so that one unit wins and is the only one with a nonzero output.

4. Send the output from the winning F_2 unit back down to F_1 where it stimulates the appearance of a **top-down template** pattern.

5. Compare the top-down template to the initial input vector. If the patterns match to within a specified amount (called the **vigilance parameter**) a resonant condition has been attained; continue with step 7.

6. Failing to achieve resonance, disable the winning F_2 unit preventing it from competing further, reset all units to their initial values, and begin a new matching cycle with step 1.

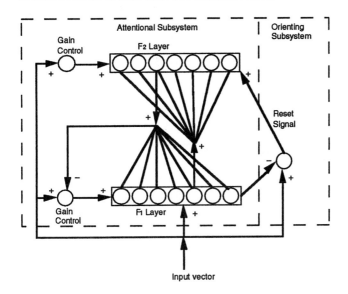

Figure 7.1 This figure illustrates the ART1 system diagram. The two major subsystems are the attentional subsystem and the orienting subsystem. F_1 and F_2 represent two layers of units in the attentional subsystem. Units on each layer are fully interconnected to the units on the other layer. Not shown are interconnects among the units on each layer. Other connections between components are indicated by the arrows. A plus sign indicates an excitatory connection and a minus sign indicates an inhibitory connection. The function of the various subsystems is discussed in the text.

7. Upon resonance, modify weights on both layers to encode the pattern.

8. Reset all units, clear the input vector, and begin at step 1 with a new input vector.

There is one subtlety involving ART networks in general that merits a slight digression. In the above algorithm, learning takes place in step seven, after resonance is established. In a *real* ART network, that is, one that is not a software simulation, weight modification is not turned on or off depending on the existence of a resonant condition; instead weights are always subject to modification, even during a matching cycle that leads to a mismatch and a reset condition. What keeps the network from learning mismatches is that the time scale over which significant changes in weight values occurs is much longer than the time scale over which the matching cycles occur. In other words, during a matching cycle in which a particular F_2 unit wins, but the resulting top-down template mismatches the input pattern, weights on the winning unit and from the winning unit, can undergo modification; but the matching process and subsequent reset occur so quickly that the weights do not have a chance to change significantly before the reset has removed the offending unit from consideration. Significant weight modification occurs only during a resonant condition, in which data passage between layers is stable for a considerable period of time.

A not so subtle, but equally important part of ART is the **gain control** mechanism. The gain control system works in concert with what is called the **2/3 rule**. If you refer back to Figure 7.1, you will notice that the units on the F_1 layer have three possible sources of inputs: bottom-up inputs, top-down inputs, and inputs from the gain control system (the same is true of the F_2 layer, but that fact is not obvious from the diagram since the top-down inputs are missing). The 2/3 rule states that, for a given unit to have a nonzero output, it must be receiving an input from two, and only two, out of the possible three input paths. The gain control is configured such that any output from F_2 sends an inhibitory signal to the gain control system, which completely shuts it off; therefore in the presence of an output from F_2, the gain control is disabled.

Disabling the gain control when F_2 is active has the effect of preventing any output from F_1 in the presence of an input from F_2 alone, that is, when there is no bottom-up input to F_1. In the algorithm for ART1 processing, it would appear that F_2 could never be active unless preceded by activity on F_1. However, the basic ART structure was intended to be a building block in a hierarchical structure, meaning that in some circumstances, the F_2 layer may be active from influences other than the associated F_1 layer. If we allowed the F_1 layer to respond to F_2 activity alone, then a resonant condition could ensue without any inputs to the F_1 layer from below, a condition that does not make sense within the context of trying to encode input patterns. You can find more details about gain control and the 2/3 rule in Chapter 8 of *Neural Networks*.

The orienting subsystem receives the same inputs as does the F_1 layer, but also receives as inputs, the outputs of the F_1 layer. If these two input vectors match to within the criterion specified by the vigilance parameter, nothing happens; or rather, the orienting subsystem remains inhibited. If, on the other hand, the orienting subsystem input vectors do not match, there will be a net excitatory signal to the orienting subsystem, resulting in a reset signal to the F_2 layer. The effect of the reset signal depends on the state of the individual F_2 unit. If the unit currently has a nonzero output, that unit is disabled for the duration of the current input vector. If the unit does not have a nonzero output, the unit ignores the reset signal.

7.1.2 ART1 Processing Equations

The equations that describe the dynamics of the activity values on the F_1 and F_2 layers are identical in their general form.

$$\dot{x}_k = -x_k + (1 - Ax_k)J_k^+ - (B + Cx_k)J_k^- \tag{7.1}$$

J_k^+ is an excitatory input to the kth unit, and J_k^- is an inhibitory input. A, B, and C, are positive constants. To distinguish between layers, we shall adopt the convention that the subscript, i, will always refer to a unit on the F_1 layer, and the subscript, j, will always refer to a unit on the F_2 layer. Furthermore, we shall append a 1 or a 2 subscript to various quantities to identify the relevant layer; for example, A_1 refers to the constant A defined specifically for the F_1 layer. Similarly, we shall use x_{1i} and x_{2j} to refer to the activities on F_1 and F_2 units respectively. When it becomes necessary to label a particular unit, we shall use v_i for F_1 units and v_j for F_2 units.

Figure 7.2 illustrates the various quantities that relate to units on the F_1 layer. Figure 7.3 provides the same information for an F_2 unit.

Processing on F_1 We can write the total excitatory input to F_1 units as

$$J_i^+ = I_i + D_1V_i + B_1G \tag{7.2}$$

where D_1 and B_1 are positive constants, G is the output of the gain control system, and V_i is the net-input contribution from the top-down connections from F_2. We calculate V_i by the usual method of the dot product of the input vector and the weight vector.

$$V_i = \sum_j u_j z_{ij} \tag{7.3}$$

The value of G is 1 as long as an input pattern is present from below and there is no output from F_2, and is zero if there is an output from

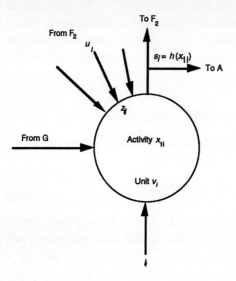

Figure 7.2 This figure shows a processing element, v_i, on the F_1 layer of an ART1 network. The activity of the unit is x_{1i}. It receives a binary input value, I_i from below, and an excitatory signal, G, from the gain control. In addition, the top-down signals, u_j, from F_2 are gated (multiplied by) weights, z_{ij}. Outputs, s_i, from the processing element go up to F_2 and across to the orienting subsystem, A.

F_2. We shall set the inhibitory input to F_1 units equal to unity. With the above definitions, the equation for the activity on F_1 units becomes

$$\dot{x}_{1i} = -x_{1i} + (1 - A_1 x_{1i})(I_i + D_1 V_i + B_1 G) - (B_1 + C_1 x_{1i}) \qquad (7.4)$$

Before any inputs are present on the F_1 layer, $G = 0$, and $V_i = 0$, for all i. We can substitute these conditions into Eq. (7.4) and solve for the equilibrium values of the activities.

$$x_{1i} = \frac{-B_1}{(1 + C_1)} \qquad (7.5)$$

Notice that the equilibrium activities are negative, meaning that the units are kept in a highly inhibited state.

During the initial stages of processing, that is, when an input is present from below, but there has yet been no response from F_2, V_i remains at zero, but the gain control has become active: $G = 1$. The

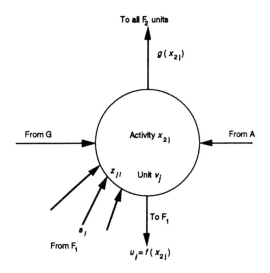

Figure 7.3 This figure shows a processing element, v_j, on the F_2 layer of an ART1 network. The activity of the unit is x_{2j}. The unit v_j receives inputs from the F_1 layer, the gain control system, G, and the orienting subsystem, A. Bottom-up signals, s_i, from F_1 are gated by the weights, z_{ji}. Outputs, u_j, are sent back down to F_1. In addition, each unit receives a positive feedback term from itself, $g(x_{2j})$, and sends an identical signal through an inhibitory connection to all other units on the layer.

equilibrium activities under these conditions are

$$x_{1i} = \frac{I_i}{1 + A_1(I_i + B_1) + C_1} \tag{7.6}$$

The unit activity will be nonzero in the case of $I_i = 1$, and will be zero if $I_i = 0$. The activity of the gain control brings the unit activities up to a zero value, ready to fire if the unit receives a nonzero input from below.

When F_2 finally responds, sending a top-down input to F_1, the gain control becomes inactive. In this case, the equilibrium activity values become

$$x_{1i} = \frac{I_i + D_1 V_i - B_1}{1 + A_1(I_i + D_1 V_i) + C_1} \tag{7.7}$$

The activity on any particular unit can now be either positive or negative, depending on the value of the numerator in Eq. (7.7). We assume that we want a positive activity if the unit receives both a top-down input and a nonzero bottom-up input ($I_i = 1$). This assumption translates into a condition on the quantities in the numerator, namely

$$V_i > \frac{B_1 - 1}{D_1} \tag{7.8}$$

We implement this condition in the network by initializing the weights on the top-down connections to be at least the value of the right hand side of Eq. (7.8). In other words

$$z_{ij} > \frac{B_1 - 1}{D_1} \tag{7.9}$$

In the complete analysis of processing of F_1, a condition relating the values of B_1 an D_1 arises. We state that condition here, but you can find the details in Chapter 8 of *Neural Networks*.

$$\max\{D_1, 1\} < B_1 < D_1 + 1 \tag{7.10}$$

At any point in the calculation, the output of an F_1 unit will be 1 if the unit has a positive activity.

$$s_i = h(x_{1i}) = \begin{cases} 1 & x_{1i} > 0 \\ 0 & x_{1i} \leq 0 \end{cases} \tag{7.11}$$

Processing on F_2   The processing of F_2 units is more complicated than that performed on F_1, yet it is much easier to implement in a computer simulation. The complication arises because F_2 is a competitive layer in which each unit sends inhibitory signals to all other units on the layer, while the unit itself receives a positive feedback signal from itself. This arrangement goes by the name of **on-center, off-surround**, and is the exact scheme that we used in the Hopfield network to ensure that only one of a certain group of units was allowed to turn on. On such a competitive layer, the equations describing the processing are complicated by the fact that they are coupled differential equations, making it impossible to find simple equilibrium values for the activities as we did on the F_1 layer.

On the other hand, because the layer is a winner-take-all competitive layer, all that we need do is calculate the net inputs for all of the units, select the one with the largest net-input value, and declare that unit the winner. The winning unit will have an output signal of unit strength, and all other units will remain inactive. We calculate the net input to the F_2 units in the usual manner

$$T_j = \text{net}_j = \sum_i s_i z_{ji} \qquad (7.12)$$

Then the outputs are given by

$$u_i = f(x_{2j}) = \begin{cases} 1 & T_j = \max_k \{T_k\} \forall k \\ 0 & \text{otherwise} \end{cases} \qquad (7.13)$$

We shall give the winning F_2 unit a special designation: v^J.

We must also impose an initial condition on the values of the weights on the F_2 units. The condition is

$$0 \le z_{ji}(0) \le \frac{L}{L-1+M} \qquad (7.14)$$

where $L > 1$, and M is equal to the number of units on the F_1 layer. Once again, we shall not digress into the rather lengthy discussion of how we derive this condition. Suffice it to say that this condition helps to ensure that a unit, which has encoded a particular pattern, continues to win over uncommitted units in the F_2 layer when that particular pattern is presented to the network.

Maintaining Vigilance in ART1   The orienting subsystem determines whether top-down templates, encoded in the network weights, match input patterns presented to the network. The degree of match is also an important consideration. The parameter, ρ, called the vigilance parameter, specifies the degree to which one pattern must be similar to another in order to be considered a match for the pattern. To examine how vigilance works, we must first make a definition or two. Given a binary vector, $\mathbf{X}$, we define the magnitude of $\mathbf{X}$ by the following expression

$$|\mathbf{X}| = \sum_i X_i \qquad (7.15)$$

In other words, the magnitude of a binary vector is equal to the number of nonzero components in that vector.

We can also define the value of the output vector of the F_1 units by the following:

$$S = \begin{cases} I & F_2 \text{ is inactive} \\ I \cap V^J & F_2 \text{ is active} \end{cases} \tag{7.16}$$

Eq. (7.16) states that the output of F_1 will be identical to the input vector, I, if no top-down signal is present from F_2, and will be equal to the intersection of the input vector and the top-down template pattern, V^J, received from the winning F_2 unit, when F_2 is active.

Provided we select a value for ρ which is less than or equal to one, we can describe the matching condition as

$$\frac{|S|}{|I|} \geq \rho \tag{7.17}$$

If Eq. (7.17) holds, then the network will take the top-down template as a match to the current input pattern.

Defining a vigilance criterion in this manner endows the network with an important property called **self-scaling**. This property, illustrated in Figure 7.4, enables the network to ignore minor differences in patterns, such as might arise due to random noise, and yet remain sensitive to major differences.

Weight Updates on ART1 Weight updates on both layers of an ART1 network are easy to describe in terms of the final results, but somewhat more complex to derive. As we have done previously, we present only the final results here. The example calculation in the next section will serve to illustrate how the particular weight-update equations serve to encode input patterns in the network.

Weight updates occur only on the winning F_2 unit, and on those connections from the winning F_2 unit down to the F_1 units. Using the subscript J to denote the index of the winning F_2 unit, we can express the weight updates on the two layers as follows. For F_1 units,

$$z_{iJ} = \begin{cases} 1 & \text{if } v_i \text{ is active} \\ 0 & \text{if } v_i \text{ is inactive} \end{cases} \tag{7.18}$$

and for the winning F_2 unit,

$$z_{Ji} = \begin{cases} \frac{L}{L-1+|S|} & \text{if } v_i \text{ is active} \\ 0 & \text{if } v_i \text{ is inactive} \end{cases} \tag{7.19}$$

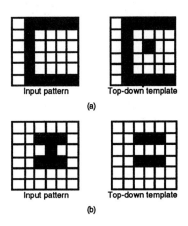

Figure 7.4 This figure illustrates the self-scaling property of ART1 networks. (a) For a value of $\rho = 0.8$, the existence of the extra feature in the center of the top-down pattern on the right is ignored by the orienting subsystem, which considers both patterns to be of the same class. (b) For the same value of ρ, these bottom-up and top-down patterns will cause the orienting subsystem to send a reset to F_2.

We have now assembled all of the equations and conditions necessary to build an ART1 network. Let's proceed to a step-by-step calculation as a demonstration of some of the processing characteristics of this network.

7.1.3 ART1 Processing Example

In this section, we shall walk through an example that illustrates some of the characteristics of the learning process in an ART1 example. This particular example follows the one that we give in Section 8.2.3 of *Neural Networks*. First, we initialize some of the network parameters and define the input vectors that we will use later.

Network Initialization and Function Definitions   The dimension of the F_1 layer is

f1dim = 5;

The dimension of the F_2 layer is

f2dim = 6;

We set the system vigilance parameter at a high value to ensure exact matches.

```
rho = 0.9;
```

The input vectors to layer F_1 are arbitrary, though we shall exploit some relationships between some of them later on. Here is a list of the 10 input vectors.

```
in = {{0, 0, 0, 1, 0}, {0, 0, 1, 0, 1}, {1, 0, 0, 0, 1},
   {1, 1, 1, 1, 1}, {1, 1, 0, 0, 0}, {0, 1, 0, 1, 1},
   {0, 0, 0, 0, 1}, {0, 1, 1, 1, 1}, {1, 0, 1, 1, 0},
   {0, 1, 1, 1, 0}};
```

The vector magnitude for ART1 networks has a different definition than the standard vector magnitude.

```
vmag1[v_] := Count[v,1]
```

The function resetflag1 tells us whether the matching condition established by the vigilance parameter has been met or not.

```
resetflag1[outp_,inp_] := If[vmag1[outp]/vmag1[inp]<rho,True,False]
```

where outp refers to the output of F_1 and inp refers to the input vector.

We shall also use a function that returns the index of the winning unit in a competitive layer whose outputs are assembled into a vector, p. This function assumes that the winning unit is the one having an activation of val.

```
winner[p_,val_] := First[First[Position[p,val]]]
```

To keep track of which F_2 elements have been inhibited by the orienting subsystem, we maintain a list as follows: (1 for not inhibited, 0 for inhibited)

```
droplistinit = Table[1,{f2dim}]
```

```
{1, 1, 1, 1, 1, 1}
```

```
droplist = droplistinit
```

```
{1, 1, 1, 1, 1, 1}
```

The output functions for the two layers have identical definitions. For the F_1 layer:

```
h[x_] := If[x>0,1,0]
```

```
s[x_] := Map[h,x]
```

and for the F_2 layer back to F_1:

```
f[x_] := If[x>0,1,0]
```

```
u[x_] := Map[f,x]
```

The F_1 layer has several parameters, which we define as follows:

```
a1=1;  b1=1.5;  c1=5;  d1=0.9;
```

The top-down weights on connections from F_2 units to F_1 units comprise a matrix, which we denote z12, having one row for each unit on F_1, and one column for each unit on F_2. According to Eq. (7.9), the initial weights must be greater than $(B_1 - 1)/D_1$. This fact explains the addition of 0.2 to the weight initialization equation in the following.

```
MatrixForm[z12 = Table[
    Table[N[(b1-1)/d1 + .2,3],{f2dim}],{f1dim}]]
```

0.756	0.756	0.756	0.756	0.756	0.756
0.756	0.756	0.756	0.756	0.756	0.756
0.756	0.756	0.756	0.756	0.756	0.756
0.756	0.756	0.756	0.756	0.756	0.756
0.756	0.756	0.756	0.756	0.756	0.756

The only parameter required on the F_2 layer is L from Eq. (7.14); we define that parameter here.

```
el = 3;
```

Weights on connections from F_1 units to F_2 units comprise the matrix, z21, having one row for each F_2 unit and one column for each F_1 unit. The subtraction of 0.1 is optional, since the weights may be initialized identically to $L/(L-1+M)$ from Eq. (7.14).

```
MatrixForm[z21 = Table[
    Table[N[(el/(el-1+f1dim)-0.1),3],{f1dim}],{f2dim}]]
```

0.329	0.329	0.329	0.329	0.329
0.329	0.329	0.329	0.329	0.329
0.329	0.329	0.329	0.329	0.329
0.329	0.329	0.329	0.329	0.329
0.329	0.329	0.329	0.329	0.329
0.329	0.329	0.329	0.329	0.329

The initial activities of the F_1 units are all negative, according to Eq. (7.5).

```
xf1 = Table[-b1/(1+c1),{f1dim}]
```

{-0.25, -0.25, -0.25, -0.25, -0.25}

The function compete takes as its argument the list of activities on the F_2 layer, and returns a new list in which only the unit with the largest activity retains a nonzero activity; in other words, this function implements competition on F_2.

```
compete[f2Activities_] :=
  Module[{i,x,f2dim,maxpos},
    x=f2Activities;
    maxpos=First[First[Position[x,Max[f2Activities]]]];
    f2dim = Length[x];
    For[i=1,i<=f2dim,i++,
        If[i!=maxpos,x[[i]]=0;Continue]  (* end of If *)
      ]; (* end of For *)
    Return[x];
    ]; (* end of Module *)
```

Processing Sequence   To begin, we select the first input vector in the list.

```
in[[1]]
```

{0, 0, 0, 1, 0}

With positive inputs from below, the F_1 activities rise.

```
xf1 = N[in[[1]]/(1+a1*(in[[1]]+b1)+c1),3]
```

{0, 0, 0, 0.118, 0}

The only unit with a nonzero activity, however, is the one with a nonzero input from below. The output of F_1 is

```
sf1 = s[xf1]
```

{0, 0, 0, 1, 0}

The dot product between the weights and input values from below determines the net inputs to the F_2 units.

```
t= N[z21 . sf1,3]
```

{0.329, 0.329, 0.329, 0.329, 0.329, 0.329}

The activity on F_2 equals the net inputs in this approximation.

```
xf2 = t
```

{0.329, 0.329, 0.329, 0.329, 0.329, 0.329}

Next, we find the unit with maximum net input,

```
xf2 = compete[xf2];
```

{0.329, 0, 0, 0, 0, 0}

and compute output values of F_2

```
uf2 = u[xf2]
```

{1, 0, 0, 0, 0, 0}

We could combine the above two steps into one, but I left them separate in order to remain true to the individual steps of the sequence. Notice that the compete function, finding no clear winner of the competition, returned the first, previously uncommitted unit on the list of F_2 units.

We shall need to save the index of winning unit for later.

```
windex = winner[uf2,1]
```

1

Going back to the F_1 layer, the net inputs back to F_1 from F_2 are

```
v= N[z12 . uf2,3]
```

{0.756, 0.756, 0.756, 0.756, 0.756}

The new equilibrium activities of the F_1 units are

```
xf1 = N[(in[[1]]+ d1*v-b1)/(1+a1*(in[[1]]+d1*v)+c1),3]
```

{-0.123, -0.123, -0.123, 0.0234, -0.123}

and the new output values of F_1 are

```
sf1 = s[xf1]
```

```
{0, 0, 0, 1, 0}
```

Notice that the new output vector is identical to the input vector. We expect, therefore, that the orienting subsystem — implemented partially as the **resetflag1** function — will indicate no mismatch.

```
resetflag1[sf1,in[[1]]]
```

```
False
```

A False from **resetflag1** indicates that resonance has been reached; therefore, we can adjust the weights on both layers. The following procedure sets the **windex** element of each weight vector on F_1 equal to 1 if the output of the corresponding F_1 unit is equal to 1.

```
z12=Transpose[z12];
z12[[windex]]=sf1;   (* just use the values in sf1 *)
MatrixForm[z12=Transpose[z12]]
```

0	0.756	0.756	0.756	0.756	0.756
0	0.756	0.756	0.756	0.756	0.756
0	0.756	0.756	0.756	0.756	0.756
1	0.756	0.756	0.756	0.756	0.756
0	0.756	0.756	0.756	0.756	0.756

As you can see, the weights on the F_1 units have encoded the input vector, but the encoding is distributed over the entire set of units. Since unit 1 was the winner on F_2, weights from that unit back to each F_1 unit are the only ones to be changed. On the other hand, only the winning unit on F_2 has its weights updated. Again you will see that the first unit on F_2 has encoded the input vector.

```
z21[[windex]] = N[el/(el-1+vmag1[sf1]) sf1,3]
```

```
{0, 0, 0, 1., 0}
```

Now let's repeat the matching process for an input vector that is orthogonal to **in[[1]]**.

```
in[[2]]
```

{0, 0, 1, 0, 1}

```
xf1 = N[in[[2]]/(1+a1*(in[[2]]+b1)+c1),3]
```

{0, 0, 0.118, 0, 0.118}

```
sf1 = s[xf1]
```

{0, 0, 1, 0, 1}

```
t= N[z21 . sf1,3]
```

{0, 0.657, 0.657, 0.657, 0.657, 0.657}

```
xf2 = t
```

{0, 0.657, 0.657, 0.657, 0.657, 0.657}

Notice that since the first unit on F_2 has encoded a vector orthogonal to the current input vector, the net input to that unit is zero.

```
xf2 = compete[xf2]
```

{0, 0.657, 0, 0, 0, 0}

Once again, compete returned the first uncommitted unit, since none of the units was a clear winner. Continuing on,

```
uf2 = u[xf2]
```

{0, 1, 0, 0, 0, 0}

```
windex = winner[uf2,1]
```

2

```
v= N[z12 . uf2,3]
```

{0.756, 0.756, 0.756, 0.756, 0.756}

```
xf1 = N[(in[[2]]+ d1*v-b1)/(1+a1*(in[[2]]+d1*v)+c1),3]
```

{-0.123, -0.123, 0.0234, -0.123, 0.0234}

```
sf1 = s[xf1]
```

{0, 0, 1, 0, 1}

```
resetflag1[sf1,in[[2]]]
```

False

Once again, we have resonance in one pass through the network. Since unit 2 on F_2 is the winner, the second weight values on the F_1 units encode the new input vector.

```
z12=Transpose[z12];
z12[[window]]=sf1;   (* just use the values in sf1 *)
MatrixForm[z12=Transpose[z12]]
```

0	0	0.756	0.756	0.756	0.756
0	0	0.756	0.756	0.756	0.756
0	1	0.756	0.756	0.756	0.756
1	0	0.756	0.756	0.756	0.756
0	1	0.756	0.756	0.756	0.756

and, the second unit on F_2 also encodes the input vector. Notice, however, that the nonzero weight values are not equal to one in this case, since vmag1[sf1] is not equal to one. Nevertheless, the pattern of the weights is identical to the input vector.

```
z21[[window]] = N[el/(el-1+vmag1[sf1]) sf1,3]
```

{0, 0, 0.75, 0, 0.75}

The entire weight matrix on F_2 is

```
MatrixForm[z21]
```

0	0	0	1.	0
0	0	0.75	0	0.75
0.329	0.329	0.329	0.329	0.329
0.329	0.329	0.329	0.329	0.329
0.329	0.329	0.329	0.329	0.329
0.329	0.329	0.329	0.329	0.329

Now let's try an input vector that is a subset of the input vector, in[[2]], namely in[[7]].

```
in[[7]]
```

{0, 0, 0, 0, 1}

```
xf1 = N[in[[7]]/(1+a1*(in[[7]]+b1)+c1),3]
```

{0, 0, 0, 0, 0.118}

```
sf1 = s[xf1]
```

{0, 0, 0, 0, 1}

```
t= N[z21 . sf1,3]
```

{0, 0.75, 0.329, 0.329, 0.329, 0.329}

```
xf2 = t
```

{0, 0.75, 0.329, 0.329, 0.329, 0.329}

```
xf2 = compete[xf2]
```

{0, 0.75, 0, 0, 0, 0}

Even though unit 2 has already encoded a vector different than the current input vector, there is enough similarity between the encoded vector and the input vector to allow unit 2 to win the competition. Trace through the following six steps very carefully.

```
uf2 = u[xf2]
```

{0, 1, 0, 0, 0, 0}

```
windex = winner[uf2,1]
```

2

```
v= N[z12 . uf2,3]
```

{0, 0, 1., 0, 1.}

```
xf1 = N[(in[[7]]+ d1*v-b1)/(1+a1*(in[[7]]+d1*v)+c1),3]
```

{-0.25, -0.25, -0.087, -0.25, 0.0506}

```
sf1 = s[xf1]
```

{0, 0, 0, 0, 1}

```
resetflag1[sf1,in[[7]]]
```

False

It may seem surprising that, even though unit 2 previously encoded a vector that does not match the current input vector within the vigilance parameter, there is still no reset. This behavior is characteristic of ART1, in that the appearance of a subset vector, following the encoding of a superset vector, may cause the unit encoding the superset vector to recode its weights to match the subset vector. The weight matrices now appear as follows:

```
z12=Transpose[z12];
z12[[windex]]=sf1;   (* just use the values in sf1 *)
MatrixForm[z12=Transpose[z12]]
```

0	0	0.756	0.756	0.756	0.756
0	0	0.756	0.756	0.756	0.756
0	0	0.756	0.756	0.756	0.756
1	0	0.756	0.756	0.756	0.756
0	1	0.756	0.756	0.756	0.756

```
z21[[windex]] = N[el/(el-1+vmag[sf1]) sf1,3]
```

{0, 0, 0, 0, 1.}

```
MatrixForm[z21]
```

0	0	0	1.	0
0	0	0	0	1.
0.329	0.329	0.329	0.329	0.329
0.329	0.329	0.329	0.329	0.329
0.329	0.329	0.329	0.329	0.329
0.329	0.329	0.329	0.329	0.329

Now let's put the superset vector back in to see what happens.

`in[[2]]`

`{0, 0, 1, 0, 1}`

`xf1 = N[in[[2]]/(1+a1*(in[[2]]+b1)+c1),3]`

`{0, 0, 0.118, 0, 0.118}`

`sf1 = s[xf1]`

`{0, 0, 1, 0, 1}`

`t= N[z21 . sf1,3]`

`{0, 1., 0.657, 0.657, 0.657, 0.657}`

`xf2 = t`

`{0, 1., 0.657, 0.657, 0.657, 0.657}`

`xf2 = compete[xf2]`

`{0, 1., 0, 0, 0, 0}`

Once again, unit two wins the competition. The ART1 network will not turn out to be very useful if this unit again recodes itself to the superset vector. If that situation prevailed, we would not be able to encode both a superset and a subset vector at the same time; a serious limitation in a network that uses only binary vectors as inputs. Let's see what happens.

`uf2 = u[xf2]`

`{0, 1, 0, 0, 0, 0}`

`windex = winner[uf2,1]`

`2`

`v= N[z12 . uf2,3]`

`{0, 0, 0, 0, 1.}`

`xf1 = N[(in[[2]]+ d1*v-b1)/(1+a1*(in[[2]]+d1*v)+c1),3]`

{-0.25, -0.25, -0.0714, -0.25, 0.0506}

```
sf1 = s[xf1]
```

{0, 0, 0, 0, 1}

```
resetflag1[sf1,in[[2]]]
```

True

Fortunately, this time we get a reset. To implement the second part of the orienting subsystem, the part that inhibits units that have won but caused a reset, we use the droplist.

```
If[resetflag[sf1,in[[2]]]==True,
      droplist[[windex]]=0,Continue]
```

0

```
droplist
```

{1, 0, 1, 1, 1, 1}

We shall see momentarily how we employ this droplist. For the moment, let's reestablish the input vector and begin another matching cycle.

```
in[[2]]
```

{0, 0, 1, 0, 1}

```
xf1 = N[in[[2]]/(1+a1*(in[[2]]+b1)+c1),3]
```

{0, 0, 0.118, 0, 0.118}

```
sf1 = s[xf1]
```

{0, 0, 1, 0, 1}

```
t= N[z21 . sf1,3]
```

{0, 1., 0.657, 0.657, 0.657, 0.657}

```
xf2 = N[t droplist,3] (* here is where we inhibit units *)
```

{0, 0, 0.657, 0.657, 0.657, 0.657}

By multiplying the activity vector on F_2 by the droplist vector, we effectively inhibit those units that correspond to positions on droplist having a zero value, thus removing them from the competition.

```
xf2 = compete[xf2]
```

{0, 0, 0.657, 0, 0, 0}

Having eliminated the second unit from the competition, compete returns the third unit as the winning unit.

```
uf2 = u[xf2]
```

{0, 0, 1, 0, 0, 0}

```
windex = winner[uf2,1]
```

3

```
v= N[z12 . uf2,3]
```

{0.756, 0.756, 0.756, 0.756, 0.756}

```
xf1 = N[(in[[2]]+ d1*v-b1)/(1+a1*(in[[2]]+d1*v)+c1),3]
```

{-0.123, -0.123, 0.0234, -0.123, 0.0234}

```
sf1 = s[xf1]
```

{0, 0, 1, 0, 1}

```
resetflag1[sf1,in[[2]]]
```

False

Since the third unit was not previously encoded, we do not get a reset, and the superset vector is encoded by the third unit. Now both superset and subset vectors are encoded in the network independently, as the following weight matrices show.

```
z12=Transpose[z12];
z12[[windex]]=sf1;   (* just use the values in sf1 *)
MatrixForm[z12=Transpose[z12]]
```

0	0	0	0.756	0.756	0.756
0	0	0	0.756	0.756	0.756
0	0	1	0.756	0.756	0.756
1	0	0	0.756	0.756	0.756
0	1	1	0.756	0.756	0.756

```
z21[[windex]] = N[el/(el-1+vmag[sf1]) sf1,3]
```

{0, 0, 0.75, 0, 0.75}

```
MatrixForm[z21]
```

0	0	0	1.	0
0	0	0	0	1.
0	0	0.75	0	0.75
0.329	0.329	0.329	0.329	0.329
0.329	0.329	0.329	0.329	0.329
0.329	0.329	0.329	0.329	0.329

If other subset vectors had been previously encoded in the network, then we may have had other resets until all units encoding subset vectors had been disabled by the orienting subsystem. At the end of the matching cycle, the droplist vector will have zeros in all positions corresponding to units that won the competition of F_2, but which resulted in a reset. Thus, before beginning the next matching cycle with a new input vector, you must remember to reinitialize droplist as follows

```
droplist = droplistinit;
```

Experiment with the other input vectors in the list. You will learn more about how ART1 operates by this experimentation than you will by reading about it.

7.1.4 The Complete ART1 Network

By collecting the various processing steps into one procedure, we can build a complete ART1 simulator. We will write a separate procedure to initialize the weights.

To initialize the weights, we need to know the dimensions of the two layers, and the values of the parameters B_1, D_1, and L. In addition, this routine takes two additional parameters, del1 and del2, which can be used to alter the initial values of the weights slightly. Be sure to select del1 and del2 within the constraints of the weight initialization equations, Eqs. (7.9) and (7.14).

```
art1Init[f1dim_,f2dim_,b1_,d1_,el_,del1_,del2_] :=
  Module[{z12,z21},
    z12 = Table[
     Table[(b1-1)/d1 + del1,{f2dim}],{f1dim}];
    z21 = Table[
     Table[(el/(el-1+f1dim)-del2),{f1dim}],{f2dim}];
    Return[{z12,z21}];
    ]; (* end of Module *)
```

For the example that we shall perform later in this section we shall set the dimension of the F_1 layer to 25, and the dimension of the F_2 layer to five. For the other parameters, we shall use the same values that we used in the example of the previous section.

```
{topDown,bottomUp} =
  art1Init[25,5,1.5,0.9,3,0.2,0.1];
```

As before, all weights on F_1 are initialized to a value of 0.756. Weights on F_2 are initialized to a value of 0.111.

The ART1 simulator in Listing 7.1 requires all of the inputs provided to the art1Init routine, as well as the additional parameters A_1 and C_1, the vigilance parameter, rho, the two weight matrices, and a list of input vectors to be encoded. The network will process the list of input patterns until all patterns have been encoded and the network has stabilized. As with art1Init, the function returns the weight matrices and a list called matchList which we can use to determine the sequence of codings and recodings performed by the network. The function also provides a running commentary so that you can follow the processing. Previously defined functions, vmag1, resetflag1, compete, and winner, are also required. Let's verify the code by using the same three input vectors that we did for the example in the previous section.

```
{topDown,bottomUp} = art1Init[5,6,1.5,0.9,3,0.2,0.1];

ins = { {0,0,0,1,0},{0,0,1,0,1},{0,0,0,0,1} };

{td,bu,mlist} = art1[5,6,1,1.5,5,0.9,3,0.9,topDown,bottomUp,ins];
```

```
art1[f1dim_,f2dim_,a1_,b1_,c1_,d1_,el_,rho_,f1Wts_,f2Wts_,inputs_] :=
  Module[{droplistinit,droplist,notDone=True,i,nIn=Length[inputs],reset,
          n,sf1,t,xf2,uf2,v,windex,matchList,newMatchList,tdWts,buWts},
    droplistinit = Table[1,{f2dim}];   (* initialize droplist *)
    tdWts=f1Wts; buWts=f2Wts;
    matchList =    (* construct list of F2 units and encoded input patterns *)
        Table[{StringForm["Unit ",n]},{n,f2dim}];
    While[notDone==True,newMatchList = matchList; (* process until stable *)
      For[i=1,i<=nIn,i++,in = inputs[[i]];        (* process inputs in sequence *)
        droplist = droplistinit;reset=True;       (* initialize *)
        While[reset==True,                        (* cycle until no reset *)
            xf1 = in/(1+a1*(in+b1)+c1);           (* activities *)
            sf1 = Map[If[#>0,1,0]&,xf1];          (* F1 outputs *)
            t= buWts . sf1;                       (* F2 net-inputs *)
            t = t droplist;                       (* turn off inhibited units *)
            xf2 = compete[t];                     (* F2 activities *)
            uf2 = Map[If[#>0,1,0]&,xf2];          (* F2 outputs *)
            windex = winner[uf2,1];               (* winning index *)
            v= tdWts . uf2;                          (* F1 net-inputs *)
            xf1 =(in+ d1*v-b1)/(1+a1*(in+d1*v)+c1);  (* new F1 activities *)
            sf1 = Map[If[#>0,1,0]&,xf1];          (* new F1 outputs *)
            reset = resetflag1[sf1,in,rho];       (* check reset *)
            If[reset==True,droplist[[windex]]=0;  (* update droplist *)
                  Print["Reset with pattern ",i," on unit ",windex],Continue];
            ]; (* end of While reset==True *)
        Print["Resonance established on unit ",windex," with pattern ",i];
      tdWts=Transpose[tdWts];   (* resonance, so update weights,top down first *)
          tdWts[[windex]]=sf1;
          tdWts=Transpose[tdWts];
          buWts[[windex]] = el/(el-1+vmag1[sf1]) sf1; (* then bottom up *)
      matchList[[windex]] =                       (* update matching list *)
                  Reverse[Union[matchList[[windex]],{i}]];
        ]; (* end of For i=1 to nIn *)
      If[matchList==newMatchList,notDone=False;   (* see if matchList is static *)
            Print["Network stable"],
            Print["Network not stable"];
            newMatchList = matchList;];]; (* end of While notDone==True *)
    Return[{tdWts,buWts,matchList}];
  ]; (* end of Module *)
```

Listing 7.1

```
Resonance established on unit 1 with pattern 1
Resonance established on unit 2 with pattern 2
Resonance established on unit 2 with pattern 3
Network not stable
Resonance established on unit 1 with pattern 1
Reset with pattern 2 on unit 2
Resonance established on unit 3 with pattern 2
Resonance established on unit 2 with pattern 3
Network not stable
Resonance established on unit 1 with pattern 1
Resonance established on unit 3 with pattern 2
Resonance established on unit 2 with pattern 3
Network stable
```

The network exhibits the same behavior that we saw in the previous section. On the first cycle through the patterns, unit two of F_2 was recoded to the subset vector after previously encoding the superset vector. On the second cycle through, unit two caused a reset on the second pattern that was subsequently encoded on unit 3. A third cycle produced no changes so the network was declared stable. The match list is

TableForm[mlist]

```
Unit 1   1
Unit 2   3   2
Unit 3   2
Unit 4
Unit 5
Unit 6
```

To interpret this list, you must recognize that the patterns encoded by each unit are listed from left to right with the most recent pattern appearing first on the left (after the unit number which is the first number next to "Unit"). If a pattern appears on more than one unit's list, the unit with that pattern farthest to the left is the one that currently encodes the pattern; for example, pattern two appears on the list of both unit two and unit three. Since the encoding for unit three is more recent, that unit currently encodes pattern two. This list may get difficult to interpret if there are a large number of patterns and recodings, but it is simple to implement here and serves the immediate illustrative purpose.

You can compare the new weight vectors to verify that the calculations were correct. The top-down weights are

```
N[MatrixForm[td],3]
```

0	0	0	0.756	0.756	0.756
0	0	0	0.756	0.756	0.756
0	0	1.	0.756	0.756	0.756
1.	0	0	0.756	0.756	0.756
0	1.	1.	0.756	0.756	0.756

and the bottom-up weights are

```
N[MatrixForm[bu],3]
```

0	0	0	1.	0
0	0	0	0	1.
0	0	0.75	0	0.75
0.329	0.329	0.329	0.329	0.329
0.329	0.329	0.329	0.329	0.329
0.329	0.329	0.329	0.329	0.329

which are identical to the results we obtained earlier.

To end this discussion of ART1, I shall construct for you a list of input vectors that correspond to the first six letters of the alphabet. To gain facility with ART1, you should experiment with this input list, varying the network parameters and especially the vigilance parameter. You might also try constructing a noisy version of these letters to see how the network responds, once trained with the noise-free letters. The letters are five-by-five pixel representations and appear in Listing 7.2. To view these input patterns in a more illuminating manner, we can employ the density plotting capability of *Mathematica* as we did in Chapter 1; for example:

```
ListDensityPlot[Reverse[Partition[letterIn[[6]],5]]]
```

```
letterIn = { {0,0,1,0,0,
          0,1,0,1,0,
          1,0,0,0,1,        (* A *)
          1,1,1,1,1,
          1,0,0,0,1},
         {1,1,1,1,0,
          1,0,0,0,1,
          1,1,1,1,1,        (* B *)
          1,0,0,0,1,
          1,1,1,1,0},
         {1,1,1,1,1,
          1,0,0,0,0,
          1,0,0,0,0,        (* C *)
          1,0,0,0,0,
          1,1,1,1,1},
         {1,1,1,1,0,
          1,0,0,0,1,
          1,0,0,0,1,        (* D *)
          1,0,0,0,1,
          1,1,1,1,0},
         {1,1,1,1,1,
          1,0,0,0,0,
          1,1,1,1,0,        (* E *)
          1,0,0,0,0,
          1,1,1,1,1},
         {1,1,1,1,1,
          1,0,0,0,0,
          1,1,1,1,0,        (* F *)
          1,0,0,0,0,
          1,0,0,0,0}     };
```

Listing 7.2

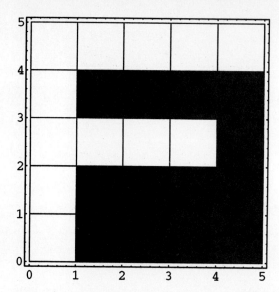

These six patterns have sufficient similarities between several letter pairs that relatively minor changes in the vigilance parameter can drastically affect how the network encodes them. Let's look at two examples. First, consider $\rho = 0.9$, which for all intents means perfect matching for this example; and use the same parameters to initialize the weights that we used in the previous example.

```
{topDown,bottomUp} =
    art1Init[25,6,1.5,0.9,3,0.2,0.1];

{td,bu,mlist} = art1[25,6,1,1.5,5,0.9,3,0.9,topDown,bottomUp,letterIn];
```

```
Resonance established on unit 1 with pattern 1
Reset with pattern 2 on unit 1
Resonance established on unit 2 with pattern 2
Reset with pattern 3 on unit 2
Reset with pattern 3 on unit 1
Resonance established on unit 3 with pattern 3
Resonance established on unit 2 with pattern 4
Reset with pattern 5 on unit 3
Reset with pattern 5 on unit 2
Reset with pattern 5 on unit 1
Resonance established on unit 4 with pattern 5
Resonance established on unit 4 with pattern 6
```

```
Network not stable
Resonance established on unit 1 with pattern 1
Reset with pattern 2 on unit 2
Reset with pattern 2 on unit 4
Reset with pattern 2 on unit 3
Reset with pattern 2 on unit 1
Resonance established on unit 5 with pattern 2
Resonance established on unit 3 with pattern 3
Resonance established on unit 2 with pattern 4
Reset with pattern 5 on unit 3
Reset with pattern 5 on unit 4
Reset with pattern 5 on unit 5
Reset with pattern 5 on unit 2
Reset with pattern 5 on unit 1
Resonance established on unit 6 with pattern 5
Resonance established on unit 4 with pattern 6
Network not stable
Resonance established on unit 1 with pattern 1
Resonance established on unit 5 with pattern 2
Resonance established on unit 3 with pattern 3
Resonance established on unit 2 with pattern 4
Resonance established on unit 6 with pattern 5
Resonance established on unit 4 with pattern 6
Network stable
```

This network required a total of 15 resets during the encoding process. Recall from several paragraphs ago that the initial values of the F_2-layer weights are 0.111 in this example. The larger these weights, the more favored is an uncommitted node over a previously committed node in the competition on F_2. Let's see what happens if we increase the initial values of these weights considerably. We can effect this change by increasing the value of the L parameter, in this case we let $L = 25$, then each weight on F_2 has a initial value of

```
N[25/(25-1+25),3]
```

```
0.51
```

```
{topDown,bottomUp} = art1Init[25,6,1.5,0.9,25,0.2,0.1];
```

```
{td,bu,mlist} = art1[25,6,1,1.5,5,0.9,25,0.9,topDown,bottomUp,letterIn];
```

```
Resonance established on unit 1 with pattern 1
Resonance established on unit 2 with pattern 2
Reset with pattern 3 on unit 2
Resonance established on unit 3 with pattern 3
Resonance established on unit 2 with pattern 4
Reset with pattern 5 on unit 3
Reset with pattern 5 on unit 2
Resonance established on unit 4 with pattern 5
Resonance established on unit 4 with pattern 6
Network not stable
Resonance established on unit 1 with pattern 1
Reset with pattern 2 on unit 2
Reset with pattern 2 on unit 4
Reset with pattern 2 on unit 3
Resonance established on unit 5 with pattern 2
Resonance established on unit 3 with pattern 3
Resonance established on unit 2 with pattern 4
Reset with pattern 5 on unit 3
Reset with pattern 5 on unit 5
Reset with pattern 5 on unit 4
Reset with pattern 5 on unit 2
Resonance established on unit 6 with pattern 5
Resonance established on unit 4 with pattern 6
Network not stable
Resonance established on unit 1 with pattern 1
Resonance established on unit 5 with pattern 2
Resonance established on unit 3 with pattern 3
Resonance established on unit 2 with pattern 4
Resonance established on unit 6 with pattern 5
Resonance established on unit 4 with pattern 6
Network stable
```

The parameter change reduced the number of resets from 15 down to 10. There are a great many more such experiments that you can perform to gain experience with the ART1 network.

7.2 ART2

Superficially, the main difference between ART1 and ART2 is that ART2 accepts input vectors whose components can have any real number as their value. In its execution, the ART2 network is considerably different from the ART1 network.

Aside from the obvious fact that binary and analog patterns differ in the nature of their respective components, ART2 must deal with additional complications. For example, ART2 must be able to recognize the underlying similarity of identical patterns superimposed on constant backgrounds having different levels. Compared in an absolute sense, two such patterns may appear entirely different when, in fact, they should be classified as the same pattern.

The price for this additional capability is primarily an increase in complexity on the F_1 processing level. The ART2 F_1 level comprises several sublevels and several gain-control systems. Processing on F_2 is the same for ART2 as it was for ART1. As partial compensation for the added complexity on the F_1 layer, the weight update equations are a bit simpler for ART2 than they were for ART1. In a software simulation, however, weight updates have the same complexity in either network.

7.2.1 ART2 Architecture

Figure 7.5 illustrates the architecture of the ART2 network; the similarities to and differences from ART1 should be apparent from that diagram. Both networks have attentional and orienting subsystems, as well as gain control systems.

You should be aware that there are many variations of the ART2 network. The version shown in Figure 7.5 matches the one in *Neural Networks*, but I do not intend to imply that this particular version is the best; it is merely a starting point for your own investigations.

7.2.2 ART2 Processing Equations

The equations governing the dynamics of the ART2 network are almost identical to those for ART1. Moreover, since the processing done on the F_2 layer of ART2 is identical to that of the ART1 F_2 layer, we shall be concerned primarily with the F_1 layer in the ensuing discussion. On each

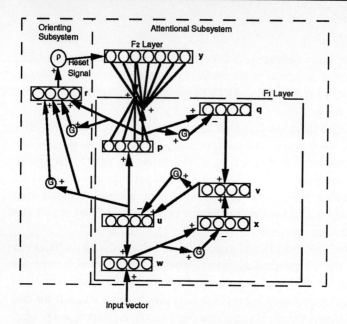

Figure 7.5 This figure shows the ART2 architecture. The overall structure is the same as that of ART1. The F_1 layer has been divided into six sub-layers, **w, x, u, v, p,** and **q.** Each node labeled G is a gain-control unit that sends an inhibitory signal to each unit on the layer it feeds. All sublayers on F_1, as well as the **r** layer of the orienting subsystem, have the same number of units. Individual sublayers on F_1 are connected unit-to-unit; that is, the layers are not fully interconnected, with the exception of the bottom-up connections to F_2 and the top-down connections from F_2.

of the F_1 sublayers, the processing equations take the form

$$\dot{x}_k = -Ax_k + (1 - Bx_k)J_k^+ - (C + Dx_k)J_k^- \qquad (7.20)$$

where A, B, C, and D, are constants, and the definitions of J_k^+ and J_k^- depend on the particular sublayer. In all cases we shall set $B = C = 0$. Since we shall, once again, be interested in the asymptotic solutions, we can solve Eq. (7.20) in that case to find equilibrium values for the activities.

$$x_k = \frac{J_k^+}{A + DJ_k^-} \qquad (7.21)$$

Table 7.1 summarizes the values of A, D, J_k^+, and J_k^- for the six sublayers of F_1, as well as for the units in the **r** layer of the orienting

Quantity Layer	A	D	J_i^+	J_i^-
w	1	1	$I_i + au_i$	0
x	e	1	w_i	$|\mathbf{w}|$
u	e	1	v_i	$|\mathbf{v}|$
v	1	1	$f(x_i) + bf(q_i)$	0
p	1	1	$u_i + \sum_j g(y_j)z_{ij}$	0
q	e	1	p_i	$|\mathbf{p}|$
r	e	1	$u_i + cp_i$	$|\mathbf{u}| + |c\mathbf{p}|$

Table 7.1 This table summarizes the factors in Eq. (7.21) for each of the sublayers on F_1, and the r layer. I_i is the ith component of the input vector. a, b, and c are constants. e is a small, positive constant used to prevent division by zero in the case where the magnitude of the vector quantities is zero. y_j is the activity of the jth unit of the F_2 layer. f and g are functions that are described in the text.

subsystem.

Using the definitions from Table 7.1, we can write the equilibrium equations for each of the sublayers on F_1 as follows:

$$w_i = I_i + au_i \tag{7.22}$$

$$x_i = \frac{w_i}{e + |\mathbf{w}|} \tag{7.23}$$

$$v_i = f(x_i) + bf(q_i) \tag{7.24}$$

$$u_i = \frac{v_i}{e + |\mathbf{v}|} \tag{7.25}$$

$$p_i = u_i + \sum_j g(y_j)z_{ij} \tag{7.26}$$

$$q_i = \frac{p_i}{e + |\mathbf{p}|} \tag{7.27}$$

The function $f()$ acts as a thresholding function that the F_1 layer uses as a filter for noise. A sigmoid function would work well in this case, but we shall use a simpler, linear threshold function:

$$f(x) = \begin{cases} 0 & 0 \le x \le \theta \\ x & x > \theta \end{cases} \tag{7.28}$$

where θ is a positive constant less than one.

Processing on F_2 is identical to that on ART1. We determine a net-input value for each unit,

$$T_j = \sum_i p_i z_{ji} \tag{7.29}$$

then determine a winning unit according to which has the largest net-input value.

$g(y)$ is the output function for the units on the F_2 layer. Since the F_2 layer is a winner-take-all competitive layer, just as in ART1, $g(y)$ has a particularly simple form

$$g(y_j) = \begin{cases} d & T_j = \max_k\{T_k\} \forall k \\ 0 & \text{otherwise} \end{cases} \tag{7.30}$$

where d is a positive constant less than one.

With the above definition of the output function on F_2, and knowing the fact that F_2 is a winner-take-all competitive layer, we can rewrite the equation for processing on the **p** sublayer of F_1 as

$$p_i = \begin{cases} u_i & \text{if } F_2 \text{ is inactive} \\ u_i + dz_{iJ} & \text{if the } J\text{th node on } F_2 \text{ is active} \end{cases} \tag{7.31}$$

The weight-update equations on ART2 turn out to be simpler than those on ART1. Once again, only weights to or from the winning F_2 unit get updated, and only after resonance has been established. If v_J is the winning F_2 node, then weights are modified according to

$$z_{iJ} = z_{Ji} = \frac{u_i}{1-d} \tag{7.32}$$

Our choice of initial values for the weights is driven by performance considerations, much as it was on ART1. From the discussion of the orienting subsystem in the next section, we shall find that setting the top-down weights initially to zero, $z_{ij}(0) = 0$, prevents reset during the time when a new F_2 node is being recruited to encode a new input pattern. Weights on F_2 are initialized with fairly large values in order to bias the network toward the selection of a new, uncommitted node, which, as in ART1, helps to keep the number of matching cycles to a minimum. There are a number of alternate ways to initialize the bottom-up weights. We shall stay with the method described in Chapter 8 of *Neural Networks*.

$$z_{ji}(0) \leq \frac{1}{(1-d)\sqrt{M}} \tag{7.33}$$

Similar considerations lead to a condition relating the parameters c and d.

$$\frac{cd}{1-d} \leq 1 \tag{7.34}$$

We are almost ready to begin an example calculation. First, we must examine the orienting subsystem in some detail, as the matching process on ART2 is not quite as straightforward as it was on ART1.

7.2.3 ART2 Orienting Subsystem

From Table 7.1 we can construct the equation for the activities of the nodes on the **r** layer of the orienting subsystem.

$$r_i = \frac{u_i + cp_i}{|\mathbf{u}| + |c\mathbf{p}|} \tag{7.35}$$

where we have assumed that $e = 0$. The condition for reset is

$$\frac{\rho}{|\mathbf{r}|} > 1 \tag{7.36}$$

where ρ is the vigilance parameter as in ART1.

Notice that two F_1 sublayers, **p**, and **u**, participate in the matching process. As top-down weights change on the **p** layer during learning, the activity of the units on the **p** layer also changes. The **u** layer remains stable during this process, so including it in the matching process prevents reset from occurring while learning of a new pattern is taking place.

Since $|\mathbf{r}| = (\mathbf{r} \cdot \mathbf{r})^{1/2}$, we can write

$$|\mathbf{r}| = \frac{[1 + 2|c\mathbf{p}| \cos(\mathbf{u}, \mathbf{p}) + |c\mathbf{p}|^2]^{1/2}}{1 + |c\mathbf{p}|} \tag{7.37}$$

using Eq. (7.35), where $\cos(\mathbf{u}, \mathbf{p})$ is the cosine of the angle between $\mathbf{u}$ and $\mathbf{p}$.

First, note that if $\mathbf{u}$ and $\mathbf{p}$ are parallel, then the above equation reduces to $|\mathbf{r}| = 1$, and there will be no reset. As long as there is no output from F_2, Eq. (7.26) shows that $\mathbf{u} = \mathbf{p}$, and there will be no reset in this case.

Suppose now that F_2 does have an output from some winning unit, and that the input pattern needs to be learned, or encoded, by the F_2 unit. We also do not want a reset in this case. From Eq. (7.26) we see that $\mathbf{p} = \mathbf{u} + d\mathbf{z}_J$, where $\mathbf{z}_J$ is the weight vector on the winning F_2 unit. If we initialize all of the top-down weights, z_{ij}, to zero, then the initial output from F_2 will have no effect on the value of $\mathbf{p}$; that is, $\mathbf{p}$ will remain equal to $\mathbf{u}$.

During the learning process itself, $\mathbf{z}_J$ becomes parallel to $\mathbf{u}$ according to Eq. (7.32). Thus, $\mathbf{p}$ also becomes parallel to $\mathbf{u}$, and again $|\mathbf{r}| = 1$ and there is no reset. As with ART1, a sufficient mismatch between the bottom-up input vector and the top-down template results in a reset. In ART2, the bottom-up pattern is taken at the $\mathbf{u}$ sublevel of F_1 and the top-down template is taken at $\mathbf{p}$.

7.2.4 Example ART2 Calculation

Since the calculations that are done on F_2 are the same for ART2 as they were for ART1, we shall not spend time describing them here. On the other hand, what happens to an input vector, as it passes through the various F_1 layers of the ART2 network, is far from obvious. Moreover, there are many variations on the F_1 architecture. We shall not concern ourselves with the second issue here, but rather, we shall spend a bit of time looking at the calculations on the particular F_1 layer described in the previous section.

The simulation of F_1 requires that we calculate the vector magnitude on several of the sublayers. We shall use the standard definition of the magnitude of a vector:

```
vmag2[v_] := Sqrt[v . v]
```

The parameters and other functions needed are as follows. We assume $e = 0$ in all cases.

```
f1dim = 5;  (* F1 dimension *)
```

```
f2dim = 6;  (* F2 dimension *)
```

```
rho = 0.9;  (* we want close matches for now *)

fv[x_] := If[x>theta,x,0]
f[x_]  := Map[fv,x]  (* output function on v layer *)

theta = 0.2;  (* threshold value *)

a1=10; b1=10; c1=0.1; (* F1 parameters *)
```

Even though there is no output from F_2 at this time, we shall define the F_2 output function and initialize the weight vectors in anticipation of continuing on with the F_2 calculation later.

```
d=0.9;
g[x_] := If[x>0,d,0]

z12 = Table[Table[0 ,{f2dim}],{f1dim}]; (* top-down *)

z21 = MatrixForm[N[Table[Table[0.5/((1-d)*Sqrt[f1dim] ),
      {f1dim}],{f2dim}],4]]
```

2.236	2.236	2.236	2.236	2.236
2.236	2.236	2.236	2.236	2.236
2.236	2.236	2.236	2.236	2.236
2.236	2.236	2.236	2.236	2.236
2.236	2.236	2.236	2.236	2.236
2.236	2.236	2.236	2.236	2.236

Let's define a set of three input vectors.

```
inputs = { {0.2, 0.7, 0.1, 0.5, 0.4},
           {0.8, 2.8, 0.4, 2.0, 1.6},
           {0.1, 0.3, 1.2, 2.0, 4.0}  };
```

Notice that the second input vector is a multiple of the first, while the third bears little resemblance to either of the first two.

Initialize the sublayer outputs to zero vectors.

```
ClearAll[w,x,u,v,p,q,r];
w=x=u=v=p=q=r=Table[0,{f1dim}];
```

We begin the calculation with the first input vector.

```
w = inputs[[1]] + a u
```

{0.2, 0.7, 0.1, 0.5, 0.4}

x is a normalized version of **w**.

`x = w / vmag2[w]`

{0.205196, 0.718185, 0.102598, 0.512989, 0.410391}

`v = f[x] + b f[q]`

{0.205196, 0.718185, 0, 0.512989, 0.410391}

Notice that the third component of **v** is zero, since the third component of x did not meet the threshold criterion. Since there is no top-down signal from F_2, the remaining three sublayers, **u**, **p**, and **q**, all have the same outputs.

`u = v / vmag2[v]`

{0.206284, 0.721995, 0, 0.515711, 0.412568}

`p = u`

{0.206284, 0.721995, 0, 0.515711, 0.412568}

`q = p / vmag2[p]`

{0.206284, 0.721995, 0, 0.515711, 0.412568}

We cannot stop the F_1 calculation yet, however, since both **u** and **p** are now nonzero. These sublayers provide feedback to other layers, so we must iterate the F_1 sublayers.

`w = inputs[[1]] + a u`

{2.26284, 7.91995, 0.1, 5.65711, 4.52568}

`x = w / vmag2[w]`

{0.206276, 0.721965, 0.00911578, 0.515689, 0.412551}

`v = f[x] + b f[q]`

{2.26912, 7.94191, 0, 5.6728, 4.53824}

```
u = v / vmag2[v]
```

{0.206284, 0.721995, 0, 0.515711, 0.412568}

```
p = u
```

{0.206284, 0.721995, 0, 0.515711, 0.412568}

```
q = p / vmag2[p]
```

{0.206284, 0.721995, 0, 0.515711, 0.412568}

A third iteration results in

```
w = inputs[[1]] + a u
```

{2.26284, 7.91995, 0.1, 5.65711, 4.52568}

```
x = w / vmag2[w]
```

{0.206276, 0.721965, 0.00911578, 0.515689, 0.412551}

```
v = f[x] + b f[q]
```

{2.26912, 7.94191, 0, 5.6728, 4.53824}

```
u = v / vmag2[v]
```

{0.206284, 0.721995, 0, 0.515711, 0.412568}

```
p = u
```

{0.206284, 0.721995, 0, 0.515711, 0.412568}

```
q = p / vmag2[p]
```

{0.206284, 0.721995, 0, 0.515711, 0.412568}

which does not change the results. We shall stop at two iterations through F_1 for all of our calculations.

Let's now apply the second input vector to F_1. Recall, the second input vector is a multiple of the first. Reinitialize the sublayer outputs first.

```
ClearAll[w,x,u,v,p,q,r];
w=x=u=v=p=q=r=Table[0,{f1dim}];
```

```
w = inputs[[2]] + a u
```

{0.8, 2.8, 0.4, 2., 1.6}

```
x = w / vmag2[w]
```

{0.205196, 0.718185, 0.102598, 0.512989, 0.410391}

```
v = f[x] + b f[q]
```

{0.205196, 0.718185, 0, 0.512989, 0.410391}

```
u = v / vmag2[v]
```

{0.206284, 0.721995, 0, 0.515711, 0.412568}

```
p = u
```

{0.206284, 0.721995, 0, 0.515711, 0.412568}

```
q = p / vmag2[p]
```

{0.206284, 0.721995, 0, 0.515711, 0.412568}

Run a second iteration to ensure stability.

```
w = inputs[[2]] + a u
```

{2.86284, 10.0199, 0.4, 7.15711, 5.72568}

```
x = w / vmag2[w]
```

{0.206199, 0.721695, 0.0288103, 0.515497, 0.412397}

```
v = f[x] + b f[q]
```

{2.26904, 7.94164, 0, 5.6726, 4.53808}

```
u = v / vmag2[v]
```

{0.206284, 0.721995, 0, 0.515711, 0.412568}

```
art2F1[in_,a_,b_,d_,tdWts_,f1d_,winr_:0] :=
  Module[{w,x,u,v,p,q,i},
    w=x=u=v=p=q=Table[0,{f1d}];
    For[i=1,i<=2,i++,
      w = in + a u;
      x = w / vmag2[w];
      v = f[x] + b f[q];
      u = v / vmag2[v];
      p = If[winr==0,u,u + d Transpose[tdWts][[winr]] ];
      q = p / vmag2[p];
      ]; (* end of For i *)
    Return[{u,p}];
    ] (* end of Module *)
```

Listing 7.3

p = u

{0.206284, 0.721995, 0, 0.515711, 0.412568}

q = p / vmag2[p]

{0.206284, 0.721995, 0, 0.515711, 0.412568}

After the **v** layer, the results are identical for the two input vectors. We can conclude that the F_1 layer performs several functions on an input vector: Vectors are normalized to the same ambient background level, noise is eliminated using a threshold condition, and the final vector is normalized to a length of one. Incidentally, the noise-reduction process described above often goes by the name of **contrast enhancement**, since, as you can see by comparing the original input vector, after reduction to a common background level, to the final output vector, values above the threshold have been enhanced, while values below the threshold have been reduced to zero.

For later use, we shall assemble the F_1 sublayers into a single function, art2F1 in Listing 7.3. The function returns the values of **u** and **p**, since these are used later. **in** is the input vector, **a**, **b**, **c**, and **d**, are the layer parameters defined above, **tdWts** is the top-down weight matrix, **f1d** is the dimension of F_1, and **winr** is the index of the winning F_2 unit. If

winr is zero — as it is by default — p will be equal to u. Let's try this
function on the third input vector to verify that claim.

```
{u,p} = art2F1[inputs[[3]],a1,b1,c1,d,z12,f1dim];

u

{0, 0, 0.259161, 0.431934, 0.863868}

p

{0, 0, 0.259161, 0.431934, 0.863868}
```

We can now assemble the functions into a complete ART2 simulator. That
development is the subject of the final section of this chapter.

7.2.5 The Complete ART2 Simulator

We can pattern the ART2 simulator after the ART1 simulator. In fact to
construct the ART2 simulator, I began with the ART1 code. Also, as we
did before, we shall initialize the weights in a separate routine.

```
art2Init[f1dim_,f2dim_,d_,del1_] :=
  Module[{z12,z21},
   z12 = Table[Table[0 ,{f2dim}],{f1dim}];
   z21 = Table[Table[del1/((1.0-d)*Sqrt[f1dim] ) //N,
           {f1dim}],{f2dim}];
   Return[{z12,z21}];
   ]; (* end of Module *)
```

The parameter del1 determines what fraction less than the maximum
value to which the top-down weights are initialized; see Eq. (7.33).
   The simulator requires the winner and compete routines that we devel-
oped previously for ART1, but the routine to determine the reset flag is
slightly different. The reset routine for ART2 is

```
resetflag2[u_,p_,c_,rho_]:=
   Module[{r,flag},
     r = (u + c p) / (vmag2[u] + vmag2[c p]);
     If[rho/vmag2[r] > 1,flag=True,flag=False];
     Return[flag];
     ];
```

```
art2[f1dim_,f2dim_,a1_,b1_,c1_,d_,theta_,rho_,f1Wts_,f2Wts_,inputs_] :=
  Module[{droplistinit,droplist,notDone=True,i,nIn= Length[inputs],reset,
          u,p,t,xf2,uf2,v,windex,matchList,newMatchList,tdWts,buWts},
    droplistinit = Table[1,{f2dim}];    (* initialize droplist *)
    tdWts = f1Wts; buWts = f2Wts;
    u = p = Table[0,{f1dim}];
            (* construct list of F2 units and encodedinput patterns *)
      matchList = Table[{StringForm["Unit ``",n]},{n,f2dim}];
    While[notDone==True,newMatchList = matchList;  (* process until stable *)
      For[i=1,i<=nIn,i++,            (* process each input pattern in sequence *)
        droplist = droplistinit;   (* initialize droplist for new input *)
        reset=True;
        in = inputs[[i]];          (* next input pattern *)
        windex = 0;                (* initialize *)
        While[reset==True,            (* cycle until no reset *)
          {u,p} = art2F1[in,a1,b1,d,tdWts,f1dim,windex];
          t= buWts . p;                 (* F2 net-inputs *)
          t = t droplist;          (* turn off inhibited units *)
          xf2 = compete[t];          (* F2 activities *)
          uf2 = Map[g,xf2];          (* F2 outputs *)
          windex = winner[uf2,d];    (* winning index *)
           {u,p} = art2F1[in,a1,b1,d,tdWts,f1dim,windex];
          reset = resetflag2[u,p,c1,rho];  (* check reset *)
          If[reset==True,droplist[[windex]]=0;    (* update droplist *)
                Print["Reset with pattern ",i," on unit ",windex],Continue];
          ]; (* end of While reset==True *)
    Print["Resonance established on unit ",    windex," with pattern ",i];
    tdWts=Transpose[tdWts];  (* resonance, so update weights *)
        tdWts[[windex]]=u/(1-d);  tdWts=Transpose[tdWts];
        buWts[[windex]] = u/(1-d);
        matchList[[windex]] =    (* update matching list *)
      Reverse[Union[matchList[[windex]],{i}]];
        ]; (* end of For i=1 to nIn *)
    If[matchList==newMatchList,notDone=False;  (* see if matchList is static *)
          Print["Network stable"],Print["Network not stable"];
          newMatchList = matchList];
      ]; (* end of While notDone==True *)
  Return[{tdWts,buWts,matchList}];
  ];   (* end of Module *)
```

Listing 7.4

The complete ART2 simulator appears in Listing 7.4. To run the network with the inputs and parameters defined in the previous section, first initialize the weights

```
{f1W, f2W} = art2Init[5,6,0.9,0.5];
```

```
MatrixForm[f1W]
```

```
0  0  0  0  0  0
0  0  0  0  0  0
0  0  0  0  0  0
0  0  0  0  0  0
0  0  0  0  0  0
```

```
MatrixForm[f2W]
```

```
2.23607  2.23607  2.23607  2.23607  2.23607
2.23607  2.23607  2.23607  2.23607  2.23607
2.23607  2.23607  2.23607  2.23607  2.23607
2.23607  2.23607  2.23607  2.23607  2.23607
2.23607  2.23607  2.23607  2.23607  2.23607
2.23607  2.23607  2.23607  2.23607  2.23607
```

then use these weights and the various parameters in the calling sequence for the art2 function

```
outputs = art2[5,6,10,10,0.1,0.9,0.2,0.999,
                    f1W,f2W,inputs];
```

```
Resonance established on unit 1 with pattern 1
Resonance established on unit 1 with pattern 2
Reset with pattern 3 on unit 1
Resonance established on unit 2 with pattern 3
Network not stable
Resonance established on unit 1 with pattern 1
Resonance established on unit 1 with pattern 2
Resonance established on unit 2 with pattern 3
Network stable
```

```
TableForm[outputs[[3]]]
```

```
Unit 1   2   1
Unit 2   3
Unit 3
Unit 4
Unit 5
Unit 6
```

As we should expect, unit one encoded both the first and second patterns. The third pattern was encoded by unit 2. We also might guess what the weight matrices look like. The top-down matrix is

`MatrixForm[N[outputs[[1]],3]]`

```
2.06   0      0   0   0   0
7.22   0      0   0   0   0
0      2.59   0   0   0   0
5.16   4.32   0   0   0   0
4.13   8.64   0   0   0   0
```

and the bottom-up matrix is

`MatrixForm[N[outputs[[2]],3]]`

```
2.06   7.22   0      5.16   4.13
0      0      2.59   4.32   8.64
2.24   2.24   2.24   2.24   2.24
2.24   2.24   2.24   2.24   2.24
2.24   2.24   2.24   2.24   2.24
2.24   2.24   2.24   2.24   2.24
```

As with the ART1 network, facility with this ART2 network can only come by experience. Moreover, the sublayer structure on F_1 provides fertile ground for additional experimentation.

Summary

The ART1 and ART2 networks that we studied in this chapter represent a class of network architectures based on adaptive resonance theory. Among other characteristics, these networks retain their ability to learn new information without having to be retrained on old information as well as the new. Moreover, these networks know when presented information is new and automatically incorporate this new information. You should view the ART1 and ART2 networks as building blocks. Hierarchical structures based on combinations of these networks can exhibit complex behavior. As with the other neural networks in this book, the ART1 and ART2 networks should be used as starting points for your own experimentation.

Chapter 8

Genetic Algorithms

Whether or not you believe in an evolutionary development of life on this planet, the theory of natural selection offers some compelling arguments that individuals with certain characteristics are better able to survive and pass on those characteristics to their progeny. We can think of natural selection as nature's way of searching for better and better organisms. A genetic algorithm (GA) is a general search procedure based on the ideas of genetics and natural selection.

The solution methodology of a GA is reminiscent of sexual reproduction in which the genes of two parents combine to form those of their children. Our basic premise will be that we can create a population of individuals that somehow represent possible solutions to a problem we are trying to solve. These individuals have certain characteristics that make them more or less fit as members of the population, and we shall associate this fitness with procreational probability. The most fit members will have a higher probability of mating than the less fit members. The power of GAs lies in the fact that as members of the population mate, they produce offspring that have a significant chance of retaining the desirable characteristics of their parents, perhaps even combining the best characteristics of both parents. In this manner, the overall fitness of the population can potentially increase from generation to generation as we discover better solutions to our problem.

I intend this chapter to be a brief introduction to GAs. In the first section, we shall look at a few of the fundamental ideas behind GAs and do a simple example calculation. In the second section, we shall develop the code for a basic GA (BGA) that solves a simple optimization problem. In the final section, we shall look at one method of applying GAs to the problem of learning in a neural network.

8.1 GA Basics

In the introduction to this chapter, I used the words *chance, perhaps,* and *potentially,* all contributing to the probabilistic flavor of GAs. Often people attempt to disprove evolutionary theory on the basis that mere chance could not possibly have resulted in the complex organisms that exist today. Usually a person offers some calculation that, in essence, proves that no matter how many monkeys sit at typewriters for an infinite time, the probability that one will type (*insert your favorite book title here*) is vanishingly small. Supposedly, by inference, any theory of evolution based on probability and random mutations is similarly doomed to failure.

I am not going to attempt to argue the pros and cons of evolution, but I do want to point out that the theory of natural selection that we will use here, while having probabilistic elements, is far from being based on chance mutations. In fact there is a very nice demonstration, described by Richard Dawkins in his book *The Blind Watchmaker,* that illustrates the philosophical differences between the theory of natural selection and the theory of randomness.[1] The following presentation is in the spirit of the one given by Dawkins.

Consider the following experiment. Set 10 monkeys down at 10 typewriters and allow each monkey to type 18 lower-case letters. We shall call that set of phrases a generation. If none of the monkeys has typed the expression "tobeornottobe," then begin again with a new sheet of paper for each monkey. Let's simulate the experiment by having *Mathematica* produce a few generations of monkey prose. The *Mathematica* function FromCharacterCode converts a list of ascii integers into their appropriate characters. We use that function to generate text from a randomly-generated list of character codes.

```
generate[] := TableForm[Map[FromCharacterCode,
  Table[Random[Integer,{97,122}],{i,1,10},{j,1,13}]]]
```

```
generate[]
```

```
vbkafmujpdneg
nifcmmuucqonf
ymwasqzsagpnp
ikowydtridswq
ilqsrqxahklvs
jogvhcjuzzxcj
xctkuwachkbwr
skfqtjbrjrrpq
kqrelgjcobhbj
alqlbsezaibdy
```

```
generate[]
```

```
ywporsuuapyfh
owqozltdvbgpu
```

---

[1]Richard Dawkins. *The Blind Watchmaker.* New York: W. W. Norton & Company, 1987.

```
qxzsaymyozwdt
uummtfbgezlir
edkpejxjhkowk
qmhefxgdsblgt
tkxlovoyglvnx
mbzkdxtlrlvvc
jowseiaersfel
momgjesfwwgbf
```

generate[]

```
hdahgwcjzagag
uvgmxanpjpkqi
ikksflflyzqgh
oqozewohuaema
vtnxclgtcwuvz
axjoakjjnflqe
etvlqillzceja
xxanjvmiooltj
uxeijweevpous
urvkzgrxscyxb
```

We could go on, but you probably get the picture: Not one of these strings has any noticeable resemblance to the target string. Occasionally the proper letter does appear in the proper location in one of the strings, but it is likely to take a very long time before our pseudomonkeys generate the correct sequence purely by chance. Since there are 26 possible letters for each of 13 locations in the string, the probability that a single monkey will type the correct phrase is

$(1./26)\hat{ }13$

```
           -19
4.03038 10
```

which is about two chances out of a billion billion. We agree, therefore, that pure chance is probably not a sufficient operator to drive evolutionary changes; but we have not been describing natural selection with this example.

Let's change the generation process somewhat. At first, we generate ten sequences at random, as before. For subsequent generations, however, we base the generation on the string which, however slightly, best matches the desired string. Then we allow each letter to change with some fixed probability. From the resulting generation, we choose the most closely matching string to form a new generation, and so on.

Begin by defining the phrase as a text string.

```
tobe = "tobeornottobe"
```

tobeornottobe

Convert the string to a generic variable, keyPhrase.

```
keyPhrase = ToCharacterCode[tobe]
```

{116, 111, 98, 101, 111, 114, 110, 111, 116, 116, 111, 98, 101}

Generate an initial population of 10 random phrases, but leave them in ascii code form for use by the program.

```
initialPop = Table[Random[Integer,{97,122}],{i,1,10},{j,1,13}]
```

{{119, 105, 118, 110, 120, 117, 116, 110, 111, 116, 115,
   106, 112}, {105, 113, 104, 111, 118, 114, 98, 119,
   107, 121, 114, 98, 104},
  {99, 108, 103, 107, 98, 112, 102, 116, 102, 107, 115,
   119, 104}, {101, 97, 118, 97, 97, 120, 117, 117, 97,
   106, 116, 111, 98}, {114, 118, 110, 110, 122, 117,
   113, 101, 114, 98, 100, 121, 103},
  {108, 110, 99, 112, 97, 106, 106, 120, 114, 103, 111,
   104, 108}, {104, 102, 116, 108, 106, 119, 115, 105,
   111, 105, 104, 114, 112},
  {116, 117, 107, 98, 119, 98, 108, 119, 122, 122, 110,
   116, 116}, {102, 106, 117, 110, 114, 117, 103, 109,
   119, 99, 122, 106, 110},
  {102, 114, 115, 122, 106, 107, 101, 117, 111, 119, 100,
   120, 109}}

Just out of curiosity, lets convert this population to strings to see what they look like.

```
TableForm[Map[FromCharacterCode,initialPop]]
```

wivnxutnotsjp

```
iqhovrbwkyrbh
clgkbpftfkswh
eavaaxuuajtob
rvnnzuqerbdyg
lncpajjxrgohl
hftljwsioihrp
tukbwblwzzntt
fjunrugmwczjn
frszjkeuowdxm
```

We will need a few more functions to implement this demonstration. The first, **flip[prob]**, implements a biased coin toss; that is, a coin toss that will come up heads with probability **prob**, instead of 50-50.

```
flip[x_] := If[Random[]<=x,True,False]
```

The function **mutateLetter** will result in a change to a given letter with a probability **pmute**.

```
mutateLetter[pmute_,letter_] :=
  If[flip[pmute],Random[Integer,{97,122}],letter];
```

newGenerate in Listing 8.1 is the main program that produces each group of new phrases. Let's produce 50 new generations to see how well this scheme works.

```
newGenerate[0.1,keyPhrase,initialPop,50]
```

```
Generation 1: iqhovrbwkyrbh Fitness= 2
Generation 2: tqhovrbwkyrbh Fitness= 3
Generation 3: tohovrbrkyrbh Fitness= 4
Generation 4: tohovrbrktrbh Fitness= 5
Generation 5: tohovrboktrbh Fitness= 6
Generation 6: tohocrboktrbh Fitness= 6
Generation 7: tobocrboktrbh Fitness= 7
Generation 8: tobocrnoktrbh Fitness= 8
Generation 9: toboornoktrbh Fitness= 9
Generation 10: toboornoktrbh Fitness= 9
Generation 11: toboornoktobh Fitness= 10
Generation 12: toboornoktobh Fitness= 10
Generation 13: toboornoktobh Fitness= 10
Generation 14: toboornoktobo Fitness= 10
```

```
newGenerate[pmutate_,keyPhrase_,pop_,numGens_] :=
  Module[{i,newPop,parent,diff,matches,
          index,fitness},
    newPop=pop;
  For[i=1,i<=numGens,i++,
    diff = Map[(keyPhrase-#)&,newPop];
    matches = Map[Count[#,0]&,diff];
    fitness = Max[matches];
    index = Position[matches,fitness];
    parent = newPop[[First[Flatten[index]]]];
    Print["Generation ",i,": ",
            FromCharacterCode[parent],
            " Fitness= ",fitness];
    newPop =
      Table[Map[mutateLetter[pmutate,#]&,parent],
            {100}];
    ]; (* end of For *)
  ]; (* end of Module *)
```

Listing 8.1

```
Generation 15: toboornoktobo Fitness= 10
Generation 16: toboornoktobe Fitness= 11
Generation 17: toboornoktobe Fitness= 11
Generation 18: tobeornoktobe Fitness= 12
Generation 19: tobeornoktobe Fitness= 12
Generation 20: tobeornoktobe Fitness= 12
Generation 21: tobeornoktobe Fitness= 12
Generation 22: tobeornoktobe Fitness= 12
Generation 23: tobeornottobe Fitness= 13
```

After only 23 generations, the population produced the desired phrase. In all fairness to the random method, we should go back and produce 230 random phrases and then see if we have a match. Please feel free to run the experiment. If you come up with anything that is even close, I would like to hear about it: You have phenomenal luck, and we should collaborate on some lottery tickets.

We have seen that the addition of randomness in the natural-selection process does not lead to chaos, but rather to order and meaning, but we have not yet added mating and reproduction to the process. Let's move on to the discussion of a more complete genetic algorithm.

8.2 A Basic Genetic Algorithm (BGA)

In this section we shall develop an algorithm that has all of the characteristic processing normally associated with a true GA. Although we will build a very simple algorithm, it has application in a number of areas. More complex GAs will have the same high-level structure, but will differ in the details of the computations performed. Before we actually perform the development of the GA in Section 8.2.2, a review of the relevant vocabulary is in order. Like neural networks, GAs are inspired by certain results from biology.

8.2.1 GA Vocabulary

In a biological organism, the structure that encodes the prescription that specifies how the organism is to be constructed is called a **chromosome**. One or more chromosomes may be required to specify the complete organism. The complete set of chromosomes is called a **genotype**, and the resulting organism is called a **phenotype**.

Each chromosome comprises a number of individual structures called **genes**. Each gene encodes a particular feature of the organism, and the location, or **locus**, of the gene within the chromosome structure, determines what particular characteristic the gene represents. At a particular locus, a gene may encode any of several different values of the particular characteristic it represents; eye color, for example, may be green, blue, hazel, etc. The different values of a gene are called **alleles**.

The development of a new generation involves sexual reproduction between two parent phenotypes resulting in child phenotypes. During this reproduction, the chromosomes of the parents are combined to form the chromosomes of the children. The children inherit certain characteristics from each of their parents. If, for example, the child inherits the best characteristics from each of its parents, then it will supposedly be more fit to survive and reproduce, thus passing the favorable characteristics on to its progeny.

In a GA, chromosomes are typically represented by a string of some variable type. In the example of the previous section, the chromosome is a string of ascii values. Since there is only one chromosome per organism, the chromosome and the genotype were the same. Each position in the chromosome string is a gene which can take on different ascii values, which themselves are the alleles. The phenotype is the string of characters decoded from the genotype. In the BGA that we shall develop in the next section, the chromosomes comprise binary numbers. In this case, the alleles are zero and one. You may, of course, eschew the biological terminology and speak instead of strings, positions on the string, and values, instead of chromosomes, genes, and alleles.

There is one aspect of the theory of GAs that we shall not treat in this chapter, but which is, nonetheless, an important topic in the development of the theoretical basis for GAs. That topic is **schemata**. Briefly stated, schemata are subsets of the chromosome string which have similar alleles at specific locations. We can view schemata as building blocks that are combined during the reproduction process to produce a new chromosome. Assuming that the schemata represent certain favorable characteristics, then combining these schemata in an offspring should result in an increase in survival probability for that offspring. Part of the theory of GAs is involved with demonstrating how GAs manipulate these schemata from one generation to the next in order to form individuals whose fitness increases from generation to generation.

8.2.2 A BGA Algorithm

In this section we shall construct a GA that solves a specific problem and in the process illustrate many of the techniques required to solve other, real-world problems. Most problems to which GAs apply, have the characteristic that something or some quantity needs to be optimized. We can identify that quantity with the fitness, or survival probability, of an individual.

Describing the actual BGA requires only a few statements.

1. Begin with a population of individuals generated at random.

2. Determine the fitness of each individual in the current population.

3. Select parents for the next generation with a probability proportional to their fitness.

4. Mate the selected parents to produce offspring to populate the new generation.

5. Repeat items 2–4.

The Fitness Function Let's begin our example by defining a quantity that determines an individual's fitness. Consider the function

```
f[x_] := 1+Cos[x]/(1+0.01 x^2)
```

We shall assume that this function measures the fitness of an individual phenotype, x. The phenotype, x, is a numerical value which we decode from a chromosome. Let's examine the behavior of the fitness function.

```
Plot[f[x],{x,-45,45},PlotPoints->200];
```

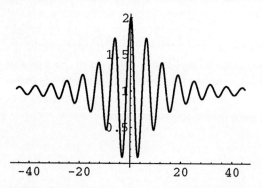

Notice that the optimal value of this function occurs at $x = 0$, but notice also that there are many local maxima which are suboptimal. A traditional hill-climbing technique, unless it were fortuitously to begin somewhere on the central peak, would quickly reach one of the suboptimal peaks and would get stuck there.

Chromosome Representation Each phenotype is a value decoded from a chromosome. We shall use chromosomes with binary alleles for this example. We choose to represent a chromosome as a ten-digit binary string, and we shall restrict the phenotypes to values between -40 and 40. Therefore, the chromosome $\{0,0,0,0,0,0,0,0,0,0\}$ must decode to the value -40, and the chromosome $\{1,1,1,1,1,1,1,1,1,1\}$ must decode to the value 40.

The binary number 1111111111 is equal to decimal 1023. If we multiply this number by 80/1023

`N[80.0/1023,10]`

`0.07820136852`

and subtract 40, we get the number 40.

`1023 (80.0/1023) -40`

`40.`

Similarly treated, 0000000000 yields -40.

`0 (80.0/1023) -40`

`-40`

The function decodeBGA embodies this conversion procedure. The function first converts the binary number into a decimal number as follows, using 1010101010 as an example. First, determine the locations of the 1s in the string.

`pList = Flatten[Position[{1,0,1,0,1,0,1,0,1,0},1]]`

`{1, 3, 5, 7, 9}`

Then, calculate the power of 2 represented by each of these locations.

`values = Map[2^(10-#)&,pList]`

`{512, 128, 32, 8, 2}`

Add these values.

`decimal = Apply[Plus,values]`

`682`

Incidentally, an elegant way of accomplishing the conversion of a binary number to a decimal number is to use a technique called Horner's rule. That technique is embodied in the following function:

`Horner[u_List,base_:2] := Fold[base #1 + #2 &,0,u]`

```
decodeBGA[chromosome_] :=
  Module[{pList,lchrom,values,phenotype},
    lchrom = Length[chromosome];
      (* convert from binary to decimal *)
    pList = Flatten[Position[chromosome,1] ];
    values = Map[2^(lchrom-#)&,pList];
    decimal = Apply[Plus,values];
      (* scale to proper range *)
    phenotype = decimal (0.078201368852394916911)-40;
    Return[phenotype];
    ];   (* end of Module *)
```

Listing 8.2

which works for arbitrary bases. We can test the function on the same binary number.

```
Horner[{1,0,1,0,1,0,1,0,1,0}]
```

682

Finally, convert to a number between -40 and 40.

```
pheonotype = decimal (0.078201368852394916911) -40
```

13.3333

The complete function is in Listing 8.2. One thing to notice about our choice of chromosomal representation is that the optimal phenotype ($x = 0$) is not represented by any chromosome. The largest negative phenotype has the chromosome $\{0, 1, 1, 1, 1, 1, 1, 1, 1, 1\}$,

```
decodeBGA[{0,1,1,1,1,1,1,1,1,1}]
```

-0.0391007

The smallest positive phenotype has the chromosome $\{1, 0, 0, 0, 0, 0, 0, 0, 0, 0\}$,

```
decodeBGA[{1,0,0,0,0,0,0,0,0,0}]
```

0.0391007

We could adjust our representation slightly, but in a real problem, we will not have advanced knowledge of the actual optimal values. Bear this issue in mind when designing a representation scheme.

The function f[x] determines the fitness of a particular phenotype. For example,

f[-0.0391007]

1.99922

The details of statements 3 and 4 require a little more discussion. The details of how we implement those statements comprise the essence of the particular GA that we are developing.

Parent Selection   In keeping with the ideas of natural selection, we presume that individuals with a higher fitness are more likely to mate than individuals with a lower fitness. One way to accomplish this scenario is to select parents with a probability in direct proportion to their fitness values, which may seem to be an obvious choice, but it is certainly not the only way parents can be selected.

The method we shall use is called the **roulette-wheel method**. In principle, we construct a roulette wheel on which each member of the population is given a sector whose size is proportional to the individual's fitness. Then we spin the wheel and whichever individual comes up becomes a parent.

We can describe the implementation of this method as follows:

1. Construct a list of the fitnesses of all individuals in the population.

2. Generate a random number between zero and the total of all of the fitnesses in the population.

3. Return the first individual whose fitness, added to the fitness of all other elements before it, from the list in step 1, is greater than or equal to the random number from step 2.

Let's walk through an example. First, construct a random population with ten individuals.

```
MatrixForm[pop =
   Table[Random[Integer,{0,1}],{i,10},{j,10}]]
```

```
1  1  0  0  1  0  0  1  1  0
0  0  0  1  0  0  0  1  0  1
0  1  0  0  1  0  0  1  1  1
1  0  1  1  1  0  1  1  0  1
1  1  1  0  0  0  0  0  1  1
1  0  1  1  0  0  0  1  0  1
1  0  1  1  0  0  1  0  0  0
1  0  0  0  1  0  1  1  1  0
1  1  1  1  0  1  0  1  1  0
0  1  1  1  0  0  1  1  0  1
```

Then decode the population by mapping the decodeBGA function onto pop.

pheno = Map[decodeBGA,pop]

{23.0303, −34.6041, −16.9306, 18.5728, 30.303, 15.4448,
   15.6794, 3.63636, 36.7937, −3.94917}

The fitness of the individuals is found from

fitList = Map[f,pheno]

{0.919582, 0.923009, 0.911761, 1.21619, 1.04341, 0.714787,
   0.710969, 0.222705, 1.04247, 0.40201}

We use the function FoldList to add each element of fitList to all of the
successive elements.

fitListSum =   FoldList[Plus,First[fitList],Rest[fitList]]

{0.919582, 1.84259, 2.75435, 3.97055, 5.01396, 5.72875,
   6.43972, 6.66242, 7.70489, 8.1069}

The total of all fitness values is the last element in the above list

fitSum = Last[fitListSum]

8.1069

The function selectOne in Listing 8.3 takes the folded list of fitness values
and returns the index of the individual who came up on a single spin of
the roulette wheel. The two parents are

parent1Index = selectOne[fitListSum,fitSum]

```
selectOne[foldedFitnessList_,fitTotal_] :=
  Module[{randFitness,elem,index},
     randFitness = Random[] fitTotal;
     elem = Select[foldedFitnessList,#>=randFitness&,1];
     index = Flatten[Position[foldedFitnessList,First[elem]]];
     Return[First[index]];
     ]; (* end of Module *)
```

Listing 8.3

9

```
parent2Index = selectOne[fitListSum,fitSum]
```

6

```
parent1 = pop[[parent1Index]]
```

{1, 1, 1, 1, 0, 1, 0, 1, 1, 0}

```
parent2 = pop[[parent2Index]]
```

{1, 0, 1, 1, 0, 0, 0, 1, 0, 1}

These two parents have fitnesses of 1.04247 and 0.714787 respectively. Of course, if you execute the above two statements, you may get different parents. We can now proceed to the reproduction process.

Reproduction: Crossover and Mutation   In Section 8.1 we looked at an example of reproduction involving only random mutation of genes from a single parent; a case of asexual reproduction. In this section we look at sexual reproduction in which each parent contributes part of its genetic structure to the offspring. Crossover is the name that we give to this sharing of genes. Mutation, in this scenario, occurs at a much lower probability than in the previous example.

There are many different crossover methods, and often each new application requires the development of a special crossover mechanism. We shall restrict our attention here to a method called single-point crossover. Figure 8.1 illustrates the results of single-point crossover on a pair of chromosomes.

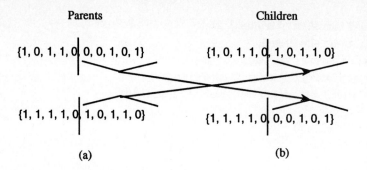

Figure 8.1 This figure illustrates the crossover operation. (a) Two parents are selected according to their fitness, and a crossover point, illustrated by the vertical line, is chosen by a uniform random selection. (b) The children's chromosomes are formed by combining opposite parts of each parent's chromosome.

After we select two parents for mating, we perform a biased coin flip with a certain probability of heads that will determine whether to proceed with the crossover. If the coin toss is successful, we choose, at random, a particular locus which we call the **crossover point**. Two children are produced by splicing the genes up to the crossover point from one parent with the genes beyond the crossover point from the other parent, as Figure 8.1 shows. If the coin toss is not successful, we simply return the parents themselves as the new children. The theory of GAs shows how this crossover mechanism can result in a population whose overall fitness increases with time as the desirable features of each parent are combined in their progeny. It can happen, however, that crossover results in children who are less fit than their parents. The mutation process can help to combat the effects of a destructive crossover.

Crossover is a powerful method for natural selection, but as we pointed out in the previous paragraph, crossover may not always work the way we want it to. By subjecting each of the genes in a chromosome to a small probability of mutation, we can, on occasion, reverse the results of a bad crossover. Suppose during crossover, a chromosome which has an allele of 1 at a particular location which is very favorable to survival, has that allele changed to a 0 during reproduction. Mutation can flip the gene back to a 1. Of course, since all of the genes are subjected to muta-tion, we could end up with the opposite situation where a favorable gene is altered. For this reason we need to keep the probability of mutation to

```
crossOver[pcross_,pmutate_,parent1_,parent2_] :=
  Module[{child1,child2,crossAt,lchrom},
            (* chromosome length *)
    lchrom = Length[parent1];
  If[ flip[pcross],
          (* True: select cross site at random *)
      crossAt = Random[Integer,{1,lchrom-1}];
          (* construct children *)
      child1 = Join[Take[parent1,crossAt], Drop[parent2,crossAt]];
      child2 = Join[Take[parent2,crossAt],   Drop[parent1,crossAt]],
        (* False: return parents as children *)
      child1 = parent1;
      child2 = parent2;
    ]; (* end of If *)
        (* perform mutation *)
    child1 = Map[mutateBGA[pmutate,#]&,child1];
    child2 = Map[mutateBGA[pmutate,#]&,child2];
    Return[{child1,child2}];
  ]; (* end of Module *)
```

Listing 8.4

a very small value, perhaps as low as one chance in a thousand for any particular gene.

Since the chromosomes are binary strings, I have written the mutation algorithm in terms of an XOR function. Moreover, since *Mathematica* does not equate True and False with 1 and 0 respectively, I have had to write my own XOR function:

```
myXor[x_,y_] := If[x==y,0,1];
```

```
mutateBGA[pmute_,allel_] := If[flip[pmute],myXor[allel,1],allel];
```

The procedure in Listing 8.4, which comprises both the crossover and mutation algorithms, returns two children to be added to the next generation of the population. Let's see if we make any progress after one crossover-mutation operation.

```
MatrixForm[children = crossOver[0.75,0.001,parent1,parent2]]
```

```
1  1  1  1  0  0  0  1  0  1
1  0  1  1  0  1  0  1  1  0
```

`decodeList = Map[decodeBGA,children]`

{35.4643, 16.7742}

`newfitness = Map[f,decodeList]`

{0.95461, 0.87324}

We gained ground in one case, but lost ground in the other. On the whole, however, the average fitness of the children

`(newfitness[[1]]+newfitness[[2]])/2`

0.913925

is greater than that of their parents

`(1.04247+0.714787)/2`

0.878628

The results could have turned out differently, however, since this process does contain an element of chance.

There is one further issue to discuss before putting everything together. That issue concerns how we are going to go about populating the next generation.

Populating the New Generation   A simplistic approach to building a new population is to mate enough parents so that enough children are produced to completely replace their parents. This technique is called **generational replacement**. This technique allows for the most thorough mixing of genes possible in the new generation, but it has some drawbacks. There is no guarantee that all, or even most of the children will turn out better than their parents; thus generational replacement might result in a loss of individuals with the best genes. Not only could the best individuals be lost, but the population as a whole could diminish in overall fitness, and we need to be concerned with the overall population as well as the best individual.

```
initPop[psize_,csize_] :=
   Table[Random[Integer,{0,1}],{psize},{csize}];

displayBest[fitnessList_,number2Print_] :=
   Module[{i,sortedList},
      sortedList = Sort[fitnessList,Greater];
      For[i=1,i<=number2Print,i++,
         Print["fitness = ",sortedList[[i]] ];
         ]; (* end of For i *)
      ]; (* end of Module *)
```

Listing 8.5

We could counter some of the negative effects of generational replacement by retaining a certain number of the best individuals from the previous generation. We call this strategy **elitism**.

At the opposite end of the spectrum from generational replacement is **steady state reproduction**. In this method, a select number of one population are deleted and are replaced with an equal number of children. In the extreme case, only two children are replaced in each successive generation.

Other strategies may be brought to bear to address this issue, but we shall spend no additional time on the problem here. We are going to use generational replacement, but feel free to experiment on your own.

Testing the BGA In order to make the program bga as generic as possible, we need several support functions. The function initPop (Listing 8.5) provides an initial random population of appropriate size. The function displayBest (Listing 8.5) allows us to see the fitness of the best chromosomes of the current generation. The arguments of the function bga (Listing 8.6) include the crossover probability, the mutation probability, the initial population, the name of the function that defines the fitness of each phenotype, the number of generations to calculate, and the number of individuals to print out at each generation. Let's choose an initial population and run the program for several generations to see how it performs. From the graph of the function, f, you can see that the maximum value of fitness is 2.0, and that any result greater than about 1.6 must be on the central peak.

```
bga[pcross_,pmutate_,popInitial_,fitFunction_,numGens_,printNum_] :=
  Module[{i,newPop,parent1,parent2,diff,matches,
          oldPop,reproNum,index,fitList,fitListSum,
          fitSum,pheno,pIndex,pIndex2,f,children},
    oldPop=popInitial;               (* initialize first population *)
    reproNum = Length[oldPop]/2;      (* calculate number of reproductions *)
    f = fitFunction;                 (* assign the fitness function *)
  For[i=1,i<=numGens,i++,            (* perform numGens generations *)
    pheno = Map[decodeBGA,oldPop];   (* decode the chromosomes *)
    fitList = f[pheno];              (* determine the fitness of each phenotype *)
    Print[" "];                      (* print out the best individuals *)
    Print["Generation ",i," Best ",printNum];
    Print[" "];
    displayBest[fitList,printNum];
    fitListSum = FoldList[Plus,First[fitList],Rest[fitList]];
    fitSum = Last[fitListSum];       (* find the total fitness *)
    newPop = Flatten[Table[      (* determine the new population *)
      pIndex1 = selectOne[fitListSum,fitSum]; (* select parent indices *)
      pIndex2 = selectOne[fitListSum,fitSum];
      parent1 = oldPop[[pIndex1]];       (* identify parents *)
      parent2 = oldPop[[pIndex2]];
    children = crossOver[pcross,pmutate,parent1,parent2]; (* crossover and mutate *)
      children,{reproNum}],1    (* add children to list; flatten to first level *)
      ]; (* end of Flatten[Table] *)
    oldPop = newPop;              (* new becomes old for next gen *)
    ]; (* end of For i *)
    ]; (* end of Module *)
```

Listing 8.6

```
initialPopulation = initPop[100,10];

bga[0.75, 0.008, initialPopulation,f,5,10];
```

Generation 1 Best 10

```
fitness = 1.90724
fitness = 1.90724
fitness = 1.58669
fitness = 1.42534
fitness = 1.42534
fitness = 1.3598
fitness = 1.3598
fitness = 1.3334
fitness = 1.33098
fitness = 1.31726
```

Generation 2 Best 10

```
fitness = 1.96206
fitness = 1.93756
fitness = 1.90724
fitness = 1.90724
fitness = 1.90724
fitness = 1.90724
fitness = 1.78363
fitness = 1.48717
fitness = 1.46704
fitness = 1.34657
```

Generation 3 Best 10

```
fitness = 1.96206
fitness = 1.90724
fitness = 1.90724
fitness = 1.90724
fitness = 1.87132
fitness = 1.83002
fitness = 1.78363
```

```
fitness = 1.73246
fitness = 1.66991
fitness = 1.48717

Generation 4  Best 10

fitness = 1.99299
fitness = 1.99299
fitness = 1.99299
fitness = 1.90724
fitness = 1.87132
fitness = 1.83002
fitness = 1.83002
fitness = 1.78363
fitness = 1.78363
fitness = 1.78363

Generation 5  Best 10

fitness = 1.99299
fitness = 1.99299
fitness = 1.99299
fitness = 1.99299
fitness = 1.98058
fitness = 1.90724
fitness = 1.90724
fitness = 1.90724
fitness = 1.90724
fitness = 1.87132
```

Not only does the best individual become better as time goes on, but the population as a whole appears to be getting better as well. In most problems we will probably be interested in the best solution; nevertheless, as the population as a whole gets better, future generations will be produced by a better and better group of parents.

8.3 A GA for Training Neural Networks

Finding the proper weights in a neural network, such as backpropagation, is an optimization problem in itself. We search through weight space looking for weights that optimize (in this case minimize) the value of the mean squared error of the neural-network outputs for the given problem. It would seem that a GA would be well suited to this task. We shall begin to explore this idea in this section. I have chosen the XOR problem as a basis for the effort.

8.3.1 Data Representation

We shall restrict our experiments to a standard, feedforward network with two inputs, two hidden-layer units, and a single output. Each of the three units (2-hidden, 1-output) will have two weights, for a total of six in each network. The hidden- and output-layer units will have the standard sigmoidal output function, reproduced here in a simplified form.

```
sigmoid[x_] := 1./(1+E^(-x));
```

The iopairs for this problem are

```
ioPairsXOR = { {{0.1,0.1},{0.1}}, {{0.1,0.9},{0.9}},
               {{0.9,0.1},{0.9}}, {{0.9,0.9},{0.1}} };
```

Whereas in the example of the previous section each phenotype had a single chromosome, the neural-network problem is complicated by the existence of multiple weights. We must decide on a data representation suitable to account for all of the weights. Although it is possible to work directly with real-valued chromosomes, I am going to stay with a binary representation which will keep us on familiar ground and allow us to reuse a fair amount of code from the previous example. We shall represent each weight value by a 20-bit binary string, after scaling the weight to a number between −5 and +5. At issue then, is how to view the individual weights. One representation would be to concatenate all of the weights together into one long string. At the other extreme, we could treat each weight as a separate chromosome and mate it only with its counterparts in other networks.

I am going to adopt a middle-of-the-road appoach for this example. We shall concatenate the two weights on each unit to form a single chromosome; thus, our genotype will comprise three chromosomes which we label h1, h2, and o1, for the two hidden-unit chromosomes, and the output chromosome respectively. During mating, h1 chromosomes will cross with h1 chromosomes only, and so on. For the fitness function, we shall use the inverse of the mean squared error (mse), mseInv, of the network outputs over the four input patterns. We use the inverse of the mse because we want a fitness function for which the larger values represent the better fitness.

Each generation will consist of a number of neural networks. We shall represent each network as a list comprising four parts: the network fitness, its h1 chromosome, its h2 chromosome, and its o1 chromosome. Symbolically, each network has the following representation:

{ mseInv, {h1}, {h2}, {o1} }

You should begin to see why this GA may take a long time to compute. Suppose we have a population of 100 networks, each initially with randomly generated weights. To determine a new generation (if we are using generational replacement) requires 50 matings, each of which involves three crossover-mutation operations. Then we must decode the chromosomes and determine the mse for each network.

We are going to employ some time-saving measures for this example. First, we will use a steady-state population methodology, in which we replace only a few of the worst-performing individuals for each new generation. Second, since we need not evaluate the fitness of each network for each new generation, we need decode only the new children in order to assess their fitness.

8.3.2 Calculating the Generations

To set up the initial population, we compute the appropriate number of chromosomes and prepend the fitness to the list of chromosomes for each network. The function initXorPop, in Listing 8.7, accomplishes this task. The initialization program requires one routine to decode the chromosomes into weight vectors, and one routine to calculate the fitness of each of the networks. Those tasks are embodied in the two functions appearing in Listing 8.8. Notice that gaNetFitness returns the inverse of the mean squared error. The parent-selection function remains unchanged.

```
initXorPop[psize_,csize_,ioPairs_] :=
  Module[{i,iPop,hidWts,outWts,mseInv},
                (* first the chromosomes *)
    iPop = Table[
      {
        Table[Random[Integer,{0,1}],{csize}],(* h1 *)
        Table[Random[Integer,{0,1}],{csize}],(* h2 *)
        Table[Random[Integer,{0,1}],{csize}] (* o1 *)
      }, {psize} ]; (* end of Table *)
                (* then decode and eval fitness *)
                (* use For loop for clarity *)
      For[i=1,i<=psize,i++,
                (* make hidden weight matrix *)
        hidWts = Join[iPop[[i,1]],iPop[[i,2]] ];
        hidWts = Partition[hidWts,20];
        hidWts = Map[decodeXorChrom,hidWts];
        hidWts = Partition[hidWts,2];
                (* make output weight matrix *)
        outWts = Partition[iPop[[i,3]],20];
        outWts = Map[decodeXorChrom,outWts];
                (* get mse for this network *)
        mseInv = gaNetFitness[hidWts,outWts,ioPairs];
                (* prepend mseInv *)
        PrependTo[iPop[[i]],mseInv];
        ]; (* end For *)
      Return[iPop];
    ]; (* end of Module *)
```

Listing 8.7

```
decodeXorChrom[chromosome_] :=
  Module[{pList,lchrom,values,p,decimal},
    lchrom = Length[chromosome];
       (* convert from binary to decimal *)
    pList = Flatten[Position[chromosome,1] ];
    values = Map[2^(lchrom-#)&,pList];
    decimal = Apply[Plus,values];
       (* scale to proper range *)
    p = decimal (9.536752259018191355*10^-6)-5;
    Return[p];
      ];   (* end of Module *)

gaNetFitness[hiddenWts_,outputWts_,ioPairVectors_] :=
  Module[{inputs,hidden,outputs,desired,errors,
      len,errorTotal,errorSum},
    inputs=Map[First,ioPairVectors];
    desired=Map[Last,ioPairVectors];
    len = Length[inputs];
    hidden=sigmoid[inputs.Transpose[hiddenWts]];
    outputs=sigmoid[hidden.Transpose[outputWts]];
    errors= desired-outputs;
    errorSum = Apply[Plus,errors^2,2]; (* second level *)
    errorTotal = Apply[Plus,errorSum];
          (* inverse of mse *)
    Return[len/errorTotal];
    ]                 (* end of Module *)
```

Listing 8.8

We shall have to modify the generation and crossover routines somewhat to accommodate multiple crossovers for each mating and to account for the steady-state population methodology. The new crossover routing appears in Listing 8.9. To minimize the amount of decoding and encoding, the generation routine, gaXor (Listing 8.10), prints out only the fitness values for each generation. The routine also returns the final population, so that we can decode any members for our own analysis or use the population as a starting point for more generations.

You should also notice that gaXor calls decodeXorGenotype (Listing 8.11), a function that takes as its argument a list of the form { {h1}, {h2}, {o1} } and returns the weights on the hidden and output layer. In case you want to see what a particular weight value looks like encoded as a 20-bit binary chromosome, I have included the function encodeNetGa. Remember that weight values are restricted to a range of −5 to +5. You also must supply the length of the chromosome, which for this particular function, must be 20. I wrote the function this way so that you could easily change the length and range by changing the two numerical values in one statement in the routine:

```
dec = Round[(weight+5.)/(9.536752259018191355*10^-6)];
```

The function is in Listing 8.12. As an example, a weight of 0.5 would encode to a chromosome of

```
encodeNetGa[0.5,20]
```

```
{1, 0, 0, 0, 1, 1, 0, 0, 1, 1, 0, 0, 1, 1, 0, 0, 1, 1, 0, 0}
```

8.3.3 An Example Calculation

We are now in a position to try our GA. First, we populate a starting generation at random. We shall use populations of 20 individuals, in the interest of expediting the calculation.

```
pop = initXorPop[20,40,ioPairsXOR];
```

Sort the population according to fitness. Although this step is not necessary to begin the GA, it will allow us to easily determine the characteristics of the initial population.

```
pop=Sort[pop,Greater[First[#],First[#2]]&];
```

The best fitness is the inverse of the best mse.

```
crossOverXor[pcross_,pmutate_,parent1_,parent2_] :=
  Module[{child1,child2,crossAt,lchrom,
          i,numchroms,chroms1,chroms2},
          (* strip off mse *)
    chroms1 = Rest[parent1];
    chroms2 = Rest[parent2];
          (* chromosome length *)
    lchrom = Length[chroms1[[1]]];
          (* number of chromosomes in each list *)
    numchroms = Length[chroms1];
    For[i=1,i<=numchroms,i++,    (* for each chrom *)
    If[ flip[pcross],
        (* True: select cross site at random *)
      crossAt = Random[Integer,{1,lchrom-1}];
        (* construct children  *)
      chroms1[[i]] = Join[Take[chroms1[[i]],crossAt],
                    Drop[chroms2[[i]],crossAt]];
      chroms2[[i]] = Join[Take[chroms2[[i]],crossAt],
                    Drop[chroms1[[i]],crossAt]],
      (* False: don't change chroms[[i]] *)
      Continue]; (* end of If *)
      (* perform mutation *)
      chroms1[[i]] = Map[mutateBGA[pmutate,#]&,chroms1[[i]]];
      chroms2[[i]] = Map[mutateBGA[pmutate,#]&,chroms2[[i]]];
      ]; (* end of For i *)
    Return[{chroms1,chroms2}];
    ]; (* end of Module *)
```

Listing 8.9

```
gaXor[pcross_,pmutate_,popInitial_,numReplace_,ioPairs_,numGens_,printNum_] :=
  Module[{i,j,newPop,parent1,parent2,diff,matches,
          oldPop,reproNum,index,fitList,fitListSum,
          fitSum,pheno,pIndex,pIndex2,f,children,hids,outs,mseInv},
              (* initialize first population sorted by fitness value *)
        oldPop= Sort[popInitial,Greater[First[#],First[#2]]&];
        reproNum = numReplace;      (* calculate number of reproductions *)
      For[i=1,i<=numGens,i++,
        fitList = Map[First,oldPop];    (* list of fitness values*)
                                      (* make the folded list of fitness values *)
        fitListSum = FoldList[Plus,First[fitList],Rest[fitList]];
        fitSum = Last[fitListSum];      (* find the total fitness *)
      newPop = Drop[oldPop,-reproNum]; (* new population; eliminate reproNum worst *)
       For[j=1,j<=reproNum/2,j++,        (* make reproNum new children *)
                (* select parent indices *)
          pIndex1 = selectOne[fitListSum,fitSum];
          pIndex2 = selectOne[fitListSum,fitSum];
          parent1 = oldPop[[pIndex1]];    (* identify parents *)
          parent2 = oldPop[[pIndex2]];
        children = crossOverXor[pcross,pmutate,parent1,parent2];   (* crossover and mutate *)
         {hids,outs} = decodeXorGenotype[children[[1]] ]; (* fitness of children *)
         mseInv = gaNetFitness[hids,outs,ioPairs];
         children[[1]] = Prepend[children[[1]],mseInv];
         {hids,outs} = decodeXorGenotype[children[[2]] ];
         mseInv = gaNetFitness[hids,outs,ioPairs];
         children[[2]] = Prepend[children[[2]],mseInv];
         newPop = Join[newPop,children]; (* add children to new population *)
         ]; (* end of For j *)
        oldPop =   Sort[newPop,Greater[First[#],First[#2]]&];(* for next gen *)
              (* print best mse values (1/mseInv) *)
        Print[ ];Print["Best of generation ",i];
        For[j=1,j<=printNum,j++,Print[(1.0/oldPop[[j,1]])]; ];
        ]; (* end of For i*)
      Return[oldPop];
      ]; (* end of Module *)
```

Listing 8.10

```
decodeXorGenotype[genotype_] :=
  Module[{hidWts,outWts},
      hidWts = Join[genotype[[1]],genotype[[2]] ];
      hidWts = Partition[hidWts,20];
      hidWts = Map[decodeXorChrom,hidWts];
      hidWts = Partition[hidWts,2];
            (* make output weight matrix *)
      outWts = Partition[genotype[[3]],20];
      outWts = Map[decodeXorChrom,outWts];
      Return[{hidWts,outWts}];
      ];
```

Listing 8.11

`1/newpop[[1,1]]`

0.156526

The last population individual has the lowest fitness, or the largest mse.

`1/newpop[[20,1]]`

0.394886

You can see the distribution by plotting the fitness values, or alternatively, plotting the mse's. Here we plot the mse values.

`poplist = Map[First,newpop];`

`ListPlot[1/poplist]`

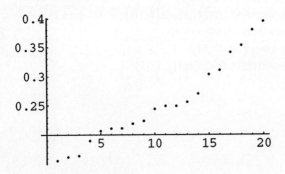

```
encodeNetGa[weight_,len_] :=
  Module[{pList,values,dec,chromosome,i},
    i=len;
    l=Table[0,{i}];
      (* scale to proper range *)
  dec = Round[(weight+5.)/(9.536752259018191355*10^-6)];
    While[dec!=0&&dec!=1,
      l=ReplacePart[l,Mod[dec,2],i];
      dec=Quotient[dec,2];
      --i;
      ];
  l=ReplacePart[l,dec,i]
    ];   (* end of Module *)
```

Listing 8.12

Let's begin the calculation by producing 100 generations where we re-place half the population at each generation.

`newpop = gaXor[0.8,0.01,pop,10,ioPairsXOR,100,1];`

Best of generation 1
0.159407
Best of generation 5
0.14867
Best of generation 10
0.125276
Best of generation 15
0.125276
Best of generation 20
0.112863
Best of generation 25
0.102992
Best of generation 30
0.102976
Best of generation 35
0.102687
Best of generation 40
0.102538

```
Best of generation 50
0.102463
Best of generation 55
0.102264
Best of generation 60
0.102223
Best of generation 65
0.101803
Best of generation 70
0.10178
Best of generation 75
0.101705
Best of generation 80
0.101669
Best of generation 85
0.101669
Best of generation 90
0.101669
Best of generation 95
0.101667
Best of generation 100
0.101644
```

You will notice a steady, but very slow, decline in the mse. At this rate, it may take hundreds of generations to reach an acceptable error. Moreover, this run of 100 generations required considerably more time than was required for the standard backpropagation method to converge on an acceptable solution. We might also ask whether we are doing any better than we would if we simply generated networks at random. To evaluate that situation, we can do just that: generate 100 populations of 20 individuals at random and see if we do as well. The function randomPop in Listing 8.13 generates the required populations.

```
randomPop[20,40,ioPairsXOR,100];
```

```
Random generation 1
0.132439
Random generation 2
0.149261
Random generation 3
```

```
randomPop[psize_,csize_,ioPairs_,numGens_] :=
  Module[{i,pop},
    For[i=1,i<=numGens,i++,
      pop = initXorPop[psize,csize,ioPairs];
      pop = Sort[pop,Greater[First[#],First[#2]]&];
      Print[ ];
      Print["Random generation ",i];
      Print[(1.0/pop[[1,1]])];
      ];
    ];
```

Listing 8.13

0.157786
Random generation 4
0.16147
Random generation 5
0.151606
Random generation 6
0.156832
Random generation 7
0.150389
Random generation 8
0.128841
Random generation 9
0.150084
Random generation 10
0.156748
Random generation 11
0.14517
Random generation 12
0.147808
Random generation 13
0.163434
Random generation 14
0.146134
Random generation 15
0.136783

Random generation 16
0.126648
Random generation 17
0.153591
Random generation 18
0.154377
Random generation 19
0.162773
Random generation 20
0.16142

and so on . . .

I have reduced the output to the first 20 generations, but the results for the remaining 80 generations are similar to those of the first 20. The best I got in 100 random generations was 0.125274; the worst was 0.186056. There is, of course, a possibility that some random population will accidently produce a very good individual. You should know, however, that generating the random population and evaluating the fitness of all of the individuals required more time per generation than the GA algorithm did. Moreover, it appears as though the GA might eventually reach an acceptable population, whereas we can never be sure about random generations.

The above development represents a first attempt, and you should not conclude that the method we employed is the best one for the task. In fact, you will find it necessary to make several modifications to the data representation in order to allow the GA to find a good solution. We could be more clever about how chromosomes are combined during the mating process. The binary representation and standard crossover algorithm are probably not the best ones for our purposes in this case. Perhaps we should maintain the chromosomes as lists of real numbers and search for more appropriate crossover mechanisms. Rather than pursue this matter further here, I will leave it to your creativity.

8.3.4 Other Uses for GAs

Even if we can generate weights for neural networks using the method of the previous sections, it is not clear that there is a particular advantage to doing so. If you look back at Chapter 3, you will recall that we implemented the guts of a backpropagation algorithm in about a dozen lines of code; the GA required many times more than that, with a similar increase in the amount of time required to produce a solution. What role then, if any, should GAs have in neural networks? I think there are several ways to use GAs effectively along with neural networks.

We could use GAs as a supplement to standard training algorithms, rather than as a replacement. As a simple example, we might choose to use the standard backpropagation algorithm to train the output layer of a neural network and use a GA to train the hidden layer. We might also be able to use a GA to help a network escape from a local minimum.

We could use GAs in a more fundamental role to help determine the particular architecture suitable for a given problem. A question that is often asked, for example, is: How many hidden-layer units should I have in my network for such-and-such a problem? Rules-of-thumb are often quoted in response to such a question, or experience is invoked as being the best teacher. We could bring a GA to bear on this issue to provide a more analytical, and perhaps, therefore, more satisfying answer. We could also use a GA to optimize the connectivity scheme among units in a network or to tune parameters such as the learning rate. Moreover, a GA might be used to find a good initial set of weights.

All of the above ignores the potential of GAs as an independent methodology for the solution of optimization problems. Although our emphasis in this book is neural networks, GAs have applicability to many other fields, and by ignoring that potential here, I hope I have not misled anyone.

Summary

In a book on neural networks, a chapter on genetic algorithms may seem out of place, even though in this we did look at a way of using the two technologies together. GAs, like some neural networks, are good at finding solutions to optimization problems when you can determine a score or cost function for each potential solution. We build a very basic GA in this chapter; many variations are possible. Whether you continue to experiment with combining GA and neural-network technologies, as we have done in this chapter, or simply use GAs for other applications, does not really matter. GAs are another tool in the problem-solving toolbox which can be brought to bear on a variety of problems. Like neural networks, GAs will not guarantee you a perfect solution, but can, in many cases, arrive at an acceptable solution without the time and expense of an exhaustive search.

Appendix A

Code Listings

Adaline and ALC

```
alcTest[learnRate_,numIters_:250] :=
Module[{eta=learnRate,wts,k,inputs,wtList,outDesired,outputs,outError},
  wts = Table[Random[],{2}];   (* initialize weights *)
  Print["Starting weights = ",wts];
  Print["Learning rate = ",eta];
  Print["Number of iterations = ",numIters];
  inputs = {0,Random[Real,{0, 0.175}]};(* initialize input vector *)
  k=1;
  wtList=Table[
    inputs[[1]] = N[Sin[Pi k/8]]+Random[Real,{0, 0.175}];
    outDesired = N[2 Cos[Pi k/8]]; (* desired output *)
    outputs = wts.inputs;    (* actual output *)
    outError = outDesired-outputs; (* error *)
    wts += eta outError inputs; (* update weights *)
    inputs[[2]]=inputs[[1]]; (* shift input values *)
    k++;   wts,{numIters}];                    (* end of Table *)
  Print["Final weight vector = ",wts];
  wtPlot=ListPlot[wtList,PlotJoined->True] (* plot the weights *)
  ]      (* end of Module *)
```

```
calcMse[ioPairs_,wtVec_] :=
    Module[{errors,inputs,outDesired,outputs},
        inputs = Map[First,ioPairs]; (* extract inputs *)
        outDesired = Map[Last,ioPairs]; (* extract desired outputs *)
        outputs = inputs . wtVec; (* calculate actual outputs *)
        errors = Flatten[outDesired-outputs];
        Return[errors.errors/Length[ioPairs]]
        ]

alcXor[learnRate_,numInputs_,ioPairs_,numIters_:250] :=
  Module[{wts,eta=learnRate,errorList,inputs,outDesired,ourError,outputs},
    SeedRandom[6460];        (* seed random number gen.*)
    wts = Table[Random[],{numInputs}];    (* initialize weights *)
    errorList=Table[      (* select ioPair at random *)
        {inputs,outDesired} = ioPairs[[Random[Integer,{1,4}]]];
        outputs = wts.inputs;    (* actual output *)
        outError = First[outDesired-outputs]; (* error *)
        wts += eta outError inputs;
        outError,{numIters}];    (* end of Table *)
    ListPlot[errorList,PlotJoined->True];
    Return[wts];
    ]; (* end of Module *)


testXor[ioPairs_,weights_] :=
    Module[{errors,inputs,outDesired,outputs,wts,mse},
        inputs = Map[First,ioPairs]; (* extract inputs *)
        outDesired = Map[Last,ioPairs]; (* extract desired outputs *)
        outputs = inputs . weights; (* calculate actual outputs *)
        errors = outDesired-outputs;
        mse=
          Flatten[errors] . Flatten[errors]/Length[ioPairs];
        Print["Inputs = ",inputs];
        Print["Outputs = ",outputs];
        Print["Errors = ",errors];
        Print["Mean squared error = ",mse]
        ]
```

```
alcXorMin[learnRate_,numInputs_,ioPairs_,maxError_] :=
  Module[{wts,eta=learnRate,errorList,inputs,outDesired,
            meanSqError,done,k,ourError,outputs,errorPlot},
    wts = Table[Random[],{numInputs}];    (* initialize weights *)
    meanSqError = 0.0;
    errorList={};
    For[k=1;done=False,!done,k++,    (* until done *)
                        (* select ioPair at random *)
      {inputs,outDesired} = ioPairs[[Random[Integer,{1,4}]]];
      outputs = wts.inputs;    (* actual output *)
      outError = First[outDesired-outputs]; (* error *)
      wts += eta outError inputs; (* update weights *)
      If[Mod[k,4]==0,meanSqError=calcMse[ioPairs,wts];
        AppendTo[errorList, meanSqError];    ];
      If[k>4 && meanSqError<maxError,done=True,Continue];    (* test for done *)
        ];                      (* end of For *)
    errorPlot=ListPlot[errorList,PlotJoined->True];
    Return[wts];
    ] (* end of Module *)
```

Backpropagation and Functional Link Network

```
Options[sigmoid] = {xShift->0,yShift->0,temperature->1};
Options[bpnTest] = {printAll->False,bias->False};

sigmoid[x_,opts___Rule] :=
    Module[{xshft,yshft,temp},
        xshft = xShift /. {opts} /. Options[sigmoid];
        yshft = yShift /. {opts} /. Options[sigmoid];
        temp = temperature /. {opts} /. Options[sigmoid];
        yshft+1/(1+E^(-(x-xshft)/temp)) //N
        ]
```

```
bpnTest[hiddenWts_,outputWts_,ioPairVectors_,opts___Rule] :=
 Module[{inputs,hidden,outputs,desired,errors,i,len=Length[inputs],
    prntAll,errorTotal,errorSum,bias},
  prntAll= printAll /. {opts} /. Options[bpnTest];
  biasVal = bias /. {opts} /. Options[bpnTest];
  inputs=Map[First,ioPairVectors];
  If[biasVal,inputs=Map[Append[#,1.0]&,inputs] ];
  desired=Map[Last,ioPairVectors];
  hidden=sigmoid[inputs.Transpose[hiddenWts]];
  If[biasVal,hidden = Map[Append[#,1.0]&,hidden] ];
  outputs=sigmoid[hidden.Transpose[outputWts]];
  errors= desired-outputs;
  If[prntAll,Print["ioPairs:"];Print[ ];Print[ioPairVectors];
             Print[ ];Print["inputs:"];Print[ ];Print[inputs];
             Print[ ];Print["hidden-layer outputs:"];
             Print[hidden];Print[ ];
             Print["output-layer outputs:"];Print[ ];
             Print[outputs];Print[ ];Print["errors:"];
             Print[errors];Print[ ]; ]; (* end of If *)
  For[i=1,i<=len,i++,Print[" Output ",i," = ",outputs[[i]]," desired = ",
      desired[[i]]," Error = ",errors[[i]]];Print[]; ];      (* end of For *)
  errorSum = Apply[Plus,errors^2,2]; (* second level *)
  errorTotal = Apply[Plus,errorSum];
  Print["Mean Squared Error = ",errorTotal/len];
  ]                 (* end of Module *)
```

```
bpnStandard[inNumber_, hidNumber_, outNumber_,ioPairs_, eta_, numIters_] :=
  Module[{errors,hidWts,outWts,ioP,inputs,outDesired,hidOuts,
          outputs, outErrors,outDelta,hidDelta},
    hidWts = Table[Table[Random[Real,{-0.1,0.1}],{inNumber}],{hidNumber}];
    outWts = Table[Table[Random[Real,{-0.1,0.1}],{hidNumber}],{outNumber}];
    errors = Table[
          (* select ioPair *)
      ioP=ioPairs[[Random[Integer,{1,Length[ioPairs]}]]];
      inputs=ioP[[1]];
      outDesired=ioP[[2]];
          (* forward pass *)
      hidOuts = sigmoid[hidWts.inputs];
      outputs = sigmoid[outWts.hidOuts];
          (* determine errors and deltas *)
      outErrors = outDesired-outputs;
      outDelta= outErrors (outputs (1-outputs));
      hidDelta=(hidOuts (1-hidOuts)) Transpose[outWts].outDelta;
          (* update weights *)
      outWts += eta Outer[Times,outDelta,hidOuts];
      hidWts += eta Outer[Times,hidDelta,inputs];
          (* add squared error to Table *)
      outErrors.outErrors,{numIters}];  (* end of Table *)
    Return[{hidWts,outWts,errors}];
    ];                              (* end of Module *)
```

```
bpnBias[inNumber_, hidNumber_, outNumber_,ioPairs_, eta_, numIters_] :=
  Module[{errors,hidWts,outWts,ioP,inputs,outDesired,hidOuts,
           outputs, outErrors,outDelta,hidDelta},
    hidWts = Table[Table[Random[Real,{-0.1,0.1}],{inNumber+1}],{hidNumber}];
    outWts = Table[Table[Random[Real,{-0.1,0.1}],{hidNumber+1}], {outNumber}];
    errorList = Table[
          (* select ioPair *)
      ioP=ioPairs[[Random[Integer,{1,Length[ioPairs]}]]];
      inputs=Append[ioP[[1]],1.0]; (* bias mod *)
      outDesired=ioP[[2]];
           (* forward pass *)
      hidOuts = sigmoid[hidWts.inputs];
      outInputs = Append[hidOuts,1.0];  (* bias mod *)
      outputs = sigmoid[outWts.outInputs];
           (* determine errors and deltas *)
      outErrors = outDesired-outputs;
      outDelta= outErrors (outputs (1-outputs));
      hidDelta=(outInputs (1-outInputs)) * Transpose[outWts].outDelta;
           (* update weights *)
      outWts += eta Outer[Times,outDelta,outInputs];
      hidWts += eta Drop[Outer[Times,hidDelta,inputs],-1];  (* bias mod *)
           (* add squared error to Table *)
      outErrors.outErrors,{numIters}];  (* end of Table *)
      Print["New hidden-layer weight matrix: "];
    Print[]; Print[hidWts];Print[];
    Print["New output-layer weight matrix: "];
    Print[]; Print[outWts];Print[];
    bpnTest[hidWts,outWts,ioPairs];   (* check how close we are *)
    errorPlot = ListPlot[errorList, PlotJoined->True];
    Return[{hidWts,outWts,errorList,errorPlot}];
     ];                           (* end of Module *)
```

```
bpnMomentum[inNumber_,hidNumber_,outNumber_,ioPairs_,eta_,
   alpha_,numIters_] :=
 Module[{hidWts,outWts,ioP,inputs,hidOuts,outputs,outDesired,
   hidLastDelta,outLastDelta,outDelta,hidDelta,outErrors},
   hidWts = Table[Table[Random[Real,{-0.5,0.5}],{inNumber}],{hidNumber}];
   outWts = Table[Table[Random[Real,{-0.5,0.5}],{hidNumber}],{outNumber}];
   hidLastDelta = Table[Table[0,{inNumber}],{hidNumber}];
   outLastDelta = Table[Table[0,{hidNumber}],{outNumber}];
   errorList = Table[
                      (* begin forward pass *)
      ioP=ioPairs[[Random[Integer,{1,Length[ioPairs]}]]];
      inputs=ioP[[1]];
      outDesired=ioP[[2]];
      hidOuts = sigmoid[hidWts.inputs]; (* hidden-layer outputs *)
      outputs = sigmoid[outWts.hidOuts]; (* output-layer outputs *)
                     (* calculate errors *)
      outErrors = outDesired-outputs;
      outDelta= outErrors (outputs (1-outputs));
      hidDelta=(hidOuts (1-hidOuts)) Transpose[outWts].outDelta;
                  (* update weights *)
      outLastDelta= eta Outer[Times,outDelta,hidOuts]+alpha outLastDelta;
      outWts += outLastDelta;
      hidLastDelta = eta Outer[Times,hidDelta,inputs]+
                        alpha hidLastDelta;
      hidWts += hidLastDelta;
        outErrors.outErrors, (* this puts the error on the list *)
        {numIters}]   ;   (* this many times, Table ends here *)
 Print["New hidden-layer weight matrix: "];
 Print[]; Print[hidWts];Print[];
 Print["New output-layer weight matrix: "];
 Print[]; Print[outWts];Print[];
 bpnTest[hidWts,outWts,ioPairs,bias->False,printAll->False];
 errorPlot = ListPlot[errorList, PlotJoined->True];
 Return[{hidWts,outWts,errorList,errorPlot}];
 ]                     (* end of Module *)
```

```
bpnMomentumSmart[inNumber_,hidNumber_,outNumber_,ioPairs_,eta_,
            alpha_,numIters_] :=
  Module[{hidWts,outWts,ioP,inputs,hidOuts,outputs,outDesired,
          hidLastDelta,outLastDelta,outDelta,hidDelta,outErrors},
    hidWts = Table[Table[Random[Real,{-0.5,0.5}],{inNumber}],{hidNumber}];
    outWts = Table[Table[Random[Real,{-0.5,0.5}],{hidNumber}],{outNumber}];
    hidLastDelta = Table[Table[0,{inNumber}],{hidNumber}];
    outLastDelta = Table[Table[0,{hidNumber}],{outNumber}];
    errorList = Table[
                      (* begin forward pass *)
      ioP=ioPairs[[Random[Integer,{1,Length[ioPairs]}]]];
      inputs=ioP[[1]];
      outDesired=ioP[[2]];
      hidOuts = sigmoid[hidWts.inputs];  (* hidden-layer outputs *)
      outputs = sigmoid[outWts.hidOuts]; (* output-layer outputs *)
                      (* calculate errors *)
      outErrors = outDesired-outputs;
      If[First[Abs[outErrors]]>0.1,
        outDelta= outErrors (outputs (1-outputs));
        hidDelta=(hidOuts (1-hidOuts)) Transpose[outWts].outDelta;
                      (* update weights *)
        outLastDelta= eta Outer[Times,outDelta,hidOuts]+
                          alpha outLastDelta;
        outWts += outLastDelta;
        hidLastDelta = eta Outer[Times,hidDelta,inputs]+
                            alpha hidLastDelta;
        hidWts += hidLastDelta,Continue]; (* end of If *)
      outErrors.outErrors, (* this puts the error on the list *)
      {numIters}]   ;   (* this many times, Table ends here *)
  Print["New hidden-layer weight matrix: "];
  Print[]; Print[hidWts];Print[];
  Print["New output-layer weight matrix: "];
  Print[]; Print[outWts];Print[];
  bpnTest[hidWts,outWts,ioPairs,bias->False,printAll->False];
  errorPlot = ListPlot[errorList, PlotJoined->True];
  Return[{hidWts,outWts,errorList,errorPlot}];
  ]                      (* end of Module *)
```

```
bpnCompete[inNumber_,hidNumber_,outNumber_,ioPairs_,eta_,numIters_] :=
 Module[{hidWts,outWts,ioP,inputs,hidOuts,outputs,outDesired,
          outInputs,hidEps,outEps,outDelta,hidPos, outPos, hidDelta,outErrors},
  hidWts = Table[Table[Random[Real,{-0.5,0.5}],{inNumber}]{hidNumber}];
  outWts = Table[Table[Random[Real,{-0.5,0.5}],{hidNumber},{outNumber}];
  errorList = Table[    (* begin forward pass *)
  ioP=ioPairs[[Random[Integer,{1,Length[ioPairs]}]]];
    inputs=ioP[[1]];
    outDesired=ioP[[2]];
    hidOuts = sigmoid[hidWts.inputs];
    outputs = sigmoid[outWts.hidOuts];
    outErrors = outDesired-outputs;    (* calculate errors *)
    outDelta= outErrors (outputs (1-outputs));
    hidDelta=(hidOuts (1-hidOuts)) Transpose[outWts].outDelta;
                  (* index of max delta *)
    outPos = First[Flatten[Position[Abs[outDelta],Max[Abs[outDelta]]]]];
    outEps = outDelta[[outPos]]; (* max value *)
    outDelta=Table[-1/4 outEps,{Length[outDelta]}]; (* new outDelta table *)
    outDelta[[outPos]] = outEps; (* reset this one  *)
                (* index of max delta *)
    hidPos = First[Flatten[Position[Abs[hidDelta],Max[Abs[hidDelta]]]]];
    hidEps = hidDelta[[hidPos]]; (* max value *)
    hidDelta=Table[-1/4 hidEps,{Length[hidDelta]}]; (* new outDelta table *)
      hidDelta[[hidPos]] = hidEps; (* reset this one  *)
    outWts +=eta Outer[Times,outDelta,hidOuts];
    hidWts += eta Outer[Times,hidDelta,inputs];
      outErrors.outErrors, (* this puts the error on the list *)
      {numIters}]   ;    (* this many times, Table ends here *)
Print["New hidden-layer weight matrix: "];
Print[ ]; Print[hidWts];Print[ ];
Print["New output-layer weight matrix: "];
Print[ ]; Print[outWts];Print[ ];
bpnTest[hidWts,outWts,ioPairs,bias->False,printAll->False];
errorPlot = ListPlot[errorList, PlotJoined->True];
Return[{hidWts,outWts,errorList,errorPlot}];
]                   (* end of Module *)
```

```
fln[inNumber_,outNumber_,ioPairs_,eta_,alpha_,numIters_] :=
  Module[{outWts,ioP,inputs,outputs,outDesired,
          outVals,outLastDelta,outDelta,outErrors},
  outVals={};
  outWts = Table[Table[Random[Real,{-0.1,0.1}],{inNumber}],{outNumber}];
  outLastDelta = Table[Table[0,{inNumber}],{outNumber}];
  errorList = Table[
                  (* begin forward pass *)
    ioP=ioPairs[[Random[Integer,{1,Length[ioPairs]}]]]];
    inputs=ioP[[1]];
    outDesired=ioP[[2]];
    outputs = outWts.inputs; (* output-layer outputs *)
                  (* calculate errors *)
    outErrors = outDesired-outputs;
    outDelta= outErrors;
                      (* update weights *)
    outLastDelta= eta Outer[Times,outDelta,inputs]+alpha outLastDelta;
    outWts += outLastDelta;
      outErrors.outErrors, (* this puts the error on the list *)
      {numIters}]   ;   (* this many times, Table ends here *)
  Print["New output-layer weight matrix: "];
  Print[]; Print[outWts];Print[];
  outVals=flnTest[outWts,ioPairs];
  errorPlot = ListPlot[errorList, PlotJoined->True];
  Return[{outWts,errorList,errorPlot,outVals}];
  ]                     (* end of Module *)
```

```
flnTest[outputWts_,ioPairVectors_] :=
  Module[{inputs,hidden,outputs,desired,errors,i,len,
            errorTotal,errorSum},
    inputs=Map[First,ioPairVectors];
    desired=Map[Last,ioPairVectors];
    len = Length[inputs];
    outputs=inputs.Transpose[outputWts];
    errors= desired-outputs;
    For[i=1,i<=len,i++,
          (*Print["Input ",i," = ",inputs[[i]]];*)
        Print[" Output ",i," = ",outputs[[i]]," desired = ",
            desired[[i]]," Error = ",errors[[i]]];Print[];
        ];           (* end of For *)
      (*Print["errors= ",errors];Print[];*)
    errorSum = Apply[Plus,errors^2,2]; (* second level *)
    (*Print["errorSum= ",errorSum];Print[];*)
    errorTotal = Apply[Plus,errorSum];
    (*Print["errorTotal= ",errorTotal];*)
    Print["Mean Squared Error = ",errorTotal/len];
    Return[outputs];
    ]              (* end of Module *)
```

Probabilistic Neural Network and Hopfield Network

```
normalize[x_List] := x/(Sqrt[x.x]]//N)


energyHop[x_,w_] := -0.5 x . w . x;


psi[inValue_,netIn_] := If[netIn>0,1,
                      If[netIn<0,-1,inValue]]
```

```
phi[inVector_List,netInVector_List] :=
   MapThread[psi[#,#2]&,{inVector,netInVector}]


makeHopfieldWts[trainingPats_,printWts_:True] :=
   Module[{wtVector},
    wtVector =
      Apply[Plus,Map[Outer[Times,#,#]&,trainingPats]];
    If[printWts,
       Print[];
       Print[MatrixForm[wtVector]];
       Print[];,Continue
       ]; (* end of If *)
    Return[wtVector];
    ] (* end of Module *)
```

```
discreteHopfield[wtVector_,inVector_,printAll_:True] :=
   Module[{done, energy, newEnergy, netInput,
             newInput, output},
    done = False;
    newInput = inVector;
    energy = energyHop[inVector,wtVector];
    If[printAll,
       Print[];Print["Input vector = ",inVector];
       Print[];
       Print["Energy = ",energy];
       Print[],Continue
       ];   (* end of If *)
    While[!done,
       netInput = wtVector . newInput;
       output = phi[newInput,netInput];
       newEnergy = energyHop[output,wtVector];
      If[printAll,
          Print[];Print["Output vector = ",output];
          Print[];
          Print["Energy = ",newEnergy];
          Print[],Continue
          ];   (* end of If *)
      If[energy==newEnergy,
          done=True,
          energy=newEnergy;newInput=output,
          Continue
          ];   (* end of If *)
       ]; (* end of While *)
    If[!printAll,
      Print[];Print["Output vector = ",output];
      Print[];
      Print["Energy = ",newEnergy];
      Print[];
      ]; (* end of If *)
    ]; (* end of Module *)
```

```
prob[n_,T_] := 1/(1+E^(-n/T)) //N;


probPsi[inValue_,netIn_,temp_] :=
 If[Random[]<=prob[netIn,temp],1,psi[inValue,netIn]];


stochasticHopfield[inVector_,weights_,numSweeps_,temp_]:=
  Module[ {input, net, indx, numUnits, indxList, output},
    numUnits=Length[inVector];
    indxList=Table[0,{numUnits}];
    input=inVector;
    For[i=1,i<=numSweeps,i++,
    Print["i= ",i];
      For[j=1,j<=numUnits,j++,
            (* select unit *)
        indx = Random[Integer,{1,numUnits}];
           (* net input to unit *)
        net=input . weights[[indx]];
           (* update input vector *)
        output=probPsi[input[[indx]],net,temp];
        input[[indx]]=output;
        indxList[[indx]]+=1;
      ]; (* end For numUnits *)
    Print[ ];Print["New input vector = "];Print[input];
    ]; (* end For numSweeps *)
  Print[ ];Print["Number of times each unit was updated:"];
  Print[ ];Print[indxList];
  ]; (* end of Module *)
```

```
pnnTwoClass[class1Exemplars_,class2Exemplars_,
                testInputs_,sig_] :=
  Module[{weightsA,weightsB,inputsNorm,patternAout,
          patternBout,sumAout,sumBout},
    weightsA = Map[normalize,class1Exemplars];
    weightsB = Map[normalize,class2Exemplars];
    inputsNorm = Map[normalize,testInputs];
    sigma = sig;
    patternAout =
        gaussOut[inputsNorm . Transpose[weightsA]];
    patternBout =
        gaussOut[inputsNorm . Transpose[weightsB]];
    sumAout = Map[Apply[Plus,#]&,patternAout];
    sumBout = Map[Apply[Plus,#]&,patternBout];
    outputs = Sign[sumAout-sumBout];
    sigma=.;
    Return[outputs];
    ]
```

Traveling Salesperson Problem

```
nOutOfN[weights_,externIn_,numUnits_,lambda_,deltaT_,
numIters_,printFreq_,reset_:False]:=
   Module[{iter,l,dt,indx,ins},
     dt=deltaT;
     l=lambda;
     iter=numIters;
     ins=externIn;
          (* only reset if starting over *)
     If[reset,ui=Table[Random[],{numUnits}];
             vi = g[l,ui],Continue];  (* end of If *)
        Print["initial ui = ",N[ui,2]];Print[];
        Print["initial vi = ",N[vi,2]];
     For[iter=1,iter<=numIters,iter++,
       indx = Random[Integer,{1,numUnits}];
       ui[[indx]] = ui[[indx]]+
          dt (vi . Transpose[weights[[indx]]] +
          ui[[indx]] + ins[[indx]]);
       vi[[indx]] = g[l,ui[[indx]]];
       If[Mod[iter,printFreq]==0,
          Print[];Print["iteration = ",iter];
          Print["net inputs = "];
          Print[N[ui,2]];
          Print["outputs = "];
          Print[N[vi,2]];Print[];
          ];  (* end of If *)
     ];  (* end of For *)
     Print[];Print["iteration = ",--iter];
     Print["final outputs = "];
     Print[vi];
     ];  (* end of Module *)
```

```
tsp[weights_,externIn_,numUnits_,lambda_,deltaT_,
numIters_,printFreq_,reset_:False]:=
   Module[{iter,l,dt,indx,ins,utemp},
     dt=deltaT;
     l=lambda;
     iter=numIters;
     ins=externIn;
           (* only reset if starting over *)
     If[reset,
        utemp = ArcTanh[(2.0/Sqrt[numUnits])-1]/l;
        ui=Table[
          utemp+Random[Real,{-utemp/10,utemp/10}],
                {numUnits}];  (* end of Table *)
               vi = g[l,ui],Continue];  (* end of If *)
         Print["initial ui = ",N[ui,2]];Print[];
         Print["initial vi = ",N[vi,2]];
     For[iter=1,iter<=numIters,iter++,
       indx = Random[Integer,{1,numUnits}];
       ui[[indx]] = ui[[indx]]+
          dt (vi . Transpose[weights[[indx]]] +
          ui[[indx]] + ins[[indx]]);
       vi[[indx]] = g[l,ui[[indx]]];
       If[Mod[iter,printFreq]==0,
          Print[];Print["iteration = ",iter];
          Print["net inputs = "];
          Print[N[ui,2]];
          Print["outputs = "];
          Print[N[vi,2]];Print[];
          ];  (* end of If *)
       ];  (* end of For *)
     Print[];Print["iteration = ",--iter];
     Print["final outputs = "];
     Print[MatrixForm[Partition[N[vi,2],Sqrt[numUnits]]]];
     ];  (* end of Module *)
```

BAM

```
makeXtoYwts[exemplars_] :=
  Module[{temp},
   temp = Map[Outer[Times,#[[2]]],#[[1]]]&,exemplars];
   Apply[Plus,temp]
   ]; (* end of Module *)


psi[inValue_,netIn_] := If[netIn>0,1,If[netIn<0,-1,inValue]];
phi[inVector_List,netInVector_List] :=
  MapThread[psi[#,#2]&,{inVector,netInVector}];


energyBAM[xx_,w_,zz_] := - (xx . w . zz)


bam[initialX_,initialY_,x2yWeights_,y2xWeights_,printAll_:False] :=
  Module[{done,newX,newY,energy1,energy2},
   done = False;
   newX = initialX;
   newY = initialY;
   While[done == False,
     newY = phi[newY,x2yWeights.newX];
     If[printAll,Print[];Print[];Print["y = ",newY]];
     energy1 = energyBAM[newY,x2yWeights,newX];
     If[printAll,Print["energy = ",energy1]];
     newX = phi[newX,y2xWeights . newY];
     If[printAll,Print[];Print["x = ",newX]];
     energy2 = energyBAM[newY,x2yWeights,newX];
     If[printAll,Print["energy = ",energy1]];
     If[energy1 == energy2,done=True,Continue];
   ]; (* end of While *)
   Print[];Print[];
   Print["final y = ",newY," energy= ",energy1];
   Print["final x = ",newX," energy= ",energy2];
   ]; (* end of Module *)
```

Elman Network

```
elman[inNumber_,hidNumber_,outNumber_,ioPairs_,eta_,alpha_,numIters_] :=
  Module[{hidWts,outWts,ioP,inputs,hidOuts,outputs,outDesired,
          i,indx,hidLastDelta,outLastDelta,outDelta,errorList={},
          ioSequence, conUnits,hidDelta,outErrors},
  hidWts = Table[Table[Random[Real,{-0.5,0.5}],{inNumber+hidNumber}],{hidNumber}];
  outWts = Table[Table[Random[Real,{-0.5,0.5}],{hidNumber}],{outNumber}];
  hidLastDelta = Table[Table[0,{inNumber+hidNumber}],{hidNumber}];
  outLastDelta = Table[Table[0,{hidNumber}],{outNumber}];
  For[indx=1,indx<=numIters,indx++,  (* begin forward pass; select a sequence *)
    ioSequence=ioPairs[[Random[Integer,{1,Length[ioPairs]}]]];
    conUnits = Table[0.5,{hidNumber}];    (* reset conUnits *)
    For[i=1,i<=Length[ioSequence],i++,      (* process the sequence in order *)
    ioP = ioSequence[[i]];         (* pick out the next ioPair *)
    inputs=Join[conUnits,ioP[[1]] ];    (* join context and input units *)
      outDesired=ioP[[2]];
      hidOuts = sigmoid[hidWts.inputs];    (* hidden-layer outputs *)
      outputs = sigmoid[outWts.hidOuts];   (* output-layer outputs *)
      outErrors = outDesired-outputs;      (* calculate errors *)
      outDelta= outErrors (outputs (1-outputs));
      hidDelta=(hidOuts (1-hidOuts)) Transpose[outWts].outDelta;
      outLastDelta= eta Outer[Times,outDelta,hidOuts]+alpha outLastDelta;
      outWts += outLastDelta;            (* update weights *)
      hidLastDelta = eta Outer[Times,hidDelta,inputs]+alpha hidLastDelta;
      hidWts += hidLastDelta;
      conUnits = hidOuts;              (* update context units *)
        (* put the sum of the squared errors on the list *)
      AppendTo[errorList,outErrors.outErrors];
      ]; (* end of For i *)
  ];    (* end of For indx *)
  Print["New hidden-layer weight matrix: "];
  Print[ ]; Print[hidWts];Print[ ];
  Print["New output-layer weight matrix: "];
  Print[ ]; Print[outWts];Print[ ];
  elmanTest[hidWts,outWts,ioPairs,hidNumber];
  errorPlot = ListPlot[errorList, PlotJoined->True];
  Return[{hidWts,outWts,errorList,errorPlot}];
  ]                  (* end of Module *)
```

```
elmanTest[hiddenWts_,outputWts_,ioPairVectors_,conNumber_,printAll_:False] :=
  Module[{inputs,hidden,outputs,desired,errors,i,j,
          prntAll,conUnits,ioSequence,ioP},
    If[printAll,Print[];Print["ioPairs:"];Print[];Print[ioPairVectors]];
             (* loop through the sequences *)
      For[i=1,i<=Length[ioPairVectors],i++,
             (* select the next sequence *)
    ioSequence = ioPairVectors[[i]];
             (* reset the context units  *)
   conUnits = Table[0.5,{conNumber}];
             (* loop through the chosen sequence *)
      For[j=1,j<=Length[ioSequence],j++,
          ioP = ioSequence[[j]];
              (* join context and input units *)
          inputs=Join[conUnits,ioP[[1]] ];
          desired=ioP[[2]];
          hidden=sigmoid[hiddenWts.inputs];
          outputs=sigmoid[outputWts.hidden];
          errors= desired-outputs;
             (* update context units *)
          conUnits = hidden;
          Print[];
          Print["Sequence ",i, " input ",j];
          Print[];Print["inputs:"];Print[];
          Print[inputs];
          If[printAll,Print[];Print["hidden-layer outputs:"];
             Print[hidden];Print[];
             ];
          Print["outputs:"];Print[];
          Print[outputs];Print[];
          Print["desired:"];Print[];Print[desired];Print[];
          Print["Mean squared error:"];
          Print[errors.errors/Length[errors]];
          Print[];
          ];  (* end of For j *)
        ];   (* end of For i *)
   ]                 (* end of Module *)
```

```
elmanComp[inNumber_,hidNumber_,outNumber_,ioPairs_,eta_,alpha_,numIters_] :=
  Module[{hidWts,outWts,ioP,inputs,hidOuts,outputs,outDesired,
          i,indx,hidLastDelta,outLastDelta,outDelta,errorList={},
          ioSequence, conUnits,hidDelta,outErrors},
  hidWts = Table[Table[Random[Real,{-0.5,0.5}],{inNumber+conNumber}],{hidNumber}];
  outWts = Table[Table[Random[Real,{-0.5,0.5}],{hidNumber}],{outNumber}];
  hidLastDelta = Table[Table[0,{inNumber+conNumber}],{hidNumber}];
  outLastDelta = Table[Table[0,{hidNumber}],{outNumber}];
  outErrors = Table[0,{outNumber}];
  For[indx=1,indx<=numIters,indx++,
   ioSequence=ioPairs[[Random[Integer,{1,Length[ioPairs]}]]]]; (* select a sequence *)
    conUnits = Table[0.5,{conNumber}];        (* reset conUnits *)
    For[i=1,i<=Length[ioSequence],i++,        (* process the sequence in order *)
      ioP = ioSequence[[i]];                   (* pick out the next ioPair *)
      inputs=Join[conUnits,ioP[[1]] ];         (* join context and input units *)
      outDesired=ioP[[2]];
      hidOuts = sigmoid[hidWts.inputs];        (* hidden-layer outputs *)
      outputs = outWts.hidOuts;                (* output-layer outputs *)
      outputs = sigmoid[outputs -   0.3 Apply[Plus,outputs] + .5 outputs];
      outErrors = outDesired-outputs;          (* calculate errors *)
      outDelta= outErrors (outputs (1-outputs));
      hidDelta=(hidOuts (1-hidOuts)) Transpose[outWts].outDelta;
      outLastDelta= eta Outer[Times,outDelta,hidOuts]+alpha outLastDelta;
      outWts += outLastDelta;                  (* update weights *)
      hidLastDelta = eta Outer[Times,hidDelta,inputs]+alpha hidLastDelta;
      hidWts += hidLastDelta;                  (* update weights *)
      conUnits = hidOuts;                      (* update context units *)
        (* put the sum of the squared errors on the list *)
      AppendTo[errorList,outErrors.outErrors];
      ]; (* end of For i *)
   ];    (* end of For indx *)
  Print["New hidden-layer weight matrix: "];
  Print[ ]; Print[hidWts];Print[ ];
  Print["New output-layer weight matrix: "];
  Print[ ]; Print[outWts];Print[ ];
  elmanCompTest[hidWts,outWts,ioPairs,conNumber];
  errorPlot = ListPlot[errorList, PlotJoined->True];
  Return[{hidWts,outWts,errorList,errorPlot}];
  ]                 (* end of Module *)
```

```
elmanCompTest[hiddenWts_,outputWts_,ioPairVectors_,conNumber_,printAll_:False] :=
Module[{inputs,hidden,outputs,desired,errors,i,j,prntAll,conUnits,ioSequence,ioP},
   If[printAll,Print[];Print["ioPairs:"];Print[];Print[ioPairVectors]];
     For[i=1,i<=Length[ioPairVectors],i++,   (* loop through the sequences *)
     ioSequence = ioPairVectors[[i]];         (* select the next sequence *)
     conUnits = Table[0.5,{conNumber}];       (* reset the context units *)
        For[j=1,j<=Length[ioSequence],j++,    (* loop through the chosen sequence *)
          ioP = ioSequence[[j]];
        inputs=Join[conUnits,ioP[[1]] ];      (* join context and input units *)
          desired=ioP[[2]];
          hidden=sigmoid[hiddenWts.inputs];
          outputs=outputWts.hidden;
          outputs=sigmoid[outputs -
             0.3 Apply[Plus,outputs] + 0.5 outputs];
          errors= desired-outputs;
             (* update context units *)
          conUnits = hidden;
          Print[];
          Print["Sequence ",i, " input ",j];
          Print[];Print["inputs:"];Print[];
          Print[inputs];
          If[printAll,Print[];Print["hidden-layer outputs:"];
             Print[hidden];Print[];
             ];
          Print["outputs:"];Print[];
          Print[outputs];Print[];
          Print["desired:"];Print[];Print[desired];Print[];
          Print["Mean squared error:"];
          Print[errors.errors/Length[errors]];
          Print[];
          ]; (* end of For j *)
       ];   (* end of For i *)
   ]              (* end of Module *)
```

Jordan Network

```
jordan[inNumber_,hidNumber_,outNumber_,ioPairs_,eta_,alpha_,mu_,numIters_] :=
  Module[{hidWts,outWts,ioP,inputs,hidOuts,outputs,outDesired,
          i,indx,hidLastDelta,outLastDelta,outDelta,errorList = {},
          ioSequence, stateUnits,hidDelta,outErrors},
  hidWts = Table[Table[Random[Real,{-0.5,0.5}],{inNumber+outNumber}],{hidNumber}];
  outWts = Table[Table[Random[Real,{-0.5,0.5}],{hidNumber}],{outNumber}];
  hidLastDelta = Table[Table[0,{inNumber+outNumber}],{hidNumber}];
  outLastDelta = Table[Table[0,{hidNumber}],{outNumber}];
  For[indx=1,indx<=numIters,indx++, (* begin forward pass *)
   ioSequence=ioPairs[[Random[Integer,{1,Length[ioPairs]}]]]; (* select a sequence *)
    stateUnits = Table[0.1,{outNumber}];   (* reset stateUnits *)
    For[i=1,i<=Length[ioSequence],i++,     (* process the sequence in order *)
     ioP = ioSequence[[i]];                (* pick out the next ioPair *)
     inputs=Join[stateUnits,ioP[[1]] ];    (* join context and input units *)
     outDesired=ioP[[2]];
     hidOuts = sigmoid[hidWts.inputs];     (* hidden-layer outputs *)
     outputs = sigmoid[outWts.hidOuts];    (* output-layer outputs *)
     outErrors = outDesired-outputs;       (* calculate errors *)
     outDelta= outErrors (outputs (1-outputs));
     hidDelta=(hidOuts (1-hidOuts)) Transpose[outWts].outDelta;
     outLastDelta= eta Outer[Times,outDelta,hidOuts]+alpha outLastDelta;
     outWts += outLastDelta;               (* update weights *)
     hidLastDelta = eta Outer[Times,hidDelta,inputs]+alpha hidLastDelta;
     hidWts += hidLastDelta;               (* update weights *)
     stateUnits = mu stateUnits + outputs; (* update state units *)
       (* put the sum of the squared errors on the list *)
     AppendTo[errorList,outErrors.outErrors];
     ]; (* end of For i *)
  ];    (* end of For indx *)
  Print["New hidden-layer weight matrix: "];
  Print[]; Print[hidWts];Print[];
  Print["New output-layer weight matrix: "];
  Print[]; Print[outWts];Print[];
  jordanTest[hidWts,outWts,ioPairs,mu,outNumber];
  errorPlot = ListPlot[errorList, PlotJoined->True];
  Return[{hidWts,outWts,errorList,errorPlot}];
  ]                    (* end of Module *)
```

```
jordanTest[hiddenWts_,outputWts_,ioPairVectors_,
        mu_, stateNumber_,printAll_:False] :=
  Module[{inputs,hidden,outputs,desired,errors,i,j,
          prntAll,stateUnits,ioSequence,ioP},
    If[printAll,Print[];Print["ioPairs:"];Print[];Print[ioPairVectors]];
      For[i=1,i<=Length[ioPairVectors],i++, (* loop through the sequences  *)
    ioSequence = ioPairVectors[[i]];   (* select the next sequence *)
    stateUnits = Table[0.1,{stateNumber}]; (* reset the context units  *)
       For[j=1,j<=Length[ioSequence],j++, (* loop through the chosen sequence *)
            ioP = ioSequence[[j]];
            inputs=Join[stateUnits,ioP[[1]] ];  (* join context and input units *)
            desired=ioP[[2]];
            hidden=sigmoid[hiddenWts.inputs];
            outputs=sigmoid[outputWts.hidden];
            errors= desired-outputs;
            stateUnits = mu stateUnits + outputs; (* update context units *)
            Print[];
            Print["Sequence ",i, " input ",j];
            Print[];Print["inputs:"];Print[];
            Print[inputs];
            If[printAll,Print[];Print["hidden-layer outputs:"];
                Print[hidden];Print[]; ];
            Print["outputs:"];Print[];
            Print[outputs];Print[];
            Print["desired:"];Print[];Print[desired];Print[];
            Print["Mean squared error:"];
            Print[errors.errors/Length[errors]];
            Print[];
            ]; (* end of For j *)
        ];   (* end of For i *)
    ]             (* end of Module *)
```

```
(* this version sets the state units equal to the desired output values,
rather than the actual output values, during the training process *)
jordan2[inNumber_,hidNumber_,outNumber_,ioPairs_,eta_,alpha_,mu_,numIters_] :=
  Module[{hidWts,outWts,ioP,inputs,hidOuts,outputs,outDesired,
          i,indx,hidLastDelta,outLastDelta,outDelta,errorList = {},
          ioSequence, stateUnits,hidDelta,outErrors},
 hidWts = Table[Table[Random[Real,{-0.5,0.5}],{inNumber+outNumber}],{hidNumber}];
 outWts = Table[Table[Random[Real,{-0.5,0.5}],{hidNumber}],{outNumber}];
 hidLastDelta = Table[Table[0,{inNumber+outNumber}],{hidNumber}];
 outLastDelta = Table[Table[0,{hidNumber}],{outNumber}];
 For[indx=1,indx<=numIters,indx++,    (* begin forward pass *)
  ioSequence=ioPairs[[Random[Integer,{1,Length[ioPairs]}]]]; (* select a sequence *)
   stateUnits = Table[0.1,{outNumber}];   (* reset stateUnits *)
   For[i=1,i<=Length[ioSequence],i++,    (* process the sequence in order *)
    ioP = ioSequence[[i]];             (* pick out the next ioPair *)
    inputs=Join[stateUnits,ioP[[1]] ];   (* join context and input units *)
    outDesired=ioP[[2]];
    hidOuts = sigmoid[hidWts.inputs];    (* hidden-layer outputs *)
    outputs = sigmoid[outWts.hidOuts];   (* output-layer outputs *)
    outErrors = outDesired-outputs;      (* calculate errors *)
    outDelta= outErrors (outputs (1-outputs));
    hidDelta=(hidOuts (1-hidOuts)) Transpose[outWts].outDelta;
    outLastDelta= eta Outer[Times,outDelta,hidOuts]+alpha outLastDelta;
    outWts += outLastDelta;          (* update weights *)
    hidLastDelta = eta Outer[Times,hidDelta,inputs]+alpha hidLastDelta;
    hidWts += hidLastDelta;          (* update weights *)
    stateUnits = mu stateUnits + outDesired;  (* update state units *)
    AppendTo[errorList,outErrors.outErrors];
    ]; (* end of For i *)
 ];    (* end of For indx *)
Print["New hidden-layer weight matrix: "];
Print[]; Print[hidWts];Print[];
Print["New output-layer weight matrix: "];
Print[]; Print[outWts];Print[];
jordan2Test[hidWts,outWts,ioPairs,mu,outNumber];
errorPlot = ListPlot[errorList, PlotJoined->True];
Return[{hidWts,outWts,errorList,errorPlot}];
]                        (* end of Module *)
```

```
jordan2Test[hiddenWts_,outputWts_,ioPairVectors_,
         mu_, stateNumber_,printAll_:False] :=
 Module[{inputs,hidden,outputs,desired,errors,i,j,
         prntAll,stateUnits,ioSequence,ioP},
   If[printAll,Print[];Print["ioPairs:"];Print[];
               Print[ioPairVectors]];
   For[i=1,i<=Length[ioPairVectors],i++,    (* loop through the sequences *)
    ioSequence = ioPairVectors[[i]];       (* select the next sequence *)
    stateUnits = Table[0.1,{stateNumber}]; (* reset the context units *)
      For[j=1,j<=Length[ioSequence],j++,    (* loop through the chosen sequence *)
         ioP = ioSequence[[j]];
        inputs=Join[stateUnits,ioP[[1]] ];    (* join context and input units *)
         desired=ioP[[2]];
         hidden=sigmoid[hiddenWts.inputs];
         outputs=sigmoid[outputWts.hidden];
         errors= desired-outputs;
         stateUnits = mu stateUnits + desired; (* update context units *)
         Print[];
         Print["Sequence ",i, " input ",j];
         Print[];Print["inputs:"];Print[];
         Print[inputs];
         If[printAll,Print[];Print["hidden-layer outputs:"];
            Print[hidden];Print[];];
         Print["outputs:"];Print[];
         Print[outputs];Print[];
         Print["desired:"];Print[];Print[desired];Print[];
         Print["Mean squared error:"];
         Print[errors.errors/Length[errors]];
         Print[];
         ]; (* end of For j *)
       ];   (* end of For i *)
    ]              (* end of Module *)
```

```
(* this is a modification of jordan2 in which the mean squared error
is calculated over the entire training pass before being added to the list *)
jordan2a[inNumber_,hidNumber_,outNumber_,ioPairs_,eta_,alpha_,mu_,numIters_] :=
  Module[{hidWts,outWts,ioP,inputs,hidOuts,outputs,outDesired,
          i,indx,hidLastDelta,outLastDelta,outDelta,errorList = {},
    cycleError,ioSequence, stateUnits,hidDelta,outErrors},
  hidWts = Table[Table[Random[Real,{-0.5,0.5}],{inNumber+outNumber}],{hidNumber}];
  outWts = Table[Table[Random[Real,{-0.5,0.5}],{hidNumber}],{outNumber}];
  hidLastDelta = Table[Table[0,{inNumber+outNumber}],{hidNumber}];
  outLastDelta = Table[Table[0,{hidNumber}],{outNumber}];
  For[indx=1,indx<=numIters,indx++,        (* begin forward pass *)
   ioSequence=ioPairs[[Random[Integer,{1,Length[ioPairs]}]]]];(* select a sequence *)
    stateUnits = Table[0.1,{outNumber}];       (* reset stateUnits *)
    cycleError = 0.0;                       (* initialize error *)
    For[i=1,i<=Length[ioSequence],i++,         (* process the sequence in order *)
      ioP = ioSequence[[i]];               (* pick out the next ioPair *)
      inputs=Join[stateUnits,ioP[[1]] ];      (* join context and input units *)
      outDesired=ioP[[2]];
      hidOuts = sigmoid[hidWts.inputs];      (* hidden-layer outputs *)
      outputs = sigmoid[outWts.hidOuts];      (* output-layer outputs *)
      outErrors = outDesired-outputs;        (* calculate errors *)
      outDelta= outErrors (outputs (1-outputs));
      hidDelta=(hidOuts (1-hidOuts)) Transpose[outWts].outDelta;
      outLastDelta= eta Outer[Times,outDelta,hidOuts]+alpha outLastDelta;
      outWts += outLastDelta;                (* update weights *)
      hidLastDelta = eta Outer[Times,hidDelta,inputs]+alpha hidLastDelta;
      hidWts += hidLastDelta;                (* update weights *)
      stateUnits = mu stateUnits + outDesired; (* update state units *)
                                          (* compute mse for this sequence *)
      cycleError=cycleError + outErrors.outErrors/Length[outErrors];
      ]; (* end of For i *)
  AppendTo[errorList,cycleError/Length[ioSequence]];
  ];     (* end of For indx *)
  Print["New hidden-layer weight matrix: "];Print[ ]; Print[hidWts];Print[ ];
  Print["New output-layer weight matrix: "];Print[ ]; Print[outWts];Print[ ];
  jordan2Test[hidWts,outWts,ioPairs,mu,outNumber];
  errorPlot = ListPlot[errorList, PlotJoined->True];
  Return[{hidWts,outWts,errorList,errorPlot}];
  ]                     (* end of Module *)
```

```
(* this is a modification of jordan2a using the Tanh function *)
jordan2aTanh[inNumber_,hidNumber_,outNumber_,ioPairs_,eta_,alpha_,mu_,numIters_] :=
  Module[{hidWts,outWts,ioP,inputs,hidOuts,outputs,outDesired,
          i,indx,hidLastDelta,outLastDelta,outDelta,errorList = {},
     cycleError,ioSequence, stateUnits,hidDelta,outErrors},
   hidWts = Table[Table[Random[Real,{-0.5,0.5}],{inNumber+outNumber}],{hidNumber}];
   outWts = Table[Table[Random[Real,{-0.5,0.5}],{hidNumber}],{outNumber}];
   hidLastDelta = Table[Table[0,{inNumber+outNumber}],{hidNumber}];
   outLastDelta = Table[Table[0,{hidNumber}],{outNumber}];
   For[indx=1,indx<=numIters,indx++,              (* begin forward pass *)
    ioSequence=ioPairs[[Random[Integer,{1,Length[ioPairs]}]]];(* select a sequence *)
     stateUnits = Table[-0.9,{outNumber}];            (* reset stateUnits *)
     cycleError = 0.0;                           (* initialize error *)
     For[i=1,i<=Length[ioSequence],i++,            (* process the sequence in order *)
       ioP = ioSequence[[i]];                    (* pick out the next ioPair *)
       inputs=Join[stateUnits,ioP[[1]] ];           (* join context and input units *)
       outDesired=ioP[[2]];
       hidOuts = Tanh[hidWts.inputs];             (* hidden-layer outputs *)
       outputs = Tanh[outWts.hidOuts];            (* output-layer outputs *)
       outErrors = outDesired-outputs;            (* calculate errors *)
       outDelta= outErrors  (1-outputs^2);
       hidDelta=(1-hidOuts^2) Transpose[outWts].outDelta;
       outLastDelta= eta Outer[Times,outDelta,hidOuts]+alpha outLastDelta;
       outWts += outLastDelta;                    (* update weights *)
       hidLastDelta = eta Outer[Times,hidDelta,inputs]+alpha hidLastDelta;
       hidWts += hidLastDelta;                    (* update weights *)
       stateUnits = mu stateUnits + outDesired;    (* update state units *)
       cycleError=cycleError + outErrors.outErrors/Length[outErrors];
       ]; (* end of For i *)
  AppendTo[errorList,cycleError/Length[ioSequence]];(* put the average mse on the list *)
  ];     (* end of For indx *)
  Print["New hidden-layer weight matrix: "];
  Print[]; Print[hidWts];Print[];
  Print["New output-layer weight matrix: "];
  Print[]; Print[outWts];Print[];
  jordan2aTanhTest[hidWts,outWts,ioPairs,mu,outNumber];
  errorPlot = ListPlot[errorList, PlotJoined->True];
  Return[{hidWts,outWts,errorList,errorPlot}];
  ]                      (* end of Module *)
```

```
jordan2aTanhTest[hiddenWts_,outputWts_,ioPairVectors_,
         mu_, stateNumber_,printAll_:False] :=
 Module[{inputs,hidden,outputs,desired,errors,i,j,
            prntAll,stateUnits,ioSequence,ioP},
   If[printAll,Print[];Print["ioPairs:"];Print[];   Print[ioPairVectors]];
   For[i=1,i<=Length[ioPairVectors],i++,        (* loop through the sequences *)
     ioSequence = ioPairVectors[[i]];            (* select the next sequence *)
      For[j=1,j<=Length[ioSequence],j++,         (* loop through the chosen sequence *)
          ioP = ioSequence[[j]];
        inputs=Join[stateUnits,ioP[[1]] ];        (* join context and input units *)
            desired=ioP[[2]];
            hidden=Tanh[hiddenWts.inputs];
            outputs=Tanh[outputWts.hidden];
            errors= desired-outputs;
            stateUnits = mu stateUnits + desired;        (* update context units *)
            Print[];
            Print["Sequence ",i, " input ",j];
            Print[];Print["inputs:"];Print[];
            Print[inputs];
            If[printAll,Print[];Print["hidden-layer outputs:"];
                Print[hidden];Print[];   ];
            Print["outputs:"];Print[];
            Print[outputs];Print[];
            Print["desired:"];Print[];Print[desired];Print[];
            Print["Mean squared error:"];
            Print[errors.errors/Length[errors]];Print[];
            ]; (* end of For j *)
        ];   (* end of For i *)
    ]                (* end of Module *)
```

ART

```
(* vmag for ART1 networks *)
vmag1[v_] := Count[v,1]

(* vmag for ART2 networks *)
vmag2[v_] = Sqrt[v . v]

(* reset for ART1 *)
resetflag1[outp_,inp_,rho_] :=
     If[vmag1[outp]/vmag1[inp]<rho,True,False]

(* reset for ART2 *)
resetflag2[u_,p_,c_,rho_]:=
   Module[{r,flag},
      r = (u + c p) / (vmag2[u] + vmag2[c p]);
      If[rho/vmag2[r] > 1,flag=True,flag=False];
      Return[flag];
      ];

winner[p_,val_] := First[First[Position[p,val]]]

compete[f2Activities_] :=
  Module[{i,x,f2dim,maxpos},
   x=f2Activities;
   maxpos=First[First[Position[x,Max[f2Activities]]]];
   f2dim = Length[x];
   For[i=1,i<=f2dim,i++,
       If[i!=maxpos,x[[i]]=0;Continue]  (* end of If *)
      ]; (* end of For *)
   Return[x];
   ]; (* end of Module *)

art1Init[f1dim_,f2dim_,b1_,d1_,e1_,del1_,del2_] :=
  Module[{z12,z21},
   z12 = Table[Table[(b1-1)/d1 + del1,{f2dim}],{f1dim}];
   z21 = Table[Table[(e1/(e1-1+f1dim)-del2),{f1dim}],{f2dim}];
   Return[{z12,z21}];
   ]; (* end of Module *)
```

```
art1[f1dim_,f2dim_,a1_,b1_,c1_,d1_,e1_,rho_,f1Wts_,f2Wts_,inputs_] :=
  Module[{droplistinit,droplist,notDone=True,i,nIn=Length[inputs],reset,
          n,sf1,t,xf2,uf2,v,windex,matchList,newMatchList,tdWts,buWts},
    droplistinit = Table[1,{f2dim}];   (* initialize droplist *)
    tdWts=f1Wts; buWts=f2Wts;
    matchList =     (* construct list of F2 units and encoded input patterns *)
          Table[{StringForm["Unit ",n]},{n,f2dim}];
    While[notDone==True,newMatchList = matchList; (* process until stable *)
      For[i=1,i<=nIn,i++,in = inputs[[i]];          (* process inputs in sequence *)
        droplist = droplistinit;reset=True;         (* initialize *)
        While[reset==True,                          (* cycle until no reset *)
          xf1 = in/(1+a1*(in+b1)+c1);               (* activities *)
          sf1 = Map[If[#>0,1,0]&,xf1];              (* F1 outputs *)
          t= buWts . sf1;                           (* F2 net-inputs *)
          t = t droplist;                           (* turn off inhibited units *)
          xf2 = compete[t];                         (* F2 activities *)
          uf2 = Map[If[#>0,1,0]&,xf2];              (* F2 outputs *)
          windex = winner[uf2,1];                   (* winning index *)
          v= tdWts . uf2;                           (* F1 net-inputs *)
          xf1 =(in+ d1*v-b1)/(1+a1*(in+d1*v)+c1);   (* new F1 activities *)
          sf1 = Map[If[#>0,1,0]&,xf1];              (* new F1 outputs *)
          reset = resetflag1[sf1,in,rho];           (* check reset *)
          If[reset==True,droplist[[windex]]=0;      (* update droplist *)
                Print["Reset with pattern ",i," on unit ",windex],Continue];
          ]; (* end of While reset==True *)
        Print["Resonance established on unit ",windex," with pattern ",i];
        tdWts=Transpose[tdWts];   (* resonance, so update weights,top down first *)
          tdWts[[windex]]=sf1;
          tdWts=Transpose[tdWts];
          buWts[[windex]] = e1/(e1-1+vmag1[sf1]) sf1; (* then bottom up *)
        matchList[[windex]] =                       (* update matching list *)
                Reverse[Union[matchList[[windex]],{i}]];
        ]; (* end of For i=1 to nIn *)
      If[matchList==newMatchList,notDone=False;     (* see if matchList is static *)
            Print["Network stable"],
            Print["Network not stable"];
            newMatchList = matchList];]; (* end of While notDone==True *)
    Return[{tdWts,buWts,matchList}];
    ]; (* end of Module *)
```

```
art2F1[in_,a_,b_,d_,tdWts_,f1d_,winr_:0] :=
  Module[{w,x,u,v,p,q,i},
    w=x=u=v=p=q=Table[0,{f1d}];
    For[i=1,i<=2,i++,
      w = in + a u;
      x = w / vmag2[w];
      v = f[x] + b f[q];
      u = v / vmag2[v];
      p = If[winr==0,u,
              u + d Transpose[tdWts][[winr]] ];
      q = p / vmag2[p];
      ]; (* end of For i *)
    Return[{u,p}];
    ] (* end of Module *)


art2Init[f1dim_,f2dim_,d_,del1_] :=
  Module[{z12,z21},
    z12 = Table[Table[0 ,{f2dim}],{f1dim}];
    z21 = Table[Table[del1/((1-d)*Sqrt[f1dim] ),
              {f1dim}],{f2dim}];
    Return[{z12,z21}];
    ]; (* end of Module *)
```

```
art2[f1dim_,f2dim_,a1_,b1_,c1_,d_,theta_,rho_,f1Wts_,f2Wts_,inputs_] :=
  Module[{droplistinit,droplist,notDone=True,i,nIn= Length[inputs],reset,
         u,p,t,xf2,uf2,v,windex,matchList,newMatchList,tdWts,buWts},
    droplistinit = Table[1,{f2dim}];     (* initialize droplist *)
    tdWts = f1Wts; buWts = f2Wts;
    u = p = Table[0,{f1dim}];
          (* construct list of F2 units and encodedinput patterns *)
      matchList = Table[{StringForm["Unit ``",n]},{n,f2dim}];
    While[notDone==True,newMatchList = matchList; (* process until stable *)
      For[i=1,i<=nIn,i++,          (* process each input pattern in sequence *)
        droplist = droplistinit;  (* initialize droplist for new input *)
        reset=True;
        in = inputs[[i]];         (* next input pattern *)
        windex = 0;               (* initialize *)
        While[reset==True,        (* cycle until no reset *)
          {u,p} = art2F1[in,a1,b1,d,tdWts,f1dim,windex];
          t= buWts . p;                (* F2 net-inputs *)
          t = t droplist;          (* turn off inhibited units *)
          xf2 = compete[t];        (* F2 activities *)
          uf2 = Map[g,xf2];       (* F2 outputs *)
          windex = winner[uf2,d];  (* winning index *)
           {u,p} = art2F1[in,a1,b1,d,tdWts,f1dim,windex];
          reset = resetflag2[u,p,c1,rho]; (* check reset *)
          If[reset==True,droplist[[windex]]=0;   (* update droplist *)
               Print["Reset with pattern ",i," on unit ",windex],Continue];
          ]; (* end of While reset==True *)
    Print["Resonance established on unit ",    windex," with pattern ",i];
    tdWts=Transpose[tdWts]; (* resonance, so update weights *)
        tdWts[[windex]]=u/(1-d); tdWts=Transpose[tdWts];
        buWts[[windex]] = u/(1-d);
        matchList[[windex]] =    (* update matching list *)
      Reverse[Union[matchList[[windex]],{i}]];
        ]; (* end of For i=1 to nIn *)
    If[matchList==newMatchList,notDone=False;   (* see if matchList is static *)
          Print["Network stable"],Print["Network not stable"];
          newMatchList = matchList];
      ]; (* end of While notDone==True *)
  Return[{tdWts,buWts,matchList}];
  ];   (* end of Module *)
```

Genetic Algorithms

```
f[x_] := 1+Cos[x]/(1+0.01 x^2)

flip[x_] := If[Random[]<=x,True,False]

newGenerate[pmutate_,keyPhrase_,pop_,numGens_] :=
  Module[{i,newPop,parent,diff,matches,
         index,fitness},
    newPop=pop;
   For[i=1,i<=numGens,i++,
     diff = Map[(keyPhrase-#)&,newPop];
     matches = Map[Count[#,0]&,diff];
     fitness = Max[matches];
     index = Position[matches,fitness];
     parent = newPop[[First[Flatten[index]]]];
     Print["Generation ",i,": ",FromCharacterCode[parent],
            " Fitness= ",fitness];
     newPop = Table[Map[mutateLetter[pmutate,#]&,parent],{100}];
     ];  (* end of For *)
    ];  (* end of Module *)

decodeBGA[chromosome_] :=
  Module[{pList,lchrom,values,phenotype},
    lchrom = Length[chromosome];
       (* convert from binary to decimal *)
    pList = Flatten[Position[chromosome,1] ];
    values = Map[2^(lchrom-#)&,pList];
    decimal = Apply[Plus,values];
       (* scale to proper range *)
    phenotype = decimal (0.078201368852394916911)-40;
    Return[phenotype];
      ];  (* end of Module *)
```

```
selectOne[foldedFitnessList_,fitTotal_] :=
  Module[{randFitness,elem,index},
      randFitness = Random[] fitTotal;
      elem = Select[foldedFitnessList,#>=randFitness&,1];
      index =
      Flatten[Position[foldedFitnessList,First[elem]]];
      Return[First[index]];
      ]; (* end of Module *)

myXor[x_,y_] := If[x==y,0,1];

mutateBGA[pmute_,allel_] :=
   If[flip[pmute],myXor[allel,1],allel];

crossOver[pcross_,pmutate_,parent1_,parent2_] :=
  Module[{child1,child2,crossAt,lchrom },
           (* chromosome length *)
      lchrom = Length[parent1];
   If[ flip[pcross],
          (* True: select cross site at random *)
        crossAt = Random[Integer,{1,lchrom-1}];
          (* construct children *)
        child1 = Join[Take[parent1,crossAt], Drop[parent2,crossAt]];
        child2 = Join[Take[parent2,crossAt],    Drop[parent1,crossAt]],
          (* False: return parents as children *)
        child1 = parent1;
        child2 = parent2;
      ]; (* end of If *)
          (* perform mutation *)
      child1 = Map[mutateBGA[pmutate,#]&,child1];
      child2 = Map[mutateBGA[pmutate,#]&,child2];
      Return[{child1,child2}];
      ]; (* end of Module *)
```

```
initPop[psize_,csize_] :=
    Table[Random[Integer,{0,1}],{psize},{csize}];

displayBest[fitnessList_,number2Print_] :=
    Module[{i,sortedList},
        sortedList = Sort[fitnessList,Greater];
        For[i=1,i<=number2Print,i++,
            Print["fitness = ",sortedList[[i]] ];
            ]; (* end of For i *)
        ]; (* end of Module *)

bga[pcross_,pmutate_,popInitial_,fitFunction_,numGens_,printNum_] :=
  Module[{i,newPop,parent1,parent2,diff,matches,
          oldPop,reproNum,index,fitList,fitListSum,
          fitSum,pheno,pIndex,pIndex2,f,children},
    oldPop=popInitial;                 (* initialize first population *)
    reproNum = Length[oldPop]/2;       (* calculate number of reproductions *)
    f = fitFunction;                   (* assign the fitness function *)
   For[i=1,i<=numGens,i++,             (* perform numGens generations *)
    pheno = Map[decodeBGA,oldPop];     (* decode the chromosomes *)
    fitList = f[pheno];                (* determine the fitness of each phenotype *)
    Print[" "];                        (* print out the best individuals *)
    Print["Generation ",i," Best ",printNum];
    Print[" "];
    displayBest[fitList,printNum];
    fitListSum = FoldList[Plus,First[fitList],Rest[fitList]];
    fitSum = Last[fitListSum];         (* find the total fitness *)
    newPop = Flatten[Table[      (* determine the new population *)
      pIndex1 = selectOne[fitListSum,fitSum]; (* select parent indices *)
      pIndex2 = selectOne[fitListSum,fitSum];
      parent1 = oldPop[[pIndex1]];          (* identify parents *)
      parent2 = oldPop[[pIndex2]];
     children = crossOver[pcross,pmutate,parent1,parent2]; (* crossover and mutate *)
      children,{reproNum}],1    (* add children to list; flatten to first level *)
      ]; (* end of Flatten[Table] *)
     oldPop = newPop;             (* new becomes old for next gen *)
    ]; (* end of For i*)
   ]; (* end of Module *)
```

```
sigmoid[x_] := 1./(1+E^(-x));

initXorPop[psize_,csize_,ioPairs_] :=
  Module[{i,iPop,hidWts,outWts,mseInv},
                (* first the chromosomes *)
    iPop = Table[
       {Table[Random[Integer,{0,1}],{csize}],(* h1 *)
        Table[Random[Integer,{0,1}],{csize}],(* h2 *)
        Table[Random[Integer,{0,1}],{csize}] (* o1 *)
       }, {psize} ]; (* end of Table *)
                (* then decode and eval fitness *)
                (* use For loop for clarity *)
      For[i=1,i<=psize,i++,
                (* make hidden weight matrix *)
          hidWts = Join[iPop[[i,1]],iPop[[i,2]] ];
          hidWts = Partition[hidWts,20];
          hidWts = Map[decodeXorChrom,hidWts];
          hidWts = Partition[hidWts,2];
                (* make output weight matrix *)
          outWts = Partition[iPop[[i,3]],20];
          outWts = Map[decodeXorChrom,outWts];
                (* get mse for this network *)
          mseInv = gaNetFitness[hidWts,outWts,ioPairs];
                (* prepend mseInv *)
          PrependTo[iPop[[i]],mseInv];
          ]; (* end For *)
      Return[iPop];
      ]; (* end of Module *)

decodeXorChrom[chromosome_] :=
  Module[{pList,lchrom,values,p,decimal},
    lchrom = Length[chromosome];
        (* convert from binary to decimal *)
    pList = Flatten[Position[chromosome,1] ];
    values = Map[2^(lchrom-#)&,pList];
    decimal = Apply[Plus,values];
        (* scale to proper range *)
    p = decimal (9.5367522590181191355*10^-6)-5;
    Return[p];
      ]; (* end of Module *)
```

```
gaNetFitness[hiddenWts_,outputWts_,ioPairVectors_] :=
  Module[{inputs,hidden,outputs,desired,errors,
     len,errorTotal,errorSum},
   inputs=Map[First,ioPairVectors];
   desired=Map[Last,ioPairVectors];
   len = Length[inputs];
   hidden=sigmoid[inputs.Transpose[hiddenWts]];
   outputs=sigmoid[hidden.Transpose[outputWts]];
   errors= desired-outputs;
   errorSum = Apply[Plus,errors^2,2]; (* second level *)
   errorTotal = Apply[Plus,errorSum];
        (* inverse of mse *)
   Return[len/errorTotal];
   ]                      (* end of Module *)


crossOverXor[pcross_,pmutate_,parent1_,parent2_] :=
  Module[{child1,child2,crossAt,lchrom,
           i,numchroms,chroms1,chroms2},
           (* strip off mse *)
     chroms1 = Rest[parent1];
     chroms2 = Rest[parent2];
           (* chromosome length *)
     lchrom = Length[chroms1[[1]]];
           (* number of chromosomes in each list *)
     numchroms = Length[chroms1];
     For[i=1,i<=numchroms,i++,    (* for each chrom *)
     If[ flip[pcross],
     crossAt = Random[Integer,{1,lchrom-1}]; (* True: select cross site at random *)
          (* construct children  *)
     chroms1[[i]] = Join[Take[chroms1[[i]],crossAt],Drop[chroms2[[i]],crossAt]];
     chroms2[[i]] = Join[Take[chroms2[[i]],crossAt],  Drop[chroms1[[i]],crossAt]],
       Continue];   (* False: don't change chroms[[i]].  End of If *)
         (* perform mutation *)
       chroms1[[i]] = Map[mutateBGA[pmutate,#]&,chroms1[[i]]];
       chroms2[[i]] = Map[mutateBGA[pmutate,#]&,chroms2[[i]]];
       ]; (* end of For i *)
     Return[{chroms1,chroms2}];
     ]; (* end of Module *)
```

```
gaXor[pcross_,pmutate_,popInitial_,numReplace_,ioPairs_,numGens_,printNum_] :=
  Module[{i,j,newPop,parent1,parent2,diff,matches,
          oldPop,reproNum,index,fitList,fitListSum,
          fitSum,pheno,pIndex,pIndex2,f,children,hids,outs,mseInv},
              (* initialize first population sorted by fitness value *)
      oldPop= Sort[popInitial,Greater[First[#],First[#2]]&];
      reproNum = numReplace;       (* calculate number of reproductions *)
     For[i=1,i<=numGens,i++,
       fitList = Map[First,oldPop];    (* list of fitness values*)
                                    (* make the folded list of fitness values *)
       fitListSum = FoldList[Plus,First[fitList],Rest[fitList]];
       fitSum = Last[fitListSum];     (* find the total fitness *)
     newPop = Drop[oldPop,-reproNum]; (* new population; eliminate reproNum worst *)
       For[j=1,j<=reproNum/2,j++,       (* make reproNum new children *)
               (* select parent indices *)
         pIndex1 = selectOne[fitListSum,fitSum];
         pIndex2 = selectOne[fitListSum,fitSum];
         parent1 = oldPop[[pIndex1]];    (* identify parents *)
         parent2 = oldPop[[pIndex2]];
       children = crossOverXor[pcross,pmutate,parent1,parent2];(*cross and mutate*)
       {hids,outs} = decodeXorGenotype[children[[1]] ]; (* fitness of children *)
       mseInv = gaNetFitness[hids,outs,ioPairs];
       children[[1]] = Prepend[children[[1]],mseInv];
       {hids,outs} = decodeXorGenotype[children[[2]] ];
       mseInv = gaNetFitness[hids,outs,ioPairs];
       children[[2]] = Prepend[children[[2]],mseInv];
       newPop = Join[newPop,children]; (* add children to new population *)
       ];  (* end of For j *)
       oldPop =    Sort[newPop,Greater[First[#],First[#2]]&];(* for next gen *)
             (* print best mse values (1/mseInv) *)
       Print[ ];Print["Best of generation ",i];
       For[j=1,j<=printNum,j++,Print[(1.0/oldPop[[j,1]])]; ];
     ];  (* end of For i*)
   Return[oldPop];
   ]; (* end of Module *)
```

```
decodeXorGenotype[genotype_] :=
    Module[{hidWts,outWts},
        hidWts = Join[genotype[[1]],genotype[[2]] ];
        hidWts = Partition[hidWts,20];
        hidWts = Map[decodeXorChrom,hidWts];
        hidWts = Partition[hidWts,2];
                (* make output weight matrix *)
        outWts = Partition[genotype[[3]],20];
        outWts = Map[decodeXorChrom,outWts];
        Return[{hidWts,outWts}];
        ];

encodeNetGa[weight_,len_] :=
  Module[{pList,values,dec,chromosome,i},
    i=len;
    l=Table[0,{i}];
      (* scale to proper range *)
   dec = Round[(weight+5.)/(9.536752259018191355*10^-6)];
   While[dec!=0&&dec!=1,
     l=ReplacePart[l,Mod[dec,2],i];
     dec=Quotient[dec,2];
     --i;
     ];
   l=ReplacePart[l,dec,i]
     ];  (* end of Module *)

randomPop[psize_,csize_,ioPairs_,numGens_] :=
  Module[{i,pop},
    For[i=1,i<=numGens,i++,
      pop = initXorPop[psize,csize,ioPairs];
      pop = Sort[pop,Greater[First[#],First[#2]]&];
      Print[ ];
      Print["Random generation ",i];
      Print[(1.0/pop[[1,1]])];
      ];
    ];
```

Bibliography

[1] Igor Aleksander, editor. *Neural Computing Architectures*. MIT Press, Cambridge, MA, 1989.

[2] James A. Anderson and Edward Rosenfeld, editors. *Neurocomputing: Foundations of Research*. MIT Press, Cambridge, MA, 1988

[3] Maureen Caudill and Charles Butler. *Naturally Intelligent Systems*. MIT Press, Cambridge, MA, 1990.

[4] Lawrence Davis, editor. *Handbook of Genetic Algorithms*. Van Nostrand Reinhold, New York, 1991.

[5] John S. Denker, editor. *Neural Networks for Computing: AIP Conference Proceedings 151*. American Institute of Physics, New York, 1986.

[6] Russell C. Eberhart and Roy W. Dobbins, editors. *Neural Network PC Tools: A Practical Guide*. Academic Press, San Diego, CA, 1990.

[7] Rolf Eckmiller and Christoph v. d. Malsburg, editors. *Neural Computers*. NATO ASI Series F: Computer and Systems Sciences. Springer-Verlag, Berlin, 1988.

[8] James A. Freeman and David M. Skapura. *Neural Networks: Algorithms, Applications, and Programming Techniques*. Addison-Wesley, Reading, MA, 1991.

[9] David E. Goldberg. *Genetic Algorithms in Search, Optimization & Machine Learning*. Addison-Wesley, Reading MA, 1989.

[10] Stephen Grossberg, editor. *Studies of Mind and Brain*. D. Reidel Publishing, Boston, MA, 1982.

[11] Stephen Grossberg, editor. *Neural Networks and Natural Intelligence*. MIT Press, Cambridge, MA, 1988.

[12] Robert Hecht-Nielsen. *Neurocomputing*. Addison-Wesley, Reading, MA, 1990.

335

[13] John Hertz, Anders Krogh, and Richard G. Palmer. *Introduction to the Theory of Neural Computation*. Addison-Wesley, Redwood City, CA, 1991.

[14] Geoffrey E. Hinton and James A. Anderson, editors. *Parallel Models of Associative Memory*. Lawrence Erlbaum Associates, Hillsdale, NJ, 1981.

[15] Tarun Khanna. *Foundations of Neural Networks*. Addison-Wesley, Reading MA, 1990.

[16] C. Klimasauskas. *The 1989 Neuro-Computing Bibliography*. MIT Press, Cambridge, MA, 1989.

[17] Teuvo Kohonen. *Self-Organization and Associative Memory*. Springer-Verlag, New York, 1984.

[18] Bart Kosko. *Neural Networks and Fuzzy Systems: A Dynamical Systems Approach to Machine Intelligence*. Prentice-Hall, Englewood Cliffs, NJ, 1992.

[19] Roman Maeder. *Programming in Mathematica*. 2nd Edition, Addison-Wesley, Reading MA, 1991.

[20] James McClelland and David Rumelhart. *Explorations in Parallel Distributed Processing*. MIT Press, Cambridge, MA, 1988.

[21] Marvin Minsky and Seymour Papert. *Perceptrons: Expanded Edition*. MIT Press, Cambridge, MA, 1988.

[22] B. Müller and J. Reinhardt. *Neural Networks: An Introduction*. Springer-Verlag, Berlin, 1990.

[23] Yoh-Han Pao. *Adaptive Pattern Recognition and Neural Networks*. Addison-Wesley, Reading, MA, 1989.

[24] David Rumelhart and James McClelland. *Parallel Distributed Processing*. MIT Press, Cambridge, MA, 1986.

[25] Patrick K. Simpson. *Artificial Neural Systems: Foundations, Paradigms, Applications, and Implementations*. Pergamon Press, New York, 1990.

[26] Philip D. Wasserman. *Neural Computing: Theory and Practice*. Van Nostrand Reinhold, New York, 1989.

[27] Bernard Widrow and Samuel D. Stearns. *Adaptive Signal Processing*. Prentice-Hall, Englewood Cliffs, NJ, 1985.

[28] Stephen Wolfram. *Mathematica: A System for Doing Mathematics by Computer*. 2nd Edition, Addison-Wesley, Reading, MA, 1991.

[29] Steven F. Zornetzer, Joel L. Davis, and Clifford Lau, editors. *An Introduction to Neural and Electronic Networks*. Academic Press, San Diego, CA, 1990.

Index

337

self-scaling, 220
short term memory (STM), 212
sigmoid function. *See* function, sigmoid
slack units, 173
spatial patterns, 185
spin, 124, 125
spin glass, 125
spurious stable state, 122, 182
stability-plasticity dilemma, 210
statistical mechanics, 151
steady state,
    population, 285
    reproduction, 277
Stearns, Samuel D., 49
stochastic processes, 116, 151
supervised learning, 43
survival probability, 267
sweep, 131, 132
synapse, 8, 9, 34, 36
synaptic,
    cleft, 34
    junction, 35
    strength, 36
synchronous updating, 120, 127

T-C problem, 75–89, 94, 97, 99, 102
Tagliarini, Gene, 156
tanh function, 203, 204
temperature, 124–126, 128–132, 134, 151
    fictitious, 127, 130
thermal,
    effects, 125

equilibruim, 26
fluctuations, 127
threshold, 33
    condition, 29, 253
    function, 18, 19, 246
    output function, 28, 65
    value, 19
    unit, 33
training, 43, 46, 108, 293
    algorithm, 68, 72
transversal filter, 49, 58
traveling salesperson problem (TSP), 154–173

units, 6, 8, 11, 16, 20, 27
    winning, 101

vector-matrix multiplication, 22
VLSI, 157

weight, 9, 10, 27, 28, 36, 44, 49, 126
    matrix, 19–27, 59, 70, 71, 162, 169, 171, 173, 174, 178–180, 196, 230, 233, 235
    space 281
    vectors, 24–27, 42, 43, 46–48, 122, 145, 238
Widrow, Bernard, 49, 54

XOR,
    function, 31–33, 275
    problem, 30, 58, 68, 89, 94, 97, 100, 103, 104, 108, 281